Questioning Our Faith in Practice

Theology in Practice

Editors-in-Chief

Bonnie J. Miller-McLemore (*Vanderbilt University*)
Elaine Graham (*University of Chester*)

Editorial Board

Tom Beaudoin (*Fordham University*)
Nadine Bowers Du Toit (*University of Stellenbosch*)
Eileen Campbell-Reed (*Union Theological Seminary*)
Danjuma Gibson (*Calvin Seminary*)
Tone Kaufman (*MF School of Theology*)
Joyce Ann Mercer (*Yale Divinity School*)
Hee-Kyu Heidi Park (*Ewha Womans University*)
Anthony Reddie (*University of South Africa*)
Phillis Sheppard (*Vanderbilt University*)
Claire E. Wolfteich (*Boston University*)

VOLUME 14

The titles published in this series are listed at *brill.com/thip*

Questioning Our Faith in Practice

Unlearning White Supremacy in Practical Theology

By

Katherine Turpin

BRILL

LEIDEN | BOSTON

Cover illustration: Tree at Smoky Sunset, used with kind permission by Ring Lake Ranch, Dubois, WY.

Library of Congress Cataloging-in-Publication Data

Names: Turpin, Katherine, 1971- author.
Title: Questioning our faith in practice : unlearning white supremacy in practical
   theology / by Katherine Turpin.
Description: Leiden : Brill, [2025] | Series: Theology in practice : 2352-9288 ;
   volume 14 | Includes bibliographical references and index.
Identifiers: LCCN 2024037686 (print) | LCCN 2024037687 (ebook) |
   ISBN 9789004714243 (paperback) | ISBN 9789004714267 (ebook)
Subjects: LCSH: Theology, Practical. | White supremacy movements–Religious
   aspects–Christianity. | Decolonization. | Postcolonial theology.
Classification: LCC BV4 .T87 2025 (print) | LCC BV4 (ebook) |
   DDC 201/.72–dc23/eng/20240925
LC record available at https://lccn.loc.gov/2024037686
LC ebook record available at https://lccn.loc.gov/2024037687

Typeface for the Latin, Greek, and Cyrillic scripts: "Brill". See and download: brill.com/brill-typeface.

ISSN 2352-9288
ISBN 978-90-04-71424-3 (paperback)
ISBN 978-90-04-71426-7 (e-book)
DOI 10.1163/9789004714267

Copyright 2025 by Koninklijke Brill BV, Leiden, The Netherlands.
Koninklijke Brill BV incorporates the imprints Brill, Brill Nijhoff, Brill Schöningh, Brill Fink, Brill mentis, Brill Wageningen Academic, Vandenhoeck & Ruprecht, Böhlau and V&R unipress.
All rights reserved. No part of this publication may be reproduced, translated, stored in a retrieval system, or transmitted in any form or by any means, electronic, mechanical, photocopying, recording or otherwise, without prior written permission from the publisher. Requests for re-use and/or translations must be addressed to Koninklijke Brill BV via brill.com or copyright.com.

This book is printed on acid-free paper and produced in a sustainable manner.

Contents

Acknowledgements   VII

1 **Questioning One's Own Faith**   1
   1   Defining Whiteness and White Supremacy   6
   2   Salvation beyond White Supremacy   15
   3   Why "Questioning"?   20
   4   "You'll Lose Your Faith"?   24
   5   How to Read This Book   29

2 **Questioning Practice**   33
   1   Practice and the Transmission of Virtue   35
   2   Practice and Symbolic Violence   44
   3   Accounting for the Ambivalent Nature of Christian Practice   47
   4   Innocence, Purity, and Complicity: Reimagining White Christian Practice   51

3 **Questioning Education**   58
   1   Teaching as Universal Mandate for Conversion   60
   2   Education, Civilization, and Imperial Force   66
   3   Pedagogical Eternalities and the Education of Children   70
   4   Education with Humility   74

4 **Questioning Intervention**   81
   1   The Role of Intervention in Practical Theological Reflection   82
   2   Agency, Assumed Control, and the White Savior   85
   3   Intervention as Religious Meaning-Making   90
   4   The Myth of Progress and Salvation as Whiteness   95
   5   From Intervention to Design for Collective Flourishing   98

5 **Questioning Leadership**   102
   1   On Leaders and Followers   104
   2   From Corporate Rock Star to Interdependent Co-collaborators   106
   3   The Paradox of Servant Leadership   109
   4   Decolonizing and Liberating Leadership   113
   5   Fragment Workers and Poetic Imagination   123

6 Questioning Congregations 128
   1   The Prominence of the Congregation in White Christianity 132
   2   Congregations as Institutions of Whiteness 136
   3   Decolonizing Community and Moving beyond Congregations 140

7 Questioning the Apologetic and Affiliative Function of Practical Theology 144
   1   What Are Apologetics and How Do Practical Theologians Get Drawn into Them? 147
   2   When Describing Practice Becomes Advocating for Practice 154
   3   Demand for Institutional Loyalty and Assimilation 157

8 Questioning Christianity 160
   1   Christian Privilege and the Racialization of Religious Identity 166
   2   Struggling with Normativity and Universality in White Theology 169
   3   Interreligious Practical Theology and Multiple Religious Belonging 176
   4   A Somewhat Less-Christian Practical Theological Reflection Cycle 178

9 Questioning Anthropocentrism 184
   1   Refuting Theologies of Human Domin[at]ion 190
   2   Restoring Connection to All Our Relations 194
   3   Legacy Fears of Heresy and Syncretism 200

Epilogue: Living the Questions 206
   1   Original Sin, Shameful Hiding, and Right Repentance 208

Bibliography 217
Index 230

Acknowledgements

Thanks to a pandemic and my second life as an academic administrator, this book took eight years to complete. Along the way so many conversation partners, supportive friends, and colleagues supported me through the process. The older I get, the more I realize how good colleagues and conversation partners are critical to whatever wisdom I might manage to get on paper.

The Iliff School of Theology in Denver, Colorado, supported me throughout the writing of this text, including allowing a year-long sabbatical in 2021–2022 that was essential to completing the first full draft of the manuscript. My Iliff faculty colleagues have been friends as well as professional colleagues. After nearly two decades of working with some of them, they have shaped my thinking and scholarship in currents now below conscious thought. Boyung Lee and Cathie Kelsey were wise and supportive deans who made my work and scholarship possible. Miguel De La Torre and Tink Tinker challenged the Iliff faculty over a decade ago to write about how whiteness defined their academic fields. It took a while, but here it is. Jennifer Leath became an important writing partner and sounding board over the course of this project, even after she moved to her new position in Canada. Our books were written together over Zoom, in outdoor walks when we were in the same city, and through the pandemic and so many life changes. Albert Hernandez and Eric Smith were also writing collaborators in the early stages of this project. Several colleagues at Iliff: Kristina Lizardy-Hajbi, Carrie Doehring, Amy Erickson, and Jeffrey Mahan read pieces of this book in early forms and offered critical feedback.

The doctoral students in practical theology I have had the privilege to work with over the years have shaped my thinking about the field and deepened my acumen within it, particularly Julie Todd, Hannah Ingram, Emily Kahm, Paula Lee, Zachary Moon, Tracy Temple, Rode Molla, Wesley Snedecker, Eunjin Jeon, Smash Caine-Conley, Tory Moir, Mana Tun, and Anthony Houston. Doctoral students who I worked with who wouldn't identify as practical theologians but have shaped my thinking nonetheless with their wisdom and partnership include Jenny Whitcher, Teresa Crist, Cari Myers, Becky David Hensley, David Scott, Heike Peckruhn, Ben Sanders, Jared Vazquez, and Mark Freeland. The opportunity to teach DMin students about practical theological research has also invited me into their practices of ministry and the challenges and creativity they experience as they live and work in the realities I tried to describe here. Your questions, conversations, and constructions made me a better scholar and teacher, and I am so grateful to have crossed paths with each one of you. The master's students at Iliff who took introductory practical theology classes with me, always starting with confusion about the oxymoronic name of the course and ending with their own important constructive projects, opened my perspective beyond the Christian tradition and congregational setting of these kinds of reflections. You invited me into your past experiences, theological reflections, and unique contexts with patience, passion, and resistance in ways that have clarified my own perspectives.

The indomitable Debbie Creamer read an early draft of this project and encouraged me not to scrap it in a period of doubt and uncertainty. The queer intergenerational scholarly family we have built has been such a source of strength and an example of why interdependence and intentional relationality are critical to survival and flourishing in academic work. Bonnie Miller-McLemore, Kathleen Cahalan, Joyce Mercer, Laura Kelly Fanucci, and Jane Patterson were also writing companions, particularly at the Episcopal House of Prayer in Collegeville, MN, where we spend several days writing together while they introduced me to the joys of pour-over coffee and gin gimlets.

Much of this manuscript was also written in the summers at Ring Lake Ranch in the Torrey Creek Valley of the Wind River Mountains just outside of Dubois, Wyoming. That community of staff, speakers, and guests and the land itself has been an extended family to my own for over a dozen years now. They have been conversation partners, comic relief, meal companions, and so much more, often as they were on vacation, and I was hiding out in the cabin to write. There are too many conversation partners who have passed through that thin place who served as gifts to my thinking to name them all, but I am particularly grateful to Amy Mears, Julie Mavity-Maddalena, Mo Morrow, Leah Vader, Alli Moore, and Kat Harrell for our extended time together in that space.

The Wabash Center has been another place where I connected with many early career scholars and collaborative leadership partners over the years of writing this. Thanks to Lucinda Huffaker, Dena Pence, Lynne Westfield, Paul Myhre, Willie Jennings, Eric Barreto, Roger Nam, Ralph Watkins, Elizabeth Drescher, Mary Hess, Mary Stimming, Joe Favazza, Patricia Killen, Ted Hiebert, Carolyn Medine, Mai-Anh Le Tran, and so many other faculty colleagues and doctoral students who shared their teaching lives and scholarly wisdom over many years of working together. Your commitments to excellence in scholarship and teaching continues to inspire my own.

Two scholarly guilds have also introduced me to many of the people who are my conversation partners here in footnotes but who also have been friends and co-conspirators in real life. The Religious Education Association and the Association of Practical Theology introduced me to so many people over the years who have influenced this book, and my years of reading conference proposals, reviewing journal articles, and serving on boards and committees for both organizations have deepened and broadened my understanding of these disciplines.

I appreciate the support of Elaine Graham and Bonnie Miller-McLemore as editors of this series, and two very fine reviewers who gave this manuscript such a constructive and thoughtful read. I have been blessed with so many good colleagues in fields that value constructive collaboration that my writing should be brilliant. All mistakes and shortcomings here are my own. I wish I could have risen to the caliber of book that you envisioned for me, but I can only offer this one humbly instead.

Krista Turpin and Jessa Decker-Smith were sister-companions along the way who made sure I had a life and conversation partners outside of the worlds of theological education. I have danced between the vocation of mother and scholar for decades now, and I don't know that I have become proficient at doing both at the same time, but I am grateful to have also gotten to companion all my children as they grew into their young adult selves in the time it took to finish this book. We had some tender and precious extra time with them in this season due to the shared quarantining of the pandemic years, and we are readjusting now as they move out of our orbit and into the unique rhythms of their own lives. Elizabeth, Christian, and Benjamin, being your mother has been an experience beyond my wildest dreams, and I am so proud of the beautiful humans you are becoming. You have all been good sports when I wanted to draw on my experience of parenting in my scholarship, and this time it was Ben's turn. Finally and most importantly, Andy, you show up every day and make our lives possible, attending to the details that allow us to stay afloat and navigate the currents of life even in the roughest waters. You make me laugh, you hold me when I cry, and you are still the first person with whom I want to share the good, the bad, and the ugly.

CHAPTER 1

Questioning One's Own Faith

I am in a moment of profoundly questioning the white United States mainline Protestant Christianity in the United States that is my heritage. I am not arrogant enough to believe that I am alone in this questioning, nor that this questioning is anything new or innovative. I have been listening carefully to and learning from the critique of white middle class colonizer Christianity by liberation theologians, womanist theologians, postcolonial theologians, and those outside of the tradition on the underside of Christian privilege for three decades, and certainly other voices have been critiquing my tradition long before I entered the conversation. The cultural power of historically white mainline denominations and evangelical churches within Christianity has been waning as a source of meaningful stories and rituals, communities of mutual support, and ideas for vibrant common life for at least as long as I have been alive, maybe longer. This is evident in the diminishing numbers of members of the younger generations ready to share in their institutions and projects, and in the overwhelming lack of impact of the stories and values of this instantiation of the Christian tradition in resisting the logic of late capitalism and white supremacy in organizing our lives together as a society.

The use of "white Western Christianity," "white settler Christianity," and "white colonizer Christianity" throughout this book is intentionally broad.[1] I use these phrases to refer to the branches of Christianity on the North American continent that emerged in the modern era that are deeply informed by the practices of colonial expansion and conquest, the logic of white and Christian supremacy that emerged from the encounter with the peoples of the "new" world, and a struggle to convert, educate, and civilize the entire spectrum of these peoples and cultures into its fold through a coordinated effort of embodied economic and cultural conquest. These inheritors would include all white mainline and evangelical protestant and Catholic movements in the United States and their European forebears.

---

1 I follow theologian and ethicist Jennifer Harvey in not capitalizing the word "white" to designate a noncritical form of racialized identity. While some movements within these faith traditions have worked to understand the legacy of white supremacy birthed in their religious traditions, on balance they have not reckoned with or embraced the undoing of this legacy, which often remains subterranean and therefore very powerful.

There are forms of Western Christianity in the United States that evolved in resistance to this colonizing project steeped in white supremacy, such as the unique forms of Christianity that evolved in African-American communities that blended the spiritual wisdom of African peoples with the teachings offered by white Western Christianity to develop something quite different. As with any dominant/oppressor culture, those who were forced to live under its structures also had to adapt or assimilate their cultural and religious practice in order to mitigate denigration, sanction, and erasure. Through the processes of internalized oppression and forced assimilation, in some instances the logics, commitments, practices, and worldview of white Western Christianity impacted the development of racially nondominant religious and cultural communities as well. The process of decolonizing Christianity in these communities has been creative and persistent for generations, and the work I am constructing here questioning the practice of my own ancestors draws heavily on the wisdom of these resistant communities in their project of detangling Christianity from the colonial project that brought it to this continent.

White settler Christianity seems to be well on its way to a diminished social role and cultural impact in U.S. culture when one considers declining numbers of affiliation with communities of faith, struggles to maintain resources and institutional support from local congregations to institutions of higher education, and participation in rituals and devotional practices. Despite this being the tradition in which I have been formed my entire life, and what I have given my adult professional work life to strengthening, I am not sure that this diminishment is not good news for the earth and its peoples. As my home tradition struggles to survive, I find myself at times no longer wanting to be a part of trying to save it. I am not sure it needs to be passed on to the next generation, and I am not in a frenzy that the numbers are decreasing, the money is drying up, the youth aren't staying in the church long term, the students aren't coming to seminary, the institutions are shutting down. I think maybe it is time.

Here's my problem: I remain a white professor of practical theology and religious education in a historically white mainline Protestant seminary. My livelihood and that of my family is wrapped up in sustaining this tradition and getting people excited about joining it. The graduate students I teach often go into an institutional system where their professional effectiveness as clergy is judged by "dashboard numbers" for their congregations tracking memberships, baptisms, financial giving, and missional involvement, a capitalistic cataloguing of success. I am a part of the refinement and professionalization of a tradition that has been deeply problematic in connecting humans with the deepest and most profound mysteries of God, but a tradition that was once highly successful in baptizing colonizing projects and concentrating power and wealth among a minority of persons on the planet.

Despite the formal diminishment of the religious institutions and affiliations related to this movement, the logics and habits of body that white settler Christianity embedded in the culture of the United States still have formative power. White Christian nationalism is a not-so-civil religion fueling the notions of policing and what passes for a criminal justice system, domination and control of women's and non-gender-conforming bodies and compulsory heterosexualities, and so much more in the contemporary United States legal and social environment, even as the religious practices and communities that birthed these ideologies are waning. So, while the originating structures and institutions are diminishing, the logics and practices born out of white colonial Christianity are alive and culturally vibrant in ways that are deeply harmful.

Hebrew Bible scholar Walter Brueggemann once said, "The crisis in the U.S. church has almost nothing to do with being liberal or conservative; it has everything to do with giving up on the faith and discipline of our Christian baptism and settling for a common, generic U.S. identity that is part patriotism, part consumerism, part violence, and part affluence."[2] He talks broadly about the US church, but he more accurately describes the European-descended settler churches that participated in the cultural and literal eradication of the original inhabitants of this land and regularly failed to resist the evils of human chattel slavery, economic and social exploitation of recent arrivals through immigration, domination of women and the development and promotion of rape culture, and hoarding of resources by the most wealthy and powerful at the direct expense of the most vulnerable. I might replace "patriotism" with "nationalism," but I stand with Brueggemann on describing the powerful evils that have been baptized by white settler Christianity.

Another prophet calling out the deficiencies of this inherited tradition is the Reverend Martin Luther King, Jr., whose naming of the tripartite evil of racism, economic exploitation, and militarism, as he began his speech to the Hungry Club Forum at the Butler Street YMCA in Atlanta in 1967, calls attention to key problematic factors. White settler Christianity has blessed these three evils by naming God's desire for racial segregation, for the blessing of prosperity on the wealthy, and for protection for those who serve in the military over against our enemies while believing that God supports our violent interventions around the world. As my colleague ethicist Miguel De La Torre sees it,

---

2   Walter Brueggemann, *A Way Other Than Our Own* (Westminster John Knox, 2016), 2–3.

"White churchgoers have historically been, and continue to be, the greatest existential hazard for humanity, especially for the dispossessed and disinherited. Since the foundation of the republic, white Christians have reigned supreme in North America by using invasion, genocide, and slavery as instruments of political control."[3] He goes on to note that the "propensity toward hyperindividualism, a call for law and order, an emphasis on charity over and against justice, an uncritical acceptance of the market economy, an emphasis on whiteness, and prominent patriarchal structural norms" are markers of white Christianity in the United States.[4]

I am entering fully into the practice of questioning my faith because I fear that it has become nearly devoid in offering anything of value in answering the questions of species survival, addressing human suffering caused by greed and exploitation in late capitalism, or decreasing racial fragility that leads to embracing despotic and immoral leaders who deny the humanity of those who are unlike them in a desperate attempt to cling to supremacist notions of white culture. Of course, those who are faithful to a God beyond the limits of this tradition and who have allowed the source of life to call their behavior into account in relationship to people unlike them and the broader earth-dwelling communities of animal, vegetable, and soil do have responses to these situations, have changed their life structures in response to them, and seek to be peacemakers and justice-creators in the world. But they are at most a countercultural minority within most of white settler Christianity. And meanwhile, a majority of white US Christians continue to support policies and cultural norms that are death-dealing, sometimes explicitly *because* of their faith in God formed by the white settler Christian traditions.

I have been writing and teaching about whether it is possible to renounce dominant culture formation since I was a doctoral student over twenty years ago. First, I wondered if the formation of Christian faith was even possible within consumer capitalism.[5] In recent years I have been working to understand the depth of formation offered by white supremacy and whether antiracist White Christian identity formation is possible. And now I am wrestling with human identity that doesn't destroy its own habitat and all other living creatures and species in the bargain, with a faith that allows for ecological

---

3 Miguel A. De La Torre, *Burying White Privilege: Resurrecting a Badass Christianity* (Eerdmans, 2018), 12.
4 De La Torre, *Burying White Privilege*, 98.
5 Katherine Turpin, *Branded: Adolescents Converting from Consumer Culture* (Pilgrim Press, 2006).

justice and appropriate human inhabitance on the planet.[6] Is this kind of counter-dominant faith formation even possible, and will it disrupt the systems in place in any meaningful way beyond just being resident aliens in the midst of their death-dealing structures?

On a more personal level, I have also wondered what it means to live in profound contention with the very systems, stories, people, and beliefs that made me who I am. I know that I love them, value them, and perceive the world most clearly through them, and yet, to recognize simultaneously that they are often morally, socially, and spiritually bankrupt creates internal dissonance. I cannot abandon my white, Christian, cisgender, heterosexual, American, capitalist, middle/upper class identity or worldview. If I could somehow "choose" to reject it and identify with another space of belonging, it would still profoundly shape the way I see the world, process information, make decisions and take on commitments in every shape and form. It has irreversibly shaped what Anishinaabe scholar of indigenous traditions Mark Freeland would call my worldview, or "an interrelated set of cultural logics that fundamentally orient a culture to space, time, the rest of life and provides a methodological prescription for relating to that life."[7] While conscious commitments and behaviors change, worldviews, because they are built into the deep structural logics of shared cultures, are much less likely to change even in an individual's lifetime, and do not shift at the behest of one person.

So perhaps this is original sin, this is human limitation, this is my lot: I know that my tradition has contributed to great violence within humanity and to the suffering of others, and I still find the things that it values beautiful, my home, the only way I know how to be. Or, as the apostle Paul so painfully confessed: "I don't know what I'm doing, because I don't do what I want to do. Instead, I do the thing that I hate."[8] This paradoxical relationship to the stories, rituals, and peoples that formed my worldview ancestrally is at the heart of this book. What does it mean to question the faith that imagined the world that you now live in? And what does it look like to not merely to push back and rage against it, like an adolescent chafing under the authority of their parents, but to be accountable to the damage it has wrought even as you know that it is fundamentally a building block of who you are? What does it mean

---

6 For a beautiful exploration of the meaning of human inhabitance in ecological religious education, see Jennifer Ayres, *Inhabitance: Ecological Religious Education* (Baylor University Press, 2019). I explore her ideas more in chapter 9.
7 Mark Freeland, *Aazheyaadizi: Worldview, Language, and the Logics of Decolonization* (Michigan State University Press, 2020), 23.
8 Rom. 7:14 (*Common English Bible*).

to question one's faith in practice? To live within the paradox of engaging in anguished questioning of and being formed by the same tradition?

1　Defining Whiteness and White Supremacy

When I talk about whiteness, I am not referring to the perceived lightness of skin in comparison to the broad range of skin tones common to the human species. Despite serious efforts to scientifically establish differences between races within the human species in the 19th and 20th centuries, no particular appearance of skin tone, genetic markers, or phenotypical differences reliably sort the human species into distinct races. That project of sorting was a social construction achieved historically through intentional cultural, legal, scientific, social, and governmental practices. Whiteness was created through a series of interventions, from theological edicts such as the Doctrine of Discovery to property laws to practices of enslavement and segregation that benefitted my ancestors while denigrating and eliminating those of other groups. This distinction between whiteness and white people is complicated to disentangle, because those societal interventions and the hierarchy they created used things like an individual's physical appearance, nation/culture of origin, and religious belonging as markers of worthiness in their sorting. When I talk about whiteness, I am not talking about the accidents of birth that make some of us have lighter skin and some of us born from European-descended ancestors. Whiteness is a coordinated historical project of organizing life together to distinguish and valorize one group of people while denigrating and eliminating others. That project is something I hope that many of us, whatever the color of our skin, can commit to dismantling.

Living with the legacy of these nefarious uses of identity categories in the project of white supremacy is hard. White folks like me perhaps have the least capacity to tolerate discussion of this legacy because many of us grew up in a time where our whiteness was the norm against which other people were raced or cultured.[9] Because we benefitted from the use of these random markers of birth to sort us into the more advantaged group, we are unused to having our racial identity linked to something undesirable or problematic that might

---

9　I have used the term "our" in the title of this book and use it here as if to assume that my readers are largely people whose identity aligns with white Christian people. Obviously, not everyone who reads this book will fit into those categories. While this is my primary audience in many ways, it is not my only audience. My assumption is that much that I say in this book will be obvious to my colleagues in practical theology who are not white.

cause feelings of guilt or shame. This fragility has led to a vigorous cultural defensiveness about whiteness, with calls of reverse racism leveled at anyone who calls attention to the benefits and advantages conferred by whiteness.[10] And these advantages are many, from everything from generational wealth to something as trivial as how many fouls are called in an NBA basketball game; whiteness has real power to confer distinction and privilege.[11] White people express concern that the teaching of history in any academically critical manner with attention to race is equated to teaching white students to feel bad about themselves.[12] Legislatures and politicians have called for a teaching of these histories that is patriotic, inadvertently equating white supremacy with the founding values of the nation that cannot be questioned.

Whiteness as a worldview is marked by several fundamental values that were played out in the invasion of this continent by European settlers and the subsequent re-shaping of its ecologies and economies into a white dominant civilization.[13] These values or patterns of being in the world undergird and permeate whiteness, providing those deep logics that are difficult to discern and to undermine because of their extensive patterning in many arenas of life. Any list like the one I am about to disclose will be insufficient, and

---

10   Robin DiAngelo, *White Fragility: Why It's So Hard for White People to Talk About Racism* (Beacon Press, 2020).

11   Alan Schwarz, "Study of N.B.A. Sees Racial Bias in Calling Fouls," *New York Times*, May 2, 2007, sec. Sports.

12   As an example, legislation in Florida originally known as House Bill 7 passed in April 2022, prohibits any teaching that: "An individual, by virtue of his or her race, color, sex, or national origin, bears personal responsibility for and must feel guilt, anguish, or other forms of psychological distress because of actions, in which the individual played no part, committed in the past by other members of the same race, color, sex, or national origin." https://www.flsenate.gov/Session/Bill/2022/7.

13   As this sentence indicates, I am writing largely from my US context in this book. While many of the settlers who constructed whiteness came from the European continent, and other colonial contexts of the European empires share some commonalities with what I describe here, the unique mix of factors that led to its dominance in the United States social order makes this a project that is grounded in North American, and particularly US realities. For an example of another scholar writing about the conundrum of being a part of the colonial project on the dominant side, see South African practical theologian Jaco Dreyer, "Knowledge, Subjectivity, (De)Coloniality, and the Conundrum of Reflexivity" in *Conundrums in Practical Theology*, eds. Joyce Ann Mercer and Bonnie Miller-McLemore (Brill, 2016), 97: "How can I, from my position as 'settler colonizer,' responsibly fulfill my duties as a practical theologian with a subjectivity tainted by colonialism and apartheid ... I did not, and still cannot, fully understand the effects of the 'inscriptions of the past,' my colonial heritage, and my whiteness on my research and knowledge-generating practices."

indeed I have made other lists in other places that included other descriptors and omitted some that I include below. For this project, I have been thinking about the following descriptors of whiteness: extractive, individualist, systematic/orderly/timely, hierarchical, patriarchal and heteronormative, supremacist, nationalist, and Christian. These combine into a particular worldview and set of cultural norms that are not seamless or uncontradicted, but that nevertheless endure and resist challenges to their organizing power. It is not a terribly flattering set of descriptors for those of us whose racial identity category most neatly falls into the category "white." But it is this combination of traits that I hope we can continue to critique and dismantle, and that is why they are at the forefront of my thinking as I set out in this project.

The connection of whiteness with the adjective *extractive* has been a relatively new term for me, but I have come to appreciate how it captures an important element in the culture of whiteness. With literal origins in the industry of mining, this word metaphorically describes how, in ways both economic and cultural, white civilizations have built their power by pulling out things of value from other civilizations and lands, whether through export of natural resources, exploitation of labor, or cultural appropriation in art and ritual. Critical media studies scholar Kim Reynolds notes, "The logic of extraction is driven by racialised violence and sustained practice of genocide of indigenous peoples,"[14] where stealing is considered good business because of the assumption of dehumanization of other peoples and environments from whom the things of value are taken. The consistent practice of appropriating the goods, labor, and beauty of other peoples for its own benefit marks one of the ways that whiteness is rooted in the colonial projects beginning in the sixteenth century. This was magnified and extended through capitalist practices of valuing profit to investors and shareholders over the creation of humane and sustainable living conditions for workers and the broader environment from which natural resources are taken in manufacturing and economic development. The creation of profit and return on investment are key values in whiteness, and these achievements often come through the extraction of value from other persons and lands.

White culture is *individualist* in that its legal systems, philosophies, and narrative genres begin with the building block of the importance of the individual. I had a seminary professor who decried claims of relativism in the heat

---

14   Kim Reynolds, "Extraction as White Supremacy | Moving towards Anti-Extraction Practices in the Arts," Creative Knowledge Resource. Accessed July 25, 2023. https://www.creativeknow.org/bopawritersforum/extraction-as-white-supremacy.

of debates about postmodernism by daring us to begin to move through the world as if we didn't have a self. His position raised the importance of the valuing of individual identity in a white Western worldview despite the claims that postmodernism had eliminated the possibility of universal truths. It is difficult to imagine what it would be like to exist in US society without an elevated notion of the individual. White criminal justice systems are based on individual intentions and behaviors and their legitimation and criminalization. White property laws, contracts, and rules of inheritance are based on the holdings of an individual. White stories of love and heroic adventure tend to focus on the experiences and narrative arcs of individuals situated minimally within broader contextual realities. Even human rights discourses favor individuals over peoples or tribal entities in their constructions. Often placed in contrast to more communitarian cultures, individualism favors solitary persons over almost any other organizing unit in policy, meaning-making, and artistic endeavors.[15]

Whiteness has been linked historically with the development of *systematic/orderly/efficient* institutions and ways of shaping time. Timeliness and punctuality are important values in white cultures, with their abiding belief that time equals money. There is an affection for schedules and charts of productivity, for keeping track of labor and possessions in highly systematized ways. The development of institutional bureaucracies and systems of administration were stylized and perfected through the colonial period, with violence encoded in the need to adapt the efforts of peoples into systems and ledgers. The niceties of relationality are sacrificed for blunt, transactional forms of interaction. Having a rational process and procedures that are delineated and followed with systematic ways of accounting for and tracking violations are part of this feature of whiteness.

Whiteness is deeply linked with being *Christian*. In the founding documents of the United States, such as the *Declaration of Independence*, the distinction was first made not between white and black persons but between Christians and "savages," the name for the first inhabitants of the continent who were seen as so deeply other as to almost be nonhuman. Certainly these persons were not afforded the political rights and respect that the colonizers were, and many of the initial colonies were linked to Christian denominational bodies and belief systems. To be white initially required adherence to the Christian

---

15 Practical theologian and religious educator Boyung Lee engages in a helpful discussion contrasting individualist and communalist forms of social organization in Boyung Lee. *Transforming Congregations through Community: Faith Formation from the Seminary to the Church* (Westminster John Knox Press, 2013), 6–10.

tradition, particularly favoring Protestant beliefs. The acronym "WASP," used both as an initial signal of the political and social elites on this continent and later as a term of resistance to critique this elitism, referred to "White Anglo-Saxon Protestant," naming primarily British heritage and affiliation with Protestant denominations as key to proximity to whiteness. Certain assumptions about class status were also enveloped in that term. Most of the persons attending Ivy League Universities well into the twentieth century were Protestant, and non-Christians were expressly limited in these institutions that networked so many of the politicians and influential business leaders in the US well into the latter half of the twentieth century.[16]

The sense that whiteness was related closely to Christianity is also evident in the racialization of the Jewish peoples and ongoing resistance to them in the form of white supremacy movements and anti-Semitism. Immigration patterns and policies favored those who were Christian, and part of the "model minority" status granted to Asian immigrants had to do with the number of them that had converted to Christianity prior to immigration. While not all Christians are white, belonging to another religious tradition, such as Islam or Judaism or Sikhism, certainly has disqualified persons from being considered white and led to racist backlash, particularly in the years following the terrorist attacks of September 11, 2001.[17]

Whiteness is *hierarchical* in that it divides peoples into categories and then ranks them in structures where some are valued, and others are demeaned. Hierarchies grant power and authority to some groups and demand obeisance from others. Patriarchy is a form of hierarchy associated with whiteness, where males are elevated and females are subordinated, but there are many good/bad binaries in whiteness that are established and then ranked. A primary one that shapes this book is white/nonwhite (including at various locales black, indigenous, brown and so on depending on which group was the dominant minority and perceived threat to white power in a particular context). Other binaries that get placed in hierarchical relationship to one another include mind/body, owner/worker, male/female, urban/rural, developed/inhabited land.

Emeritus Stanford business professor Harold Leavitt tried to articulate why hierarchies persist and regenerate themselves despite the ongoing resistance to them philosophically in recent times. He notes, "More important, though, hierarchies deliver real practical and psychological value. On a fundamental

---

16 Jerome Karabel, *The Chosen: The Hidden History of Admission and Exclusion at Harvard, Yale, and Princeton* (Houghton Mifflin, 2005).
17 One powerful account documenting this backlash can be found in Valarie Kaur, *See No Stranger* (One World, 2020).

level, they don't just enslave us, they also fulfill our deep needs for order and security. And they get big jobs done. Of course, hierarchies are terribly flawed. They inevitably foster authoritarianism and its destructive offspring: distrust, dishonesty, territoriality, toadying, and fear."[18] Efficiency, another value in white culture, is enhanced through hierarchies of power, which delimit who should make decisions and what values will be most honored without requiring negotiations. While Leavitt notes that artists, solo entrepreneurs, and homemakers largely live outside hierarchies, he believes that hierarchies provide comfort to those who work within them. He notes, "Like our families, communities, and religions, they help us define ourselves."[19] Leavitt acts as if this is a universal experience; he is not speaking of white affection for hierarchies. Perhaps there is something fundamentally human as a species about social comparison and ranking that informs the creation of hierarchies, but certainly there have been and continue to be cultures where hierarchies are less of a valued form of social organization than within whiteness.

One of the enduring forms of hierarchy in whiteness informs its nature as *patriarchal and heteronormative*, where males are given authority to lead and expected to pair with females as they are given the rights of landowner and head of family in household settings. Whiteness persistently shows a commitment to the so-called "nuclear family" with a focus on male/female monogamous pairings and their immediate offspring rather than extended kinship networks with multiple ways of combining for mutual support. There is an emphasis on caring for one's own nuclear family and preserving its legacy of possession and safety rather than focusing on a broader social arrangement or community as the primary unit of survival. Whiteness maintains gender-normed expectations for identity development and vocational expression, which is why we see so much policing of gender identity and expression and female and queer sexuality as a shorthand for "traditional" values in US culture. The bodies of women and children are heavily controlled in policy and religious values as supportive of the success and valorization of men who are in charge.

Whiteness is *supremacist and assimilationist* rooted in the historical belief in the "civilizing" influence of white settlers over original inhabitants of the US continent. Evidence of the ongoing echoes of this belief arises in the current preferential treatment of whiteness in electoral politics and representation, in the persistence of whose cultural norms are deemed "professional,"

---

18   Harold J. Leavitt, "Why Hierarchies Thrive." *Harvard Business Review*, March 1, 2003. https://hbr.org/2003/03/why-hierarchies-thrive.
19   Leavitt, "Why Hierarchies Thrive."

and in ongoing defense of the "traditional" values of the ideals of the slaveholding founders of the US as essential to maintain in contemporary culture. Religiously, a belief in the rightness of one's own tradition and the need for others to accept and adopt one's beliefs and values to ensure salvation has a supremacist and assimilationist thread in it as well. Linking whiteness to salvation gave a divine imperative to subdue and eradicate those who rejected this superior form of life.[20] The deep and abiding belief that white civilizations were superior to other cultures and forms of social organization was legitimated academically through the development of the social sciences, where a developmental approach to civilizations repeatedly articulated where European descended forms of human life together in religion and economics and education and forms of government were considered superior.

Whiteness is *nationalist* in its connection to building a nation-state by consolidating of single national power over against the diversity of social groups and ethnic origins that existed within it. In the United States a particular merging of Christian belief and militant nationalism has a long history in the notion of supporting "God and Country," whether in the motto etched on several of Yale's residential college dorms, the motto of the American Legion, or the commitment of Army chaplains.[21] Built on a phrase from the British military (For King and Country), the saying has a kind of parochial assumption of patriotism as a self-evident expression of devotional piety. While its power has risen and waned over the centuries that the United States has existed, white Christian nationalism has experienced either a resurgence or, more likely, renewed cultural legitimacy to go public since the election of Barack Obama as the first non-white President of the United States in 2008.

Supremacy serves as a constitutive ideology to the narratives of American exceptionalism, particularly the use of narratives of "the chosen people" from the Hebrew Bible reworked to include the "new Jerusalem" that was reinterpreted as the United States in early American mythology. An example of the belief in American exceptionalism, or the notion that there is no other coun-

---

20 Willie James Jennings, "Whiteness isn't Progress: How the Missionary Project Went Horrifically Wrong." *The Christian Century* 135, no. 23 (November 7, 2018): 28–31.
21 I was recently reminded of how easily this is invoked by a group of Catholic high school boys who came to the retreat center where I live. On their t-shirts for the retreat was the "Jesus Prayer" [Lord Jesus Christ, Son of God, have mercy on me, a sinner] in Greek and beneath it the words "Pro Deo et Patria." When I asked one of the leaders about the second phrase, they said it was just a saying that was important to them as a school. The weight of that phrase and its link to military practice was not at the level of awareness, simply a phrase to be evoked.

try like the United States that exists, comes from the American Legion website explaining why "For God and Country" matters so much:

> Surely no nation in history has provided such opportunity for individual freedom and quality of life alike to all its citizens. And just as surely, no nation in history has given so much and been of such positive benefit to the other nations of the world. America's very existence proclaims, protects and defends the vision that freedom and peace may be experienced throughout the world.[22]

In the United States political scene this belief in the primacy of the nation-state over all forms of human connection has been recently expressed in "America First" rhetoric and policies. When longtime activist South African activist Allan Boesak spoke recently at my school, his answer to a question of the crowd about what we should give up for Lent was a quick "American exceptionalism," as he detailed the disastrous effect that doctrine has globally. That belief in nation/country as a primary organizing value has been linked strongly with white supremacy.

All of these descriptors I am using for whiteness might also add up to and perhaps can be summed up by something like the word "colonial" or "settler" culture in the United States. The project of whiteness was an economic project as well as a cultural one. Whiteness advocated a reshaping of the world into conforming with the values of one group and in service of the economy of that group that was baked into the colonial project of expansion, invasion, and ongoing settlement for the enrichment of originating country and individuals.

Scholars have also reminded us that a key feature of whiteness is its commitment to anti-blackness, first defined by Afropessimist philosophers. Education theorist Michael Dumas summarizes this school of thought: "Antiblackness scholarship, so necessarily motivated by the question of Black suffering, interrogates the psychic and material assault on Black flesh, the constant surveillance and mutilation and murder of Black people."[23] Dumas names the dilemma that anti-blackness creates for black persons, when their very being is constructed first and foremost as problem to white people, to the nation, to the common good. While focusing on white supremacy, I do not wish to diminish the anti-blackness inherent in it, the diminishment and denigration

---

22   Tierian "Randy" Cash, "For God and Country," *The American Legion*. Accessed July 21, 2022. https://www.legion.org/magazine/243950/god-and-country.

23   Michael J. Dumas, "Against the Dark: Antiblackness in Education Policy and Discourse." *Theory into Practice* 55, no. 1 (2016): 12.

of whole peoples. In addition to anti-blackness, anti-indigeneity is also a key feature in the colonial enterprise that generated the legal and social category of whiteness.

My appeals to whiteness and white supremacy are going to be a bit broad and messy in this project, because whiteness is not a neat and tidy venture. I do not want to leave out the full range of the ways it was leveraged across social, cultural, and economic systems and practices in order to capture it precisely but artificially. What whiteness means has shifted over time. It has fingers in many ways of making sense of the world. I am using it to capture a broad range of economic, social, psychological, and cultural dimensions of life together. One of the primary strategies for success of whiteness was hiding its particularity under a cloak of universal truth. It emerged out of values developed in different cultures of European immigrants, but they also had to buy into it in a different way to establish themselves in a particular way on this continent as a part of the colonial project of expansion and investment in the American racial project.

Why, if it is so expansive and difficult to pin down, have I chosen to write about the legacy of whiteness and white supremacy in practical theology? I had a strongly formative experience as a scholar of writing with other collaborators in community for the *Opening the Field of Practical Theology* book.[24] As documented within that book, colleagues and friends such as Courtney Goto and Dale Andrews expressed frustration about being forced to write the "racial" chapters of this book, as if the other chapters and the field itself was not racialized. As Goto noted in a later work:

> However, this does not erase an unwitting division of labor that implies and reinforces an assumption that those with power and privilege in the field speak about what is privileged (often without realizing that the field itself and they are in fact privileged), while those who are historically marginalized address what is often treated as marginal ... I was also disturbed that unlike scholars of color, my white colleagues in the project and in general were not expected to account for dynamics of power, privilege, and whiteness in their research and teaching.[25]

---

24 *Opening the Field of Practical Theology: An Introduction.* Eds. Kathleen A. Cahalan and Gordon S. Mikoski (Rowman & Littlefield Publishers, 2014).
25 Courtney Goto, "Writing in Compliance with the Racialized 'Zoo' of Practical Theology," in *Conundrums in Practical Theology*, 111.

I had initially been assigned to write the chapter on "Liberationist Practical Theology," which raised questions given my focus on feminist, black, and queer liberationist perspectives as well as the Latin American theologians from which some colleagues thought the term originated and should be honored. My authority to write such a chapter given my social location as a Protestant white woman was challenged by other authors on the project even as the lack of a chapter on white practical theology was highlighted. In her follow-up to this project that reflected further upon it, Goto named the reality that the chapter I ended up co-writing with Tom Beaudoin responded to the lack of attention to the white racialization of the field but did so in a way that was depersonalized. As she notes, "However, white colleagues rarely write *confessionally* in terms of whiteness. As in other fields, white practical theologians are not expected to be articulate how their whiteness, their experience of it, and their formation in it affects their thinking, research, and writing."[26] In many ways, this project is my attempt to write confessionally about what it means to reckon with the legacy of whiteness in the field.

2 Salvation beyond White Supremacy

As I teach and write in my chosen fields of religious education and practical theology, I struggle with the need to tell a story as if Christian formation is possible in contemporary white US contexts and with the sense that engaging in it is always a good thing. Sometimes I feel as though formation in anything like faith in God following the way of Jesus in contemporary white dominant US contexts is impossible. My field of Christian education presupposes communities of stable identity, into which people can be socialized into practices that pass on the wisdom of faith. In reality, the white mainline Protestant church of which I am a participant is in a total freefall in cultural significance, membership numbers, and influence in its members' lives, a situation exacerbated by the experience of churches moving abruptly online during the pandemic days of 2020, and the resulting destabilization of funding schemes and intergenerational support that has led to continued disaffiliation with these traditions and institutions. I struggle with teaching practical theology and religious education as I recognize that any formation that might be significant or long-lasting is unlikely to happen through participation in a local congregation, and yet I know many congregations with hard-working leaders and faithful members who long for their lives together to be worthy and impactful.

---

26 Goto, "Racialized 'Zoo,'" 129.

This is not a new story. If I ask a classroom of seminarians where their primary formation in faith happened, it is often in an unusually devoted family setting, or through multiple years at camp or some sort of long-term service opportunity, through their own reading of spirituality books after a time of personal crisis or through a twelve-step recovery group. Or, conversely, they have found meaning in a Zen Buddhist meditation center, a sangha, or a yoga studio that taught embodied spiritual practices that changed their lives. The temptation in local white mainline Protestant congregations is to say if we just started this program or committed ourselves more deeply and energetically to this institution or got people to come to the church more regularly, deep counter-cultural Christian formation would be possible. But the reality of contemporary life is that the church is a sidelined institution to schools, mass media, and governmental entities that have a much greater impact on life structure than churches.[27]

When I am tempted to believe that the Christian community might have potential as a counter-cultural home for followers of Jesus who are a witness to something different in the world, I remember that 80% of my fellow white Christians willingly elected a narcissistic, racist, misogynist, and eventually criminal president into the White House, and other college-educated white folks disenchanted from the church but still enmeshed in the worldview joined them in this project. Four years later, after increased evidence of authoritarian tendencies and racist propaganda, a majority of white Christians and a super-majority of white evangelical Christians still supported his leadership. Beyond this symbolic figurehead lies an entire supporting system of political will that allows for defining shared identity through white supremacy and defensive, exclusionary practices such as separating families seeking asylum and America First policies. This is the fear that fuels theories like the "Great Replacement Theory," the notion that white people are being pushed out of dominance by immigration, racial intermarriage, and calls for representation that have the potential to dilute the bloodlines and culture that its proponents wish to sustain in the primary position of US culture. A majority of white Christians voted their belief that a strong male who will restore the country to its prior white-dominant greatness, even though he supports oppressive dictators as good leaders who love their people, has no vision for the common good beyond his own self-serving greed, and continued to support his family business with political power. What good is Christian formation if supporting

---

27   Michael Warren, *At this Time in this Place: The Spirit Embodied in the Local Assembly* (Trinity Press International, 1999).

this kind of regime and common life is the outcome of faithfulness? I have wondered if the tradition of Christianity that is predominant in my context is so steeped in white supremacy and misogyny and capitalist undergirding that it no longer has the capacity to invoke an alternative set of shared values or stories about the meaning and significance of life together.

Meanwhile, an Australian climate report exploring all possible outcomes of the current climate crisis names that human civilization is unlikely to survive past 2050 if we don't take seriously the rising temperatures on land and sea and species die off and desertification of the Amazon.[28] Many young prophets such as Greta Thunberg are begging adult leaders in government and corporations with responsibility and power to take this situation seriously so that they might have a tenable future. Millions of my fellow US residents have taken to the streets to protest police brutality, but also lack of access to health care, reasonable wages, investment in infrastructure and common life, safe places to exist and thrive, particularly during a global pandemic. Yet, my own historically white mainline denomination is fighting over how to re-organize itself while protecting the pensions of its own leadership and the property ownership of local communities since we cannot seem to agree on how to reckon with human sexuality.[29]

In that environment, I am unable to continue to write apologetics for the white Western Christianity that has contributed to the alienation from the environment, the colonialism and racism and exceptionalism that is part and parcel of what it means to be a white citizen of the United States. As theologian Willie Jennings notes, this project of imagining salvation through whiteness is a warped view of human progress that has led to death-dealing practice:

> To speak of whiteness is not to speak of particular people but of people caught up in a deformed building project aimed at bringing the world to its full maturity. What does maturity look like, maturity of mind and body, land and animal (use), landscape and building, family and govern-

---

28 David Spratt and Ian Dunlop, "Existential Climate-Related Security Risk: A Scenario Approach | PreventionWeb," June 12, 2019. https://www.preventionweb.net/publication/existential-climate-related-security-risk-scenario-approach.

29 As I was completing this book, the United Methodist Church did remove restrictions to ordination of LGBTQIA+ persons and the language of "homosexuality being incompatible with Christian teaching" from its official documents and policies after a 42-year fight. This occurred after disaffiliation from the denomination of many congregations who wished to maintain these policies and their establishment of a new denomination, the Global Methodist Church.

ment? Whiteness is a horrific answer to this question formed exactly at the site of Christian missions.[30]

In this book, I am attempting to imagine what teaching practical theology or religious education might look like without willing participation in this deformed building project, this vision of maturity as whiteness that has led to such alienation and failure in belonging, to one another, to the land, or to God. Fortunately, in imagining that different future I am joining many wise others who have already been doing this work.

I have framed this book in terms of unlearning white supremacy in practical theology, and that is a political choice as a person who benefits from the social/political advantages of whiteness and has been formed within the narratives of white supremacy as an insider. By that I do not mean to say that my family are avowed members of white supremacist organizations or that I participate in communities that actively encourage racist ways of being in the world in explicit forms, but rather that I participate in the everyday variety of white supremacy that is part and parcel of the systematic and structural racism of the United States.

Other scholars from different social and identity locations might talk about the decolonial or decolonizing nature of this project. I share with those scholars, such as my colleagues from the intersections of religious education and practical theology HyeRan Kim-Cragg, Christine Hong, and Anne Carter Walker,[31] a commitment to critiquing and undoing the strength of colonial and missionized forms of Christianity that denigrate multireligious belonging, cultural forms of being and knowing other than those valued by European-descended whiteness, distrust of our relationship with the earth and nonhuman species within it, and other racist forms of being and organizing life based in the intersection of white supremacy and settler Christianity. Kim-Cragg has noted in particular the lack of attention to colonialism as a concern in practical theology, naming that her own book: "not only calls for the inclusion of colonialism as a critical optic for practical theology but also demands a close look at how colonialism is entangled with issues of race, ethnicity, gender, class, disability, and sexual orientation."[32] I have learned much from their

---

30 Jennings, "Whiteness Isn't Progress," 28.
31 HyeRan Kim-Cragg, *Interdependence: A Postcolonial Feminist Practical Theology* (Pickwick Publications, 2018); Christine J. Hong, *Decolonial Futures: Intercultural and Interreligious Intelligence for Theological Education* (Lexington Books, 2021); and Anne Carter Walker, "Dreams (a Poem) Indigenous Futuring in the Theological Classroom (Prose)," *The Wabash Center Journal on Teaching* 4, no. 1 (2023): 7–17.
32 Kim-Cragg, *Interdependence*, 4.

work, but have not felt it appropriate to take on the label of postcolonial or decolonial for this work. I am still on the journey of questioning, and have not achieved the sense of "beyond" that Kim-Cragg centers in her work, the hope of what can be imagined and enacted beyond the past limitations of colonialism, while acknowledging the power of the ways they are still enacted.[33] I am still in the process of unlearning and disentangling from colonialism, struggling to continue to name the ways its myths and illusions are beautiful and attractive to me, fundamental to the way I see the world. But I aspire to join the decolonizing project of my colleagues with my own small contribution as one who is enmeshed in the benefits granted by white supremacy and trying to be accountable to them.

I believe that the only faithful response as a white religious educator and a practical theologian is to stop acting as if just doing the same things we have done forever more faithfully and with more control and influence over the next generation will somehow bring us closer to God. For me, being faithful means fearfully pulling the only rug I am standing on out from under my own feet and asking with fear and trembling what God would do with me, with my people, if it was not to prop up this endeavor that we've been trying to sustain and have found to be profoundly wanting. I am standing with my people, naked and ashamed, before God, knowing that the religious traditions and institutions that have been fashioned to cover me are utterly inadequate to the task, and that owning up to the shame of that legacy is part of re-establishing the possibility of deeper connections and less extractive forms of living on the planet. I am asking what it means to practice questioning my own faith. Not in a gentle "living the questions" kind of way that is the brand of post-modern white liberal Christianity that is part of my own faith-development story, but literally ceasing to trust that which has made me and trying to take apart its influence in my life and my work.

In case you are hoping for a useful ending to this project, this taking-apart is not in the service of advocating for a better solution, the next white suggestion for progress in human existence, a more faithful expression of white settler Christianity. I am trying as an intimate insider to the discourses of Christian formation and practical theology to use that intimate knowledge to notice and confess where it all goes terribly wrong as an act of repentance, and not to trust that I am the one who can creatively and imaginatively and faithfully chart a new course. I am trying to disrupt my own and my field's confidence that we have the best answers worth sharing or the next great pathway to God. This is

---

33   Kim-Cragg, *Interdependence*, pp. 7–8.

not my project. I am working to notice the ways that what I want to call good, beautiful, and truthful has been implicated in death, exploitation, control, and evil. I am about listening carefully to the prophetic voices that have named this particular perversion of salvation and taking seriously what they are saying and what it means for me as a white Christian practical theologian. And I am hoping beyond hope that salvation is bigger than whiteness, and that the God that my ancestors have witnessed to is bigger than this racialized Christian project into which I have been birthed.

3   Why "Questioning"?

From the title of the whole book to the title of each chapter, I use the term questioning in both a broad and a specific sense. In the broadest sense, I am attending to what my teaching colleague and scholar of pastoral care Carrie Doehring calls the "jarring" questions that arise in my reading of the field of practical theology. When Doehring introduces case studies or film clips or guest lectures to her students, she invites them to pay attention to the jarring questions that arise for them as they read, watch, and listen. Where do the materials make them uncomfortable, cause them to recoil, experience disgust or dismay, or create anger and irritation? She then invites them to sit with their reactions and begin to ask deeper and more curious questions of self-reflection. Which of their core values are being challenged by the speaker? What aspects of themselves are they feeling the need to defend or protect? Why are they getting hooked or triggered, and what personal and communal experiences are related to those reactions? It is in this questioning that they begin to understand their own interiority and core commitments, even as they are being asked to hold those lightly in the light of the information or person sitting before them and listening intently to their experience, insight, or expertise. For Doehring, this is an essential practice in developing the kind of self-reflexivity and empathy that allows for co-creative work with other people across difference in chaplaincy or care practices.

In one sense, the questioning that I am talking about is not an aggressive interrogation for the sake of dismantling or discrediting a source. It is more akin to Doehring's notions of attending to the jarring questions. Each chapter I have written has come from being jarred in relation to the field of practical theology, of literally being shaken or having my teeth set on edge by the discovery of my own previously hidden commitments to white supremacy often cloaked as virtuous core values instilled by my context of origin, my process of education and formation, the people I live with in community. This has led me to a process of questioning those commitments in intentional and curious ways with an eye towards uncovering the depth and persistence of these narratives in how I understood the field of practical theology as well as how they are linked to histories of colonialism and white supremacy.

In many ways, the practice of questioning in this work functions quite similarly to Courtney Goto's modeling of "taking on" the discipline of practical theology and its grounding assumptions in her 2018 book with that phrase in the title.[34] Goto speaks of "taking on" the field of practical theology in three ways: in terms of engaging seriously the values and practices at the heart of the field, in terms of reflecting on problematic assumptions with courage and vulnerability, and in terms of becoming more ethical and loving in our knowledge production in the field.[35] In other places in her project she talks about the work of "taking on" as a prophetic act understood as "an ongoing exercise of self-criticism conducted in the light of faith," borrowing from John Hull's work on prophecy.[36] She notes that Hull links prophetic work and confession, claiming that one reason to name the collective sins of the church is a faithful "effort not to reiterate *them*."[37]

One of the struggles in taking on the discipline is simply in seeing the problems inherent in it. As Goto notes, "We [practical theologians] too are trained in the languages and practices of, our discipline—all of which are grounded in implicit assumptions that potentially are harmful to those we serve and with whom we work, especially if they are never questioned."[38] Goto talks about our embracing of these harmful assumptions as a kind of idolatry, a worshiping of a wrong object as if it were a true God. Whereas Goto frames her task as "unmasking the idol *context* and advocating for its critical revision,"[39] and models beautifully and thoroughly what it means to do such a thing in depth, here I am looking at a range of hallowed concepts in the discipline of practical theology and asking what it might mean to unmask and revise them. In her spirit, I "take on" the use of practice, education, congregational life, intervention, leadership, anthropocentrism, even the primary focus on Christianity itself in the discipline. I also follow Goto in acknowledging that such a project requires "constant communal effort" and indeed a "critical mass to challenge and revise them."[40] One of the interesting observations that Goto makes is the

---

34 Courtney T. Goto, *Taking on Practical Theology* (Brill, 2018).
35 Goto, *Taking on Practical Theology*, 1.
36 Goto, *Taking on Practical Theology*, 56.
37 Goto, *Taking on Practical Theology*, 56.
38 Goto, *Taking on Practical Theology*, xiv.
39 Goto, *Taking on Practical Theology*, xv.
40 Goto, *Taking On Practical Theology*, xix.

link between the power of certain concepts or foci in the field of practical theology and "our hunger for disciplinary identity, coherence, and legitimacy" that enshrined them as idols.[41] Many scholars have already "taken on" the intense focus on methodology in the field as a way of trying to gain authority and legitimacy in the academic university. In this text, I am moving to a different focus, the way that alignment with the values of white supremacy was also important in gaining legitimacy and power with the practices in the field.

Additionally, practical theologian and my sometime co-author Tom Beaudoin described three disorientations in relation to "the theological significance of practice and the place of Christianity in practical theology," which he describes as "Questioning Practice," "Questioning Whiteness," and "Questioning Christianity."[42] I find myself forever figuring out what Beaudoin is working on nearly a decade after he has written about something, and in many ways this project is an extended version of his work in the chapter in the *Conundrums* book. He noted in that chapter, "As a field, we do not yet understand sufficiently how whiteness has been allied to the need to find practice theologically significant, although we have longstanding research from scholars of color and recent research from white scholars that can contribute to this understanding."[43] Like Beaudoin, in the pages that follow, my own "discoveries" of white supremacy in the field have often been fueled by the existing work of colleagues of color.

In a more specific sense, I am bringing seven key questions to each of the concepts heading the chapters at the heart of this book. I am writing this book as someone who has taught religious education and practical theology in the white Western Protestant Christian tradition for many years. In this book, I draw into question some of the bedrocks of those disciplines: a recent focus on practice as a framing metaphor for formation, a reliance on congregations and the institutional church as the primary vehicle for Christian life, a belief in education as a primarily benevolent endeavor, a search for transformation in our work, a framing of the formation of Christian leaders as our primary task, the commitment to propping up the life of the mainline church as the main role of my discipline in theological education, a demand for normative deployment of the Christian theological tradition, and a refusal to situate humans as but one species among many within the fragile ecosystem of the planet. For each of these concepts, I explore the following seven questions:

---

41 Goto, Taking On, xix.
42 Tom Beaudoin, "Why does practice matter theologically?" in ed. Mercer and Miller-McLemore, *Conundrums*, 10.
43 Beaudoin, "Why does practice matter theologically?," 11.

1. How and why is whatever I am questioning valued in existing literature in practical theology?
2. How is this concept or practice linked to the history and practice of whiteness/white supremacy?
3. Where are the deep origins of this practice linked to a specific ideology related to white supremacy in white Western Christianity?
4. What problem does this ideology create in the work of practical theology?
5. Why do these origins matter as they play out in the praxis of ministry or the doing of practical theology?
6. What do we fear we might lose if we give up this value or practice in the field? What is our attachment to it?
7. Where are postcolonial/decolonial scholars taking this concept in new directions in practical theology? What existing constructive moves towards a different future exist? What constructive decolonizing work has already been done related to this practice that we can learn from and build on?

While I don't take these questions on in the same order in each chapter, they have framed my reflections with each concept that I question chapter by chapter.

In one sense, starting with the academic disciplines I teach and their focus is a sideways approach to the enormity of the problems I have named thus far in this chapter. But in another sense, these are the contexts that form some element of the next generation of religious leaders in the traditions about which I am writing. This field is one of the places where I spend my life, and where I therefore regularly notice the diseased roots of these broader cultural logics and institutions impacting our work together. Consequently, I am writing about what I know within the contexts of theological education and using that to point towards how this plays out in the broader practice and ministries of white settler Christianity as it influences US dominant culture.

In writing about those traditions and disciplines and their complicity with white supremacy, I am writing about myself as well. Often, I am writing about friends in the academy that I respect and whose work has been important to me. I am writing about white Protestant Christian clergy and their work, many people that I taught and whom I love. That, too, is part of this work, and not one that I enjoy. But to look carefully at our work, at our professional advocacy for God and how it is filtered through the lens and habits learned in colonization is essential to questioning our faith.

4 "You'll Lose Your Faith"?

When I was headed off to college from my neighborhood United Methodist church in suburban Birmingham, Alabama, my beloved elders in the church questioned my decision to study psychology. "You'll lose your faith," they said. "Maybe study pre-law or education." Upon further questioning, it turned out that philosophy and religion were also on the suspect list of subjects whose further inquiry could endanger the faith they believed they had instilled in me as an adolescent. The fear of questioning, of critical inquiry and rigorous examination of beliefs, felt strange to me from these women that I knew loved and served God in their daily lives in powerful ways. What would happen if I learned more? At that point in history, this was not a broad-brushed stroke leveled against the "liberal elites" that control higher education and who wanted to indoctrinate young people as it is now. But that anti-intellectualism and fear that faithfulness required simple belief without questioning or complicating things too much was definitely present in that advice.

In recent years I have listened to a friend talk about the sacredness of small group time in the evenings with the white Catholic high school boys that he brings to Wyoming each summer to stay at the retreat center that my spouse runs. A dedicated English teacher, Greg gives three weeks of each summer (and a great deal more time in logistics and preparation) to bring rising juniors from Ohio to a retreat center in rural Wyoming on a sort of pilgrimage. The boys hike mountains and ride horses, play Euchre and Cadillac and any number of other games together, and at night they gather to share and affirm one another, to take off the masks they are used to wearing and seek to be real with one another as brothers under the fathership of God (their language, not mine). When asked to describe why he is so committed to this work, he says: "I love to see them learn that they can, that it is necessary, to speak from the heart. To hear a few of them say that maybe the person they are here is the person they want to be back home. To hear them say, unprompted, that they love each other. That time is sacred."

I am moved by Greg's testimony, and I am grateful for these young men to have the experience of vulnerability and trust with one another that critiques the form of toxic masculinity that they are more regularly formed into and that is critical to learning to love their neighbors. And part of me is so cynical. Retreat high. Uncritical use of the Christian tradition. Privileged white kids on a privileged Christian vacation. It is hard for me to remember the heart of Christian love, the basic humility and connection and trust that Greg is teaching these young men. Despite the fact that the women in my church thought there was something there to lose, I am not sure I ever had that kind of faith.

I have learned this before in teaching Sunday school with a friend who has survived the death of her four-month-old child from complications with heart surgery. Laurie's faith is immediate and urgent. She always asks the most poignant questions of the texts we read with the tweens we work with. She testifies to a God who is a real presence that helps us through life because she knows that to be true, and I feel my own attempts at faithfulness shriveled and lifeless in comparison. In 10 years of studying theology and 20 years of teaching it, what has happened to my own faith?

I think this feeling of lifelessness, this shriveling, is what we fear as the potential result in being honest about the white settler Christian tradition, about its involvement in oppression and injustice throughout history, about the way that it both forms and deforms those who are involved in it. Maybe paying attention to this will destroy our faith. And I feel the step of academic distance I use when I talk about faith and tradition. I am not talking about God like Laurie and Greg talk about God. I would not dare make claims so boldly about the maker of the universe, about the ground of all being, about the source of life abundant caring for me. I talk about the tradition, the humans that have practiced it, the wisdom and folly they have left behind in text, ritual practice, spiritual forms, habits of the heart and mind. But to rest fully in trusting belief in God? That is elusive to me because I know how complicit the avenues that brought me to my knowledge of God have been in histories of death-dealing and colonization.

Unlike the faithful women of my younger years warning me of the dangers of a psychology major, I believe that critical thinking and questioning of authoring claims are essential parts of responsible adult human behavior. I believe that there is value in maintaining humble separation between what I can trust to be true from the received tradition into which I have been formed and knowledge of some sort of absolute entity that is God. In the midst of this process, it is difficult to speak with directness about God, to continue to advocate for others to educate about this white Eurowestern Christian tradition that we have inherited.

I am not alone. The questioning of authority that is part and parcel of modern faith is well documented in contemporary literature about those so-called spiritual but not religious persons. The inability to trust anything outside oneself as an adult ... be it institutions, religious tenets, or even an elusive and transcendent God is not unique to me. However, I think we have to be careful when that questioning of authority stops by placing the locus of spiritual and religious authority internal to the individual. In other words, a person becomes the ultimate authority on what is true based on their individual judgment. Trusting an individual's judgment as authoritative is problematic because we know that implicit bias is real, that our intuition does not exist somehow outside of the shaping narratives and worldview into which we were born and that is embedded in our very language systems, and that what we think of as individuals are socially constructed selves within white dominant culture.

Thinking about the nature of authority has been helpful to me in understanding what it means to question faith. One of my teachers, practical theologian and ethicist James Fowler, noticed something about the shifts in the locus of authority over a lifetime of faith development in his work. In adolescence, Fowler noted, authority is given to those shared symbols of value and power that are identified as valuable by the people that we love and are in relationship with.[44] This is the kind of understanding of religious authority that Fowler found most common amongst even his adult research participants. For most people, their faith is a unique synthesis of the stories, myths, and symbols offered to them by their culture through their loved ones. When we are able to stay in sync with those forms of faith, we feel at home in the world.

However, for some persons, through processes of broadening experience and encounter with difference, those "home" symbols and forms of meaning-making that our loved ones shared with us lose their sense of authority through questioning and a re-settling of the locus of authority to the self.[45] Fowler's student and research collaborator Sharon Daloz Parks identified the profound nature of this questioning an experience of "shipwreck," drawing on the work of theologian H. Richard Niebuhr. An experience of disruption often related to experiences of loss, disappointments, challenges to their worldview, or deep questioning, shipwreck reshapes the meaning-making work of young adults. She notes: "If we do survive shipwreck—if we wash up on a new shore, perceiving more adequately how life really is—there is gladness. It is gladness that pervades one's whole being; there is a new sense of vitality, be it quiet or exuberant. Usually, however, there is more than relief in this gladness. There is transformation. We discover a new reality behind the loss."[46] In this transition out of conventional faith, individuals must decide what is meaningful and trustworthy through a process of consideration, rejection, affirmation, and intuition based in their life experiences and what seems valid to their internal sense of authority. Such a change is considered essential to moving from the submerged and embedded theologies we inherit into a more considered and intentional form of belief.

---

44   James W. Fowler, *Becoming Adult, Becoming Christian: Adult Development and Christian Faith*, rev. ed. (Jossey-Bass, 2000), 65.
45   Fowler, *Becoming Adult, Becoming Christian*, 71.
46   Sharon Daloz Parks, *Big Questions, Worthy Dreams: Mentoring Young Adults in their Search for Meaning, Purpose, and Faith* (Jossey-Bass, 2000), 29.

For many people, this new and powerful sense of individual judgment feels like maturity, like throwing off the limited narratives of superstition and bias from our elders and coming into our own voice and full judgment. This is, perhaps, the kind of faith that many who eschew institutional religion and trust in their own capacity to sort through many spiritual and cultural traditions to find what is meaningful for them hold. They are able, in the name of a Colorado media company disseminating spiritual wisdom for many years, to understand what Sounds True.[47]

However, in his philosophical claims about maturity of faith, Fowler did not consider this moment or internalizing authority and standing critically and reflectively in relationship to the tradition the final stage. He theorized that a further state of faith development came when we realize through our own failures that our sense of internal authority is not absolute. Through the metaphors of "second naivete" and the "second rise of the symbol" from Ricouer, Fowler believed that a further stage of faith development involved the recognition that we are authored by powers greater than us at work, that the symbols and habits of meaning-making that we engage create us as much as we create them, that we are reliant on them for our meaning-making in ways we cannot control even while they are not the only ultimate Truth.[48] We recognize that we have declared true and right based on our own intuitions and judgments may be embedded in a social formation that we do not always recognize, just as we come to recognize that marketers and logarithms can predict our commitments, buying decisions, and which echo chambers we will appreciate based on where we live and who we are around. What seems like our decisions, our judgment, our intuition, is more driven by the power of those shared narratives and symbols than we previously thought. While Fowler seems to have found the grounding of this second naivete in the reality of the God of all being in a way that was beautiful, self-correcting, and true, I often think about how it can also be in shared centers of value and power, like those that mistook whiteness for salvation, that are harmful, damaging, and misguided. And yet, knowing that makes them no less formative of our very selves in sneaky, persistent, and self-deceptive ways.

This realization feels connected to the idea of questioning our faith in practice to me. Fowler's work may have been more culturally-bound and individually-oriented than he initially realized, and his hopefulness about how the rise of second naivete was a positive movement toward a universalizing

---

47 https://www.soundstrue.com/.
48 Fowler, *Becoming Adult, Becoming Christian*, 73.

faith is not something I share.[49] For white settler Christianity, maybe it is a marker of mature faith to stop believing that we make all the choices about what is authoritative to us, about which symbols of meaning, value, and power we believe to be true. Instead, we might acknowledge that they are deeply flawed and limited and grounded in an extractive worldview that has caused a great deal of damage in the world, and yet that they are powerful and constitutive in creating us. Our sense of individual control and discernment is less stable that we might have thought, our beliefs in individualism, exceptionalism, and uniqueness are perhaps faulty. We live entangled in a worldview committed to whiteness with deep roots in colonial Christianity.

As I advocate for a faith that is fully aware of its contradictions and inherent evil in the tradition in which it is shaped, the question arises: How are you loyal to someone or something you question? What does it mean to have faith in something that you cannot fully trust? One response might be that the difference between "faith" and "knowledge" is that faith requires an element of doubt and uncertainty. To cite the biblical text:

> [1]Now faith is the assurance of things hoped for, the conviction of things not seen. [2]Indeed, by faith our ancestors received approval. [3]By faith we understand that the worlds were prepared by the word of God, so that what is seen was made from things that are not visible.[50]

Faith requires that element of the unseen, the invisible, the things hoped for but not yet received. The kind of faith that demands certainty, clarity, and control lies in values of whiteness in late capitalism, not the assurance that exists in the midst of uncertainty that this passage describes. This faith is a much more ambivalent experience resting in hope rather than certainty.

On a deeper ideological note, the demand for absolute purity and perfection in our sense of what is right and true is a value linked to white supremacy. The need for one's own beliefs to be recognized as unassailably correct arose historically from being in a minority position (think the few European-descended conquistadors, colonizers, or slaveowners trying to control much larger populations of local residents with entirely different worldviews) and declaring that your worth is greater because of your God-ordained destiny, your blood purity, your civilized ways, your superiority, the power of the church articulated through the Doctrine of Discovery. Demands that the Bible must be

---

49 Fowler, *Becoming Adult, Becoming Christian*, 75.
50 Heb. 11:1–3 (NRSV).

inerrant to be at all valuable,[51] that religious authorities must be obeyed and not questioned to be respected, that the Church is a sacrament that reveals God in its human institutional form are all harmful notions about religious traditions based in purity and control thinking. They are not faithful in containing divine mysteries beyond what can be understood, they are steeped in arrogance and notions of superiority that are a part of colonial thinking.

5 How to Read This Book

Over the years of teaching in a seminary setting, I have come to recognize that questioning our faith, recognizing the limitations and failures of what we stand on, takes courage. There is real loss in the sense of being "at home" in the traditions of our people, or certainly within our own intuitions and individual judgments about what is true and right and good. Living in this state of questioning that which forms us is difficult, particularly if we hope not to slide into the habits of "cultured despisers," but to face up to the reality of the devastation wrought by what we were taught was beautiful and of God.

The process of writing this book has led me to combine the questioning and confessional modes of my own embodied experience of working in practical theology with more analytical literature review and conceptual work within the field of practical theology. Early readers of the manuscript were at times confused by my switching back and forth between my more personal forms of reflection and the more formal voice I was taught to use in academic writing as a graduate student. Early in my dissertation writing, my advisor once said to me that he was surprised by how forceful and clear my voice was in writing, noting that it did not match my self-presentation in the classroom or everyday interactions. This is not surprising as someone who was socialized as a white woman in the United States, where being accommodating and deferential was built into my body in a way that clashed with the linear and confident argumentation of white professional norms of academic writing. In my younger female body, I learned to draw on humor, empathy, honesty, and humility as part of my teaching voice and presence. He encouraged me to adapt that written voice to my teaching setting to better establish my authority

---

51 For an interesting take on biblical inerrancy as a handmaiden to white Christian patriarchal supremacy, see Stephen Young, "Biblical Inerrancy's Long History as an Evangelical Activist for White Patriarchy," *Religion Dispatches*, February 8, 2022. https://religiondispatches.org/biblical-inerrancys-long-history-as-an-evangelical-activist-for-white-patriarchy/.

in the classroom. Part of the journey of my now quarter-century of experience in writing and in teaching is to bring together the parts of my personal life that are emotional, grounded in embodied experience, at times confident in working with materials, at times unsure and conflicted, into my academic writing voice as well. I feel like that blend of the personal and the analytical captures the wrestling I have done with the ideas of this text, trying to show the reader with examples of what I am talking about in both daily experience and in the literature of the field.

Recently my middle school son was engaging in a unit on gentrification in his social studies class, an impressive outcome of a group of public-school teachers learning about racism and how it is expressed in systemic forms and committing to teach their students about these institutionalized forms of oppression. He shared indignantly during the ride home about the suffering and dislocation caused by gentrification, telling stories about how this plays out and how it impacted working people who lost homes because of their inability to pay taxes and how it destroyed the cultural vibrancy of certain neighborhoods in Denver.

As I drove and listened gratefully to his learning about this unjust impact of efforts in what are normatively lauded policies of "economic development" and "neighborhood improvement," I had to make a choice as his parent. I wanted him to continue down the path of imagining the world through the eyes of those who are most economically vulnerable and whose cultures and communities are destroyed in the name of capitalistic improvements. I also needed him to know that our own home purchase in Denver was possible because of the gentrification we had benefitted from in our neighborhood in Decatur, Georgia (a city within the bounds of Atlanta). The story I told him went something like this: When I was in graduate school and my husband was working in urban ministry for minimum wage, we used money given as wedding gifts to purchase one of the only homes we could afford to purchase in metro Atlanta. This burned out and partially renovated small 1918 Craftsman bungalow was in a neighborhood that had been redlined and had experienced white flight forty years earlier. We lived in a neighborhood that had been economically depressed for decades, that was located in a food desert with the nearest grocery store five miles away, and that had an active gang and police presence. Our neighbors two doors down dealt in weapons and cocaine off their front porch on warm days when it was too hot to be in their unairconditioned home.

What we didn't know when we bought the house was that our white bodies, along with those of a few other couples who had moved into the neighborhood, signaled that the neighborhood was not off-limits to potential white home buyers but "transitional," and therefore a good investment for eager young professionals who were beginning to reverse white flight with urban infill at the turn of the new century. We watched in frustration as our elderly African-American neighbors were harassed by would-be house flippers, wanting to buy their paid-off homes at under market value to fix them up and sell them to people like us, often using scare tactics about rising property taxes and disrespectful and disdainful remarks about the disrepair and unsightliness of their homes. One by one most of our neighbors sold their homes, and the neighborhood gentrified. Our home sold for two and a half times what we bought it for after only a five-year period. I did not know the term "gentrification" at that point in my life, but I watched it play out in real time and benefitted greatly from it.

So, when Ben came home from school outraged at the injustice of gentrification, it was my job as his parent to tell him that the home he had lived in his whole life was purchased with the spoils of the linked historical practices of red-lining and gentrification. We discussed the power of our white bodies to impart literal economic value in a racist housing market. As a parent, that conversation felt terrible and disillusioning and painful to share with my son. I linked the story of our involvement in gentrification with the immense economic and social privilege that is afforded to those of us who have white skin. Whether we intended to, the very presence of our bodies in a neighborhood caused property values to rise, in a sick reversal of the drop in property values that African American families experienced when they moved into the same neighborhoods nearly half a century before.

My commitment to acknowledging the existence of systemic racism and economic disadvantage built into US culture meant that I pulled the rug out from beneath my son's position as one who was able to simply be appalled at the injustice he had learned about. I asked him to also take responsibility as one who had benefitted greatly from those same circumstances, to understand himself as being on the oppressor's side in the story of injustice he had learned that day, to live in the complex position of being the very thing that he hated, to borrow a phrase from the apostle Paul. This is not a heroic tale of justice. We did not redistribute the monies we gained from gentrification to our neighbors who were pressured into selling their homes or invest them in affordable housing and continue to struggle with our own situation. This moment of truth telling was, in honest terms, the least I could do. To acknowledge that our financial stability as a family was predicated on the process that he found abhorrent and to ask that he carry that responsibility of that knowledge alongside his newfound sense of the injustice of it was part of understanding how the social hierarchies of racial injustice work.

In many ways, the kind of conversation I had with my son is central to the primary task of this book. It is a work of deep listening, confession, and analysis, a project that blends the personal, the political, and the scholarly. I am trying to take responsibility for the ways that the tradition I inherited and have worked within is based on the spoils of generational injustice and harm to other peoples and the earth. If you are ready to put this book down, I get it. I have been putting down writing it for years. It is not easy to live with this level of questioning and dismantling as a voluntary practice. But if we are to have a chance to get out of the way and to learn of another way of living together that is not based in the quiet notion that while everyone is equal in the sight of God, whiteness is just a better way to go about being human, this is essential work.

CHAPTER 2

Questioning Practice

In a recent summer, I visited significant cultural sites on the Wind River Reservation in Riverton and Ft. Washakie, Wyoming. This reservation is a geographic neighbor to Ring Lake Ranch, an ecumenical retreat center that my spouse directs near Dubois, Wyoming. The retreat center sits on land that was traditionally significant to the Tukadeka (Sheepeater) or Mountain Shoshone peoples, ancestors to some members of the Eastern Shoshone nation that now inhabit Ft. Washakie. Their spiritual practices left traces by the petroglyphs they etched into the rocks by the lake on which the retreat center sits. This trip to the reservation was part of a white Christian institution trying to be accountable to the intertwining of its heritage with the people from whom the land on which it is located was taken, and we spent the day learning more about the history of the reservation, the mission and fort established in the nineteenth century, and the two mission boarding schools that were dominant institutions for many years within its borders.

The educator who helped us interpret these sites, Fred Nichol, was at the time the spouse of a member of the Board of Trustees of the retreat center. As we visited St. Stephen's Mission (originally Jesuit) and the St. Stephen's Indian School on the grounds, Mr. Nichol talked about how he could speak some of the Shoshone language because of his own work on the reservation as a social worker and educator, but that he hadn't grown up with the language. His father had been forbidden to learn the language because of his grandmother's brutal treatment when she spoke her mother tongue in the Christian boarding schools she had been forced to attend.

I have studied and taught the legacy of Christian boarding schools and their participation in cultural genocide and the generational trauma that they created for nearly two decades of my teaching career. What was startling to me, and shouldn't have been, was the immediacy of the experience to my friend. It was his grandmother who experienced the brutality of Christian education firsthand, and he and his father directly experienced the erasure of culture and generational wisdom that these schools had wrought. For Mr. Nichol, his own experience of community, culture, and identity contained painful gaps because of what I unconsciously considered an historic practice of abduction and cultural erasure of young Indian children in the name of Christian progress and civilizing influence rather than a present-day ongoing cultural genocide.

The Institute of Tribal Learning at Central Wyoming Community College that we visited in Riverton, Wyoming, has a display dedicated to the loss of lives of local children and adolescents to the Carlisle boarding school in Pennsylvania. The display explains that the rate of death and disappearance of native American children from the Wind River Reservation sent to the Carlisle Industrial Indian School in Pennsylvania was higher than the death rate of Jewish people sent to the Nazi concentration camp in Auschwitz.[1] Either "lost" through permanent indentured service to the families they were loaned out to for forced labor, dead from malnourishment and mistreatment, or exposure to disease, the children never came back to the reservation once they were forcibly taken in a Christian practice of civilizing "improvement." As Mr. Nichol would explain the situation when asked about how they had died, he said simply, "Well, they died of broken hearts, didn't they, after being separated from everything and everyone they had known and loved?" Members of the local community are working to identify and return the remains of their children to the community to this day.

This legacy is almost invisible in the teaching of US history in public schools, although recent uncovering of mass unmarked graves at Canadian boarding schools is beginning to draw at least fleeting cultural attention to these histories. In listening to Mr. Nichol, I was reminded that to the people of long memories to whom this happened, it is not historical trauma or even generational trauma, it is present trauma, wrought by Christian practices of education and evangelization, in the case of Wind River Reservation, sponsored by both the Episcopalian and Roman Catholic churches in partnership with the US government.

In listening to Mr. Nichol's story, the need to teach adequately about the ambivalence of Christian religious practice as transmitting both wisdom and destruction came home to me once again. This horrifying story of cultural destruction and genocide was based in a Christian practice of evangelization and education meant to improve the American continent by bringing the "light of Christianity" and a "civilizing influence" to every inch of its land and its peoples. And yet, when I read the literature in practical theology related to formational practice, I rarely see attention given to this kind of Christian

---

1   The Carlisle Industrial Indian School was the first boarding school established by the US government designed to remove children from their homes on reservations and enact cultural genocide on students, founded in 1879 by Lieutenant Richard Henry Pratt. At the time of its founding, the position of the founder who hoped to "kill the Indian, but not the man" was considered more enlightened than campaigns at the time to eradicate indigenous persons altogether.

practice.² Instead, Christian practice is often represented as a beneficent good that should be cultivated to enliven the church.

I had actually written very briefly about the different ways that practice is understood in practical theology several years ago: "Whereas virtue-based analyses of practice tend to focus on their value as a site of formative wisdom in the norms and virtues of a social tradition, political analysis of practices also focus on the manner in which everyday practices may often unknowingly replicate or reproduce unequal distributions of resources, differential valuing of persons and experiences, and oppressive 'common sense' understandings of the world."³ The goal of this chapter is to briefly trace these competing traditions of understanding "practice" in social science and philosophy and to advocate for an understanding of formational practice in white Western Christianity that takes seriously our history of domination and colonization, such as that represented in the practice of evangelization and "education" of American Indian persons. This philosophical reflection is an attempt to draw our attention to how the ways in which we talk about practice in the fields of religious education and practical theology may erase the history of, and continued potential for, white domination in Christian practice.

Primarily, my concern is that the ways we talk about practice in the fields of practical theology and religious education softens the legacy of embodied control and links to dominating power that can be related to practice, perhaps as a part of a broader apologetic function of the two fields to support the work of the church. This recognition of the ambivalence of practice is particularly important for dominant culture Christians, whose historical heritage includes both oppressive and virtuous practice linked through the pedagogical and formational work of the church in colonizing settings. How might one theorize and engage in Christian formational practice without a sense of confidence that it is entirely beneficent, thereby unlearning white pedagogical habits of dominance?

1 Practice and the Transmission of Virtue

The timing of the contemporary turn to practice in mainline U.S. Protestantism aligns with the desire to recapture the moral and cultural influence

---

2 Lauren Winner's book *The Dangers of Christian Practice: On Wayward Gifts, Characteristic Damage, and Sin* (Yale University Press, 2018) is a notable exception to this statement within the field of spirituality, and I will explore it further in this chapter.

3 Katherine Turpin, "Liberationist Practical Theology," in *Opening the Field of Practical Theology*, eds. Kathleen A. Cahalan and Gordon S. Mikoski (Rowman & Littlefield, 2014), 157–58.

and vitality of the white church in a time of great demographic change and institutional decline. The discourse of practice in faith formational literature truly picked up steam in the late 1990's and the first decade of the 21st century. In educational and management literature the idea of "best practices" became a strategy for capturing easily replicable insights that could be scaled up as a way of improving efficacy across a large organization or even a field of business. Cameron, et al, note how this understanding of "best practice" still haunts the field of practical theology:

> A broader cultural problem is a common understanding of research as seeking 'best practice' which is difficult to challenge. Drawing analogies from health sciences there is a view that there is one best way to do something and this can be learned by copying people with the most successful practice and recording it in a protocol. This suggests that work and context are detachable, something which workers in faith-based agencies can struggle with as so much of what they do arises from their context.[4]

I still receive many requests to provide these "best practices" in religious education when I am asked to speak in churches or write for practitioners. As someone seen as practical or pragmatic, I should be able to come with a couple of good ideas that will enliven the ministry of the congregation. However, the "turn to practice" in the world of religious education, spiritual formation, and practical theology predominantly involved a shift in strategies of formation to improve the vitality of the (primarily white mainline and emergent/postevangelical) church through voluntary, embodied commitment to reclaimed and often recontextualized traditional practices of the church. It is that kind of practice that we are focused on in this chapter.

In the field of religious education, various approaches to faith formation have emerged as different theoretical conversation partners engaged scholars in the field. Developmental literature in psychology brought age-level developmentally appropriate standardized curriculum to be delivered in the schooling model, attention to anthropology brought a socialization model that involved rich participation in communities of faith, and hermeneutical theory and liberative pedagogy brought a shared praxis model with groups of believers making sense of their world and working together towards liberation

---

4   Cameron, Helen, Deborah Bhatti, Catherine Duce, James Sweeney, and Clare Watkins, *Talking About God in Practice: Theological Action Research and Practical Theology* (SCM Press, 2010), 35.

and vocational discernment.⁵ More recently a "revitalizing Christian practice" discourse as a model for faith formation emerged in conversation with neo-Aristotelian philosophies of practice. With generous funding from the Lilly Endowment, Inc., under the leadership of Craig Dykstra, and through collaborative scholarship organized by Dorothy Bass at the Valparaiso Institute, this understanding of Christianity as a way of life learned through intentional participation in historic practices of Christianity was articulated in several collaborative projects in practical theology and faith formation: Dorothy Bass, ed., *Practicing Our Faith*, Bass and Richter, eds. *Way to Live*, Bass and Dykstra, eds. *For Life Abundant*, and Volf and Bass, eds. *Practicing Theology*.⁶ Additionally, attention to practices was popularized and disseminated widely to historically white mainline and progressive evangelical churches through the written work and speaking engagements of Diana Butler Bass⁷ and Brian McLaren.⁸ The idea of participating in intentional individual and communal practice gained traction as a way of thinking about how people come to be more Christian in their lives in a time when the institutional church's power to form faithful disciples through socialization was waning. As Gordon Mikoski and Kathleen Cahalan note, "Whether in more restricted (e.g., practices of hospitality) or more expansive notions of practice (e.g., the practice of discipleship), many practical theologians, in recent decades, have emphasized the importance of understanding and proposing specifically religious practices for individuals and communities."⁹

There are many theories for why this turn to practice in faith formational literature. One element is surely as a corrective to the overly cognitive and doctrinal understandings of faith that were a legacy of white western Protestantism, sometimes articulated in terms of bridging the theory/practice divide

---

5   Thomas H. Groome, *Sharing Faith Sharing Faith: A Comprehensive Approach to Religious Education and Pastoral Ministry: The Way of Shared Praxis*, 1st ed. (HarperSanFrancisco, 1991); Anne E. Streaty Wimberly, *Soul Stories: African American Christian Education*, rev ed. (Abingdon Press, 2005).
6   See Dorothy C. Bass, ed., *Practicing Our Faith: A Way of Life for a Searching People* (Jossey-Bass, 1996); Dorothy Bass and Don C. Richter, eds., *Way to Live: Christian Practices for Teens* (Upper Room, 2002). Dorothy C. Bass and Craig Dykstra, eds., *For Life Abundant: Practical Theology, Theological Education, and Christian Ministry* (Eerdmans, 2008); Miroslav Volf and Dorothy Bass, *Practicing Theolog: Beliefs and Practices in Christian Life* (Eerdmans, 2001).
7   Since Diana Butler Bass and Dorothy Bass share a surname, I will refer to them respectively as Butler Bass and Bass throughout this chapter to maintain a distinction between them.
8   Particularly related to Diana Butler Bass, *Christianity for the Rest of Us: How the Neighborhood Church is Transforming the Faith* (HarperOne, 2006) and Brian McLaren, *Finding Our Way Again: The Return of the Ancient Practices* (Thomas Nelson, 2008).
9   Cahalan and Mikoski, "Introduction," *Opening the Field*, 2.

or in recognizing the "wisdom" or "intelligence" of embodied practice and the value of *phronesis*. Emerging attention to ritual studies, feminist and womanist theology's attention to embodiment, and other theological movements created a sense that there was more to the experience of faith than cognitive assent to doctrines. The perhaps overzealous embrace of modernity and rationality in many historically white Protestant denominations left a sense of emotional disconnect and a dissatisfaction with the lack of a sense of transcendence and connection with mystery. While their Jewish and Roman Catholic counterparts held a deeper notion of what it meant to be "observant" of the religious practices of their traditions, this had been lost in mainline Protestantism, which was perceived to be part of the loss of the vitality of these communities. A route to revitalization for the white mainline church and individual faith lives might be through "an intentional and reflexive engagement with Christian tradition as embodied within the practices of faith, with the goal of knowing God."[10]

The hopeful trajectory of attention to practice was represented by the very popular book in US mainline circles by Diana Butler Bass, *Christianity for the Rest of Us*, in which she did ethnographic research with mainline congregations that were bucking the trend of decline, often doing so through a renewed focus on practice: "All the congregations have found new vitality through an intentional and transformative engagement with Christian tradition as embodied in faith practices. Typically, they have rediscovered the riches of the Christian past and practice simple, but profound, things like discernment, hospitality, testimony, contemplation, and justice."[11] Butler Bass focuses on practices as "signposts to let us know that we are heading toward beauty, goodness, and truthfulness ... the things they do together in community that form them in God's love for the world."[12] She names several key features that allow practices to function in a time when the authority of the church was waning: "Practices require commitment (they are 'high demand'), but that commitment is typically internally and subjectively driven and not external or authoritarian."[13] She notes that a focus on practice rather than doctrinal purity "elevates the sense of intentionality throughout the congregation that leads to greater vitality and spiritual depth."[14] Practices are intentional, embodied, elicit internal authority, and support congregational vitality.

---

10   Butler Bass, *Christianity for the Rest of Us*, 305.
11   Butler Bass, *Christianity for the Rest of Us*, 7.
12   Butler Bass, *Christianity for the Rest of Us*, 11.
13   Butler Bass, *Christianity for the Rest of Us*, 306.
14   Butler Bass, *Christianity for the Rest of Us*, 306.

In the study, the congregations Butler Bass spoke with focused on their engagement with intentional practices framed in a largely positive way: "The practices that predominated discussion were: worship, hospitality, discernment, theological reflection, healing, forming diverse communities, testimony, and contemplative devotional disciplines."[15] She warns about naïve reclamation of history in the text: "Remixing the past by taking out the unpleasant bits is a dangerous thing" and expresses frustration with the evangelical version of America's Christian identity as "ignoring the fact that American Christians committed wholesale evils like slavery, the genocide of native peoples, persecution of non-Protestants, racism, and violence against women and children."[16] However, she does not connect her advocacy of practice with the idea that these historic evils might have themselves been perpetuated through intentional Christian practice.

Another issue of this moment in history was the loss of cultural dominance of white Protestants in the US context. This sense of loss comes through in Butler Bass's chapter "The Vanished Village." Whereas once the white Protestant churches had had a trifecta of formation through their control of the culture in home, church, and school,[17] the changes wrought by changes in immigration patterns and the resulting increase of more diverse racial and religious populations, secularization in schools, and the deep cultural challenges of changing family structures to the historic "mainline" in the late 60's and 70's had begun to demonstrate the loss of cultural dominance to white Protestants. Popular Christian authors in the 80's and 90's such as Stanley Hauerwas and William Willimon began to speak of post-Christendom, sometimes with the hope that this change might loosen the ties between empire and church, but also with a clear sense of loss and concern for the need to double down on formation to stop the hemorrhaging of members in those Protestant communities.[18] White historically mainline Protestants could no longer assume that the vague cultural air was going to do the work of religious formation for them because they were losing their dominant position. And they began to take embodied practice seriously as a means of engaging that religious formation more effectively with the decrease of affiliation with local communities and the resulting

---

15   Butler Bass, *Christianity for the Rest of Us*, 306.
16   Butler Bass, *Christianity for the Rest of Us*, 31.
17   Charles R. Foster, *Educating Congregations: The Future of Christian Education* (Abingdon, 1994), 37.
18   Stanley Hauerwas and William H. Willimon, *Resident Aliens: A Provocative Christian Assessment of Culture and Ministry for People Who Know that Something Is Wrong* (Abingdon, 1989).

socialization into the faith. This historical coincidence should raise questions about whether a desire to promote connection with God or a desire to regain cultural authority are the central motivating force of the turn to practice. Perhaps for historically white settler Christian traditions, the two are difficult to disentangle.

A primary philosophical understanding of religious practice draws on the neo-Aristotelian work of Alasdair MacIntyre, who understands practice as a communally based, self-critiquing transmitter of wisdom across generations. Practical theologian Don Richter claims, "The breakthrough book in this regard—that catalyzed rich conversation and a significant body of literature—was Alasdair MacIntyre's *After Virtue*."[19] Richter goes on to recount the definition of practice found in that work that has animated a great deal of research into Christian practices in the last two decades:

> By a 'practice' I am going to mean any coherent and complex form of socially established cooperative human activity through which good internal to that form of activity are realized in the course of trying to achieve those standards of excellence which are appropriate to, and partially definitive of, that form of activity, with the result that human powers to achieve excellence, and human conceptions of the ends and goods involved, are systematically extended.[20]

For many working with the idea of practice in the fields of religious education and practical theology, this quote is the primary grounding that they take from MacIntyre, often linking it to his explanation with playing sports and chess, and they walk through the various elements necessary to make a practice a good practice before they turn to the practice they are describing.

In full disclosure, I was a part of this movement to think about intentional, embodied practice in community rather than doctrinal instruction or communal socialization as a key model for education. In fact, Richter quotes my first book as an example of intentional practice in religious community that runs counter to social norms, in the case of that book, those practices embodied in consumer culture.[21] In a time when socialization into the Christian faith seemed less possible in church communities because of decreasing rates of

---

19 Richter, "Religious Practices in Practical Theology," in ed. Mikoski and Cahalan, *Opening the Field*, 204.
20 Alasdair MacIntyre, *After Virtue*, 3rd ed. (Notre Dame, 2007), 187.
21 Katherine Turpin, *Branded: Adolescents Converting from Consumer Faith* (Pilgrim Press, 2006).

participation, raising the notion of intentional spiritual practice steeped in the tradition became an attractive way of talking about faith formation and re-enlivening congregations in the face of deep formation into other value systems of late capitalism.

Part of this understanding of practice is that engaging in it shapes the character of persons, largely in virtuous ways, with the potential to allow for more depth of engagement with God. Particularly in the literature about theological education, there is much talk of the importance of forming a *habitus* as a part of doing practical theology. The version of *habitus* that it forms is perhaps most clearly articulated by Edward Farley, when he talks about "theology as *habitus*"—"a disposition, power, and act of the soul itself. And some of the writers argued that the primary character of this disposition (habit) was wisdom. The genre of theology is, therefore, an existential, personal act and relation of the human self, namely, wisdom."[22] In other places, Farley shorthands a definition of habitus as "a cognitively disposed posture that attends salvation, a knowledge of the self-disclosing God. As such, it is for the sake of God, but, specifically, for God's appointed salvific end of the human being."[23] Terry Veling uses a similar understanding of habitus, which he defines as "a disposition of the mind and heart from which our actions flow naturally, or, if you like, 'according to the Spirit' dwelling within us."[24] *Habitus* is a cultivated disposition of the heart and mind so that that attention naturally flows to God's presence and cultivates virtuous action.

Richard Osmer points to key elements of MacIntyre that are attractive to those scholars who participate in what he calls "The Neo-Aristotelian Trajectory of Practical Theology":

> MacIntyre seeks to recover Aristotle's theory of virtue and character, arguing that virtues are acquired through participation in the practices and moral vision of particular religious and moral communities. He is critical of modernity, for he believes it has eroded the capacity of such communities to shape the character of their members and fostered an individualistic, utilitarian moral outlook.[25]

---

22 Edward Farley, *Practicing Gospel* (Westminster John Knox, 2003), 16.
23 Farley, *Practicing Gospel*, 19.
24 Terry A. Veling, *Practical Theology: On Earth as It Is in Heaven* (Orbis Books, 2005), 16. Christopher Brittain humorously challenges the notion of the importance of habitus in theological education by asking "Can A Theology Student Be an Evil Genius?: On the Concept of Habitus in Theological Education," *Toronto Journal of Theology*, 2009, 141–54.
25 Osmer, "Empirical Practical Theology," *Opening the Field*, 69.

One can see how the shared frustration with MacIntyre over the erosion of communities capable of shaping the character of their members might resonate with leaders of white Western Christianity in a period where their churches are declining precipitously in membership and cultural prominence. The call for the renewal of communities of character is a key element of the work of virtue ethics, and this kind of thinking resonated with religious educators who recognized the role of formative communities in their own educational efforts.

The counter to this decline in the power of formative communities becomes imagined in terms of creating vibrant communities of practice that can shape *habitus* through serious engagement with religious practices, vibrant leaders through theological education focused on practices, and vibrant personal spirituality that leads to greater connection with God. For Dykstra, the formative power of practices ultimately rests in God's beneficent action: "While human achievement is valued in the Christian story, it has a different place and meaning. The human task is not fundamentally mastery. It is the right use of gifts graciously bestowed by a loving God for the sake of the good that God intends—*and ultimately assures* (emphasis original)."[26] Dykstra places great confidence in the involvement of God in religious practice, arguing that a gracious and loving God ultimately assures the good that God intends in practice will come to fruition. He grounds this belief in a powerful Christian theological claim about the goodness of God. Dykstra envisions this as a check on the tendency toward human mastery and control in practice (read here a Protestant aversion to the notion of salvation through works righteousness), and an assurance that God's presence in the practice will put us on the right track.

My concern with framing religious practice in such an intentional and positive way, primarily as a source of virtue and connection with God that is backed up by the gracious intervention of God to ensure positive outcomes, is that this framing conceptually aligns the work of the white mainline churches as synonymous with religious practice that is grounded in the goodness of God. "We white people are good people who offer good things that you should imitate" is dangerously close to the legacy of white supremacy and civilizing uplift ideologies at work in the boarding school story with which I began this chapter.

Christian practice has an ambivalent legacy. Scholars who have looked deeply into particular historic practices in Christianity with the goal of

---

26　Craig Dykstra, *Growing in the Life of Faith: Education and Christian Practices* (Geneva Press, 1999), 76.

reclaiming them for their positive formation of virtue, such as the practice of welcoming strangers as Christ described by Christine Pohl in her work on the practice of hospitality, discover this ambiguity of virtue and evil embedded within them. Pohl wisely indicates that we should be careful in how we talk about the "recovery" of practice: "A wholesale, indiscriminate recovery of any ancient practice is neither possible nor desirable. Certain aspects of the Christian tradition of hospitality are deeply disturbing. Only honest and serious attention to the failures, omissions, and tragedies in the story will allow us to make use of its strengths."[27] These failures, omissions, and tragedies are evident in other religious practices, like institutional secrecy about clergy sexual abuse in order to protect the holy image of clerical authority, which clearly have a harmful legacy that we would hesitate to claim as God's gracious self-giving action made manifest.

The way that the virtues-based Christian practices discourse might deal with this concern about the ambivalent legacy of practice is to say that some practices occur in communal settings, linked to founding narratives, seeking standards of excellence, with an internally formed wisdom seeking salvation, and others do not. As Bass notes her and Dykstra's normative criteria for what makes a particular practice Christian, "It has seemed to us, therefore, that to be called 'Christian' a practice must pursue a good beyond itself, responding to and embodying the self-giving dynamics of God's own creating, redeeming, and sustaining grace."[28] But this distinction that some practices are wholly Christian and implicitly benevolent while others are not seems on shaky ground. The institutional practice of protecting clergy authority through moving abusive priests and pastors within the Roman Catholic Church was a "coherent and complex form of socially established cooperative human activity" that sought a good beyond itself in maintaining the capacity for people to view clerical leaders in their ritual roles as largely holy and not pedophilic, for the good of the community who would be led by those priests as a representative of Christ. However, we know that this practice, though maintained for decades, did not contribute to the good of community but rather caused great harm to the survivors and families of the abuse of religious leaders. Yet, I think that we can give evidence to the enduring and coordinated state of this behavior as a Christian religious practice. Invoking God does not eliminate the possibility that Christian practices may be evil.

---

27 Christine D. Pohl, *Making Room: Recovering Hospitality as a Christian Tradition* (Eerdmans, 1999), 9.
28 Bass, *For Life Abundant*, 31.

To be fair, Bass, like Pohl, was aware that practices could go awry. She notes, "Because communities engage in these practices forever imperfectly—faltering, forgetting, even falling into gross distortions—theological discernment, repentance, and renewal are necessary dimensions of each practice and of the Christian life as a whole."[29] Bass also recognized that in trying to give accounts of various practices, "it is easy to idealize Christian practices and the way of life they comprise, making them seem more smooth and coherent than they actually are in the midst of everyday conditions."[30] She nevertheless argues that embracing such practices "humbly yet boldly" is how people are helped to make decisions about "what to do next within the actual complexities of contemporary society."[31] Even more strongly, Bass and Dykstra conclude the book with the following endorsement of practices: "Like faithful ministry and discipleship, practical theology pursues the telos of a life-giving way of life in awareness that the means employed in doing so—the practices of faith, including the arts of ministry—are not merely tools. Rather, they are both the goal and the path of the Christian life."[32] In this moment we see the full embrace of embodied Christian practice as not only the way to walk in a Christian way, but even more strongly, as the final destination of Christian life.

2 Practice and Symbolic Violence

Another important set of theories of practice less commonly deployed in practical theology and religious education comes from social philosophers who also understand practice as socially based, institutionalized forms of behavior that inform the construction of selves through the formation of habitus. However, these understandings of practice are more concerned with how practice reiterates domination across generations through the disciplining of bodies in institutional structure and function (as in the work of Michel Foucault), forming habitus that aligns with the interests of those with the most capital (as in the work of Pierre Bourdieu), and the demand that one performs an embodied identity recognizable within the norms of the community (as in the work of Judith Butler).[33] For the purposes of this chapter and to provide a strong con-

---

29 Bass, *For Life Abundant*, 29.
30 Bass, *For Life Abundant*, 34.
31 Bass, *For Life Abundant*, 34.
32 Bass and Dykstra, "In Anticipation," in *For Life Abundant*, 358.
33 Pierre Bourdieu, *Outline of a Theory of Practice* (Cambridge, 1977); Michel Foucault, *Discipline and Punish*, 2nd ed. (Vintage, 1995); Judith Butler, *Giving an Account of Oneself* (Fordham, 2005).

trast to the ideas of MacIntyre, I will focus on the work of French sociologist Pierre Bourdieu.

Where MacIntyre understands practice as passing down virtue through socially organized behavior, Bourdieu conceptualizes practice as maintaining structures of domination and forming people to serve the values of dominant culture even against their own best interests, often without their noticing or questioning it. Bourdieu understood people as active agents deeply formed within a particular sector of the world, what he calls not communities of practice but "social space," "field," or "fields of power."[34] In these socially organized spaces, individuals become:

> endowed with a *practical sense*, that is, an acquired system of preferences, of principles of vision and division (what is usually called taste), and also a system of durable cognitive structures (which are essentially the product of the internalization of objective structures) and of schemes of action which orient the perception of the situation and the appropriate response. The habitus is this kind of practical sense for what is to be done in a given situation—what is called in sport a 'feel' for the game.[35]

The habitus[36] works for people in the way other philosophies or psychological understandings might describe the conscience or intuition, built through intimate relationships with caregivers or personal experience throughout a lifetime. For Bourdieu, this intuition is not an individually constructed phenomenon or endowed by God as a part of human nature but rather a "a socialized body, a structured body, a body which has incorporated the immanent structures of a world or of a particular sector of that world—a field—and which structures the perception of that world as well as action in that world."[37] These institutions and sectors of the world might be mediated through smaller units or communities like the family or the church, but in the end he felt that habitus was deeply and broadly societal.[38]

---

34 Pierre Bourdieu, *Practical Reason: On the Theory of Action*, trans. Randall Johnson (Stanford, 1998), 32–33.
35 Bourdieu, *Practical Reason*, 25.
36 Since many translations of Bourdieu do not italicize the word "habitus," I am following that practice here. This also provides a convenient visual distinction between *habitus* in the virtues discourse of practice and habitus in the domination discourse of practice.
37 Bourdieu, *Practical Reason*, 81.
38 See the appendices on "The Family Spirit" and "Remarks on the Economy of the Church" in Bourdieu, *Practical Reason*.

Bourdieu is deeply suspicious of the power relations in which practice is formed, and the way in which practice generally benefits those with more economic, social, political, or cultural capital, even referring to practice as "pedagogic violence" or "symbolic violence."[39] For Bourdieu, practice creates an internalized, embodied cooperation with those "who possess a sufficient amount of one of the different kinds of capital to be in a position to dominate the corresponding field."[40] He did not understand domination as direct physical coercion by those who are dominant. Rather, systemic violence occurred in a more structural and embedded way, "the indirect effect of a complex set of actions engendered within the network of intersecting constraints."[41] The resulting effect of this socialization favors the cognitive, institutional, and economic structures of the more powerful by recruiting those with less power to see and understand the world through the lenses of the powerful through embodied practice, which serves to uphold the power of existing structures and institutions.

Bourdieu uses religious language to describe the dominant cultures that assert themselves through the logic of practice into the habitus of individuals. His word for the shared established order encoded in a person's habitus is: "doxa, an orthodoxy, a right, correct, dominant vision which has more often than not been imposed through struggles against competing visions."[42] That language of "doxa" and "orthodoxy" is not incidental, as Bourdieu felt that the church was one of the shaping institutions that impacted habitus, particularly in his home country, France. Bourdieu asserts that "cognitive structures are not forms of consciousness but *dispositions of the body*"[43] (emphasis original) that "belong to the order of *belief*" (emphasis original) that is neither conscious nor rational choice, "outside the channels of consciousness and calculation" as a form of "common sense."[44]

For Bourdieu, practice is linked with power, in particular the recruitment of bodies and selves into an orthodoxy that favors the values and aesthetics of the dominant group. In his reckoning, practice keeps nondominant bodies in line. Whereas within faith formational literature, religious practice is almost always cast as intentional, for Bourdieu, practice worked best when it did not draw attention to itself and when participants were not aware of their participation in it. The most powerful practices are those that we simply engage without

---

39 Bourdieu, *Practical Reason*, 121.
40 Bourdieu, *Practical Reason*, 34.
41 Bourdieu, *Practical Reason*, 34.
42 Bourdieu, *Practical Reason*, 56.
43 Bourdieu, *Practical Reason*, 54.
44 Bourdieu, *Practical Reason*, 55.

conscious thought nor question. As religious educator Michael Warren interpreted him, "Much of Bourdieu's social theory focuses, not on explicit norms guiding social behavior, but on the more subtle production of practices standing outside of rational calculation while entering deeply but unspokenly into behavior."[45] Warren also picked up on Bourdieu's "feel for the game" language, noting, "One does not think about the game reflexively; one just plays it."[46]

While in the field of religious education both Michael Warren and Joyce Mercer drew on Bourdieu as part of their explorations of formation, both stop short of describing the practice of religious communities using Bourdieu. They tend to use Bourdieu to describe the formative power of the broader cultural milieu in which an alternative intentional Christian formation or practice occurs as a form of resistance. Michael Warren, for example, insists that any discussion of Christian practice must be imagined within the already existing conditions of material existence, and that practice in the local congregation is at best contesting those conditions while working within them. Mercer, like Warren, sees Bourdieu as helpful to describe the formation that already exists through participation in consumer culture: "In short, this method will lead me to examine the larger 'habitus' in which belief and practice take shape—that wider social and cultural shape within which people experience and learn a way of life."[47] As such, Christian practice is subtly cast as an intentional and virtuous practice, while the formative practice linked to domination is relegated to broader secular or social forces.

3   Accounting for the Ambivalent Nature of Christian Practice

In one sense, both understandings of practice contain common themes. They are drawing on similar European philosophical traditions of formation, so that words like "practice" and "habitus" and a "feel for the game" are a part of both traditions of practice. As Dorothy Bass describes practice, it could apply to either understanding of practice outlined above:

> In spite of important differences among theories, certain features are common to many ways of understanding what a practice is, including our own. Practices are borne by social groups over time and are constantly

---

45   Michael Warren, *At this Time, In this Place: The Spirit Embodied in the Local Assembly* (Trinity Press International, 1999), 107.
46   Warren, *At this Time, In this Place*, 107.
47   Joyce Ann Mercer, *Welcoming Children: A Practical Theology of Childhood* (Chalice Press, 2005), 29.

negotiated in the midst of changing circumstances. As clusters of activities within which meaning and doing are inextricably interwoven, practices shape behavior while also fostering practice-specific knowledge, capacities, dispositions, and virtues. Those who participate in practices are formed in particular ways of thinking about and living in the world.[48]

However, one of the two understandings of practice asks pointed questions about whom the practice benefits, notices sleight of hand in misrecognition that hides these power relationships, and links the embedded, preconscious feel for the game to practices of domination. The other links practice with a goodness that points beyond itself, is assisted by God to form persons, and is intentionally engaged as the "goal and the path of Christian life." In religious education and spiritual formation discourses it is much more comfortable to talk about intentional formation of Christian habitus in communities of faith, but not so much about pedagogic violence, or the naked analysis of power, domination, and misrecognition that Bourdieu saw as intimately connected with the logic of practice, particularly religious practice.[49] I am going a step further to argue that primarily framing practice as transmitting virtue is a way of disregarding potential alignment between Christian practice and the violence of dominant culture, downplaying the possible evils transmitted through white Christian practice in the name of revitalizing the church.

How does this happen, even with those within the field who use theorists such as Bourdieu to understand religious practice? Christian Scharen is one of a few people who uses Bourdieu in his attempt to "develop a theory of ritual as a social practice, rooted in the habitus produced in communities of character and practice."[50] He is initially attentive to the ways in which practice is linked to categories of socially significant distinction: "Immediately one sees that Bourdieu is trying to describe the way in which particular social space—one's social class, nationality, religious identity, gender, whatever—becomes to some extent merged with one's embodied existence. Those social distinctions, those things that make one what one is and not another, Bourdieu

---

48   Dorothy Bass, "Ways of Life Abundant" in *For Life Abundant*, 29.
49   Bourdieu, *Practical Reason*, 95.
50   Christian Scharen, *Public Worship and Public Work: Character and Commitment in Local Congregational Life* (Liturgical Press, 2008), 65. Others who use Bourdieu quite well in the field of practical theology include Mary McClintock Fulkerson, *Places of Redemption: Theology for a Worldly Church* (Oxford, 2010); and Elaine L. Graham, *Transforming Practice: Pastoral Theology in an Age of Uncertainty* (Mowbray, 1996).

describes as 'bodily knowledge.'"[51] Scharen is focused on how Bourdieu understands the body as a primary site of learning, citing Bourdieu to note the "most serious social injunctions are addressed not to the intellect but to the body, treated as a 'memory pad.'"[52] While Bourdieu is talking about "injunctions" and "enforcement," in Scharen this language gets shifted to "apprenticeship in the community of practice," more common to the virtues ethics discourse of Stanley Hauerwas. As Scharen acknowledges, the language of "community of practice" is not used in Bourdieu.

Scharen softens the language of Bourdieu, a theorist whose primary metaphor for education is "pedagogic violence," and who thought that education served to maintain power across generations that served the dominant group. We might ask ourselves what it means to change this understanding of formation to "apprenticeship within a community of practice," effectively erasing the bold analysis of power and the warnings about violence that are a part of Bourdieu's understanding of habitus? Why do we avoid the parts of this understanding of practice that speak of the issues of control and the exercise of power that are a part of constructing habitus through embodied practice?

Bourdieu perhaps would call this the classic euphemistic language of the church, a kind of collective misrecognition that is required to maintain itself. In the field of practical theology, which intentionally understands itself in some cases as existing to build up the church, this misrecognition of the power involved in determining embodied practice may serve as a kind of habitual apologetic for the work of the church as always and entirely benevolent, linked to the goodness of God and different from other forms of practice in economic or political realms. The softening of language, the focus on how religious practice contributes to the passing on of virtue rather than its ambivalent role in sharing wisdom and maintaining domination rests in this sense that our field's job is to build up the church and not tear it down. Subtly, that critique of the potential violence and search for control in the church is passed off to non-white religious communities, to those who critique the church based on gender or sexuality, to religious studies scholars, or to secular critics of the church. Practical theology implicitly aligns itself with maintaining the power of the church through regularly describing and advocating its practices as virtuous. Maintaining the virtue discourse of practice without attention to the domination and control of bodies through embedded knowledge and pre-rational consideration that is also a part of religious practice may align the discourse of religious practice with white normativity, even white supremacy.

---

51   Scharen, *Public Worship and Public Work*, 60.
52   Bourdieu, *Logic of Practice*, 141, cited in Scharen, *Public Worship and Public Work*, 61.

Some scholars are beginning to model what taking the potential of Christian practices to participate in domination more seriously. Historian of Christian spirituality Lauren Winner, in her book *Dangers of Christian Practice*, takes up the ways that Christian practice have characteristic distortions built into them, in her theological framing, because of human sinfulness: "Therefore, because nothing created is untouched by the Fall, Christians should not be surprised when lovely and good, potentially gracious Christian gestures are damaged, or when human beings deploy those Christian gestures in the perpetuation of damage."[53] Where Winner talks more generally about the Fall as the source of these failures, I want to name this as the problem of white settler Christianity more specifically. In her historical work, Winner takes on the beloved practices of the church, not just the outlying ones. She looks specifically at instances such as anti-Semitic charges of host desecration and supercessionism related to the practice of Eucharist in the Middle Ages in Europe and the documented racist prayers of white women slaveowners for their slaves' obedience and submission. She explores baptism through the lens of how practices designed to incorporate persons into the body of Christ and erase distinctions were modified instead to preserve familial ties and extend them for the economic benefit of succeeding generations. She completes a helpful assessment of who pays attention to the distinction between the ideal descriptions of Christian practices and their justified theological accounts and the actual ways that they play out in the lives of Christians.[54]

Where I have considered practices of domination and practices of virtue as if they are perhaps separate kinds of Christian practices, Winner recognizes that all practice contains the possibility for both drawing near to God *and* creating damage:

> In this book I read Christian practices—practices of the church, like the Eucharist and prayer—under the pressure of the foregoing understanding of sin and damage, with the aim of encouraging the church to be on the lookout for the ways good Christian practices may, and inevitably sometimes will, do the very opposite of what those practices were made, in their goodness (in God's goodness, and in God's good hopes for the church), to do.[55]

---

53   Winner, *Dangers of Christian Practice*, 3.
54   Winner, *Danger of Christian Practice*, 40–42.
55   Winner, *Dangers of Christian Practice*, 4.

In her exploration of various practices like eucharist and baptism, she notices that each one has embedded within it certain characteristic damages, that they "carry with them their own deformations."[56] She also documents how these distortions of practice persist over time. Not insignificantly, this historical work ties the work of Christian practice with anti-Semitism in Europe, classism and wealth preservation, and the historic racism of chattel slavery in the United States.

Winner provides a helpful alternative to the alignment of advocating Christian practice and its collusion with white supremacy and the development of capitalism and preservation of wealth, and she is not alone in noticing that practice can be bent to dominating ends. Theologian Don Saliers notes, "Liturgical theology suffers when it fails to acknowledge 'hidden' power issues and the malformative histories of practice," calling upon the need for "an adequate descriptive account of what actually takes place" as an antidote to the problem of overly optimistic descriptions of the benefits of liturgical practice.[57] Similarly evoking the need to actually describe how practices are lived out in congregations in imperfect ways, theologian Mary McClintock Fulkerson notes that the way practice is described by her theological colleagues often overlooks "both the worldly way that communities live out their faith and the worldly way that God is among us" in favor of more cognitive and orthodox definitions of Christian faithfulness.[58] Moves towards ethnographic, qualitative, and lived religion approaches to Christian practice often chasten the optimistic and salvific descriptions of Christian practice in light of the power-laden and potentially damaging ways that these practices are lived into when observed in real human communities, particularly white Protestant congregations.

4 Innocence, Purity, and Complicity: Reimagining White Christian Practice

One of the concerns in questioning the turn to practice in the field of practical theology is the fear of losing the control that is sought in forming people into the Christian fold. Acknowledging that behind the concern for formation might be practices of domination and assimilation learned in the colonial era of settler Christianity raises questions about what it means to evangelize, or to

---

56 Winner, *Dangers of Christian Practice*, 180.
57 Don Saliers, "Afterword—Liturgy and Ethics Revised" in E. Byron Anderson, ed., *Liturgy and the Moral Self: Humanity at Full Stretch Before God* (Pueblo Books, 1998), 214–215.
58 Fulkerson, *Places of Redemption*, 6.

invite others to copy the practices of the church in a process of cultural assimilation. In her beautiful book *This Here Flesh*, Cole Arthur Riley puts it this way as she reflects on where she began to feel detached from her body through the practices of dominant culture:

> I think whiteness knows that the more detached I am from my body, the easier that body will be to colonize and use toward whiteness's own ends. It desires that my mind be fixed firmly on an immaterial realm, that I become numb to any present and material injustices. It is this belief system that indoctrinates us to sneer at social justice but bow to evangelism. After all, evangelism has the ability to exercise the same muscles as colonization—telling someone what to think and be. It can be a form of ownership in the name of heaven.[59]

Riley says this with such matter-of-factness, it is easy to breeze through it: "After all, evangelism has the ability to exercise the same muscles as colonization—telling someone what to think and be." Exercising the same muscles as colonization is a helpful way to think about the shared legacy that I am questioning between white practices of Christian formation and the legacy of white supremacy that assumed that others should take up the cultural practices that white people offer. In the face of the decline of the mainline, the fear of loss of affiliation, of joining in with the projects of white Christianity through church membership and alignment, makes us want to double down on the idea that there are best practices that could re-invigorate the church and get more people to affiliate. If we could just get people to take on the practices of Christianity, we could regain cultural legitimacy and power to control others into accepting the truths that we offer, the God that we proclaim.

One direction I thought about going with this chapter was to suggest that the fields of Christian formation abandon the idea of practice because of its ambivalent nature as both transmitting domination and virtue. I turned to some wise colleagues in the field who are using different metaphors entirely to frame religious education. For example, Courtney Goto has taken up the metaphor of play as a primary metaphor for understanding religious education as a way to facilitate "revelatory experiencing."[60] In focusing on play,

---

59 Cole Arthur Riley, *This Here Flesh: Spirituality, Liberation, and the Stories That Make Us* (Convergent Books, 2022), 59.
60 Courtney Goto, *The Grace of Playing: Pedagogies for Leaning into God's New Creation* (Pickwick Publications, 2016), 5.

she draws attention to the aesthetic and improvisational dimensions of "leaning into God's new creation," focusing on "local" and "contextually sensitive" conditions that are "conducive to revelatory experiencing" rather than practices that pass down the established wisdom of the tradition.[61] This metaphor seems highly promising in terms of pointing away from embodied formation as maintaining control across generations that is a part of the metaphor of practice in its white dominant forms. The improvisational and surprising nature of play perhaps reduces the focus on assured outcomes and re-focuses the educator on the process of opening ourselves up to the divine in surprising and engaging ways.

Practical theologian Jaco Hamman also reflects on the contradictions between the hermeneutical, strategic, and descriptive nature of practical theological reflection and the disclosive and ambiguous nature of play. He highlights this paradoxical relationship: "[P]ractical theological reflection is deliberate and planned. It follows a defined method or process. Playing calls forth imaginative spontaneity that invites the unexpected even when rules define the activity, as in a card or board game."[62] In seeking to make space for the less controlled and more improvisational and relational work of playing, he describes the "different hermeneutic" involved in play that is "not the kind of ethical project that practical theology tends to be."[63] Hamman traces the importance of play and playfulness through many subdisciplines within practical theology, from the work of Charles Gerkin in pastoral care to the work of Jerome Berryman in religious education and Margaret Guenther in spiritual direction.[64]

Mai-Ahn Le Tran explores an entirely different set of metaphors in her book *Reset the Heart*. One is contained in the subtitle: "unlearning violence and relearning hope." It seems to me that unlearning violence is so central to the work of white Western Christianity at this point in time that we should be listening deeply to her work, particularly its critique about the erasure of memory, organized forgetting, and a habitus of *dis*imagination.[65] Tran is deeply sensitive to the sleight of hand that Christian congregations have engaged to draw

---

61 Goto, *Grace of Playing*, 13.
62 Jaco Hamman, "Playing" in Bonnie J. Miller-McLemore, ed., *The Wiley-Blackwell Companion to Practical Theology* (Wiley-Blackwell, 2011), 44.
63 Hamman, "Playing" in Miller-McLemore ed. *Wiley-Blackwell Companion to Practical Theology*, 44.
64 Hamman, "Playing" in Miller-McLemore ed. *Wiley-Blackwell Companion to Practical Theology*, 47–49.
65 Mai-Anh Le Tran, *Reset the Heart: Unlearning Violence, Relearning Hope* (Abingdon, 2017), 57.

attention away from their continued participation in violence and oppression. Her metaphors of educability, redeemability, and communicability offer a new language for thinking about formation as well. Particularly the "communicability" criterion, with its ambivalent relationship to both knowledge and disease as being potentially spread, builds the potential for colonization or infection into the very metaphor she chooses.

But, in the spirit of unlearning violence that is central to Tran's work, I think that a central part of white settler Christianity's work in unlearning domination is re-thinking practice as a neutral metaphor for the work of formation. Communal practice does not automatically create connection to God or enliven the church, even when it is deeply steeped in the Christian tradition. As a human practice that draws upon the mixed human experiences of being created in the image of God and being sinners who have fallen far short from that glory, we can never form a *habitus* that is only focused on salvation and not in danger of seeking to maintain our own power. Practice, even Christian religious practice, can also be a form of symbolic violence that recruits those who are dominated by a system to perceive the world through the lenses of the most powerful. Perhaps *especially* Christian practice.

As a White Western Christian, one who takes the legacy of my people's participation in dominating forms of Christian practice seriously, taking a good hard look at the ambivalent nature of the practices that I advocate for, how they participate in domination and supremacist forms of seeing the world as well as transmit the potential for connection to God, and trying to unlearn those habitual forms of practice is critical, even when inviting others into the practice of faith. To insist solely on the virtue of Christian practice when historically retrieved carefully in the name of enlivening the church puts white dominant Christians in a potentially dangerous place where we are replicating a kind of good/bad binary with ourselves in the position of the good and others in need of replicating that good for the sake of God that fueled the missionizing projects that ended in cultural and literal genocide on the American and other continents. This understanding of the virtue of practice flirts with a reliance on purity as a sign of goodness that has been a part of the legacy of white supremacy. We cannot acknowledge that our own religious practice may be tainted or compromised, because our own supremacist logic relies on others recognizing our goodness, marked by purity, to maintain authority. It requires us to be right and to convince others to join us in our view of the world as an indicator of faithfulness.

Purity is a complicated notion, and often in contemporary Christian conversations indicates the purity movement related to sexuality that began to rise in power in the US in white evangelical and other conservative Christian communities in the mid to late 1980s as part of the backlash to the HIV/AIDS pandemic and the free-love ideologies of the 1970s. In this case, I am talking about an earlier notion of purity born in the colonial era as a racialized concept. As philosopher Alexis Shotwell notes, by tracing "debates about the nature of human races back to questions that animated and justified the Atlantic slave trade," including questions of whether humans came from a single gene or for many origins, that are basic to the notion of purity and the purity of white people in particular. "Markers of racial purity are in turn entangled and co-constituted with biopolitical practices aiming to reduce or eliminate disability, poverty, and queerness at the population level."[66] Drawing on an essay from María Lugones, Shotwell argues against purity and "the rhetorical or conceptual attempt to delineate and delimit the world into something separable, disentangled, and homogenous."[67] Instead, she hopes to argue for implication, complicity, and compromise as the only place we can begin to address the major problems such as climate destruction that we are facing. She is worried that an ethic of purity in addressing these problems leads to despair, and individual performativity of personal purity practice through saying the absolute right things, rather than what she names as "righteous politics—collective work toward a future prefigured in present practice."[68] She notes:

> To be against purity is to start from an understanding of our implication in this compromised world, to recognize the quite vast injustices informing our everyday lives, and from that understanding to act on our wish that it were not so. I believe that this orientation is at the heart of prefigurative, loving, social movement practices whose point is not only to interpret the world, but to change it. We cannot predict what might emerge from individual and collective practices of staying with the trouble, except that it holds the possibility of another world, still imperfect and impure, and another one after that.[69]

For Shotwell, we engage in practices knowing that they cannot be considered pure, innocent, or linked solely to beneficial outcomes. She is concerned that this notion of being right or personally pure leads more to conspiracy theory

---

66 Alexis Shotwell, *Against Purity: Living Ethically in Compromised Times* (University of Minnesota Press, 2016), 15.
67 Shotwell, *Against Purity*, 15.
68 Shotwell, *Against Purity*, 196.
69 Shotwell, *Against Purity*, 204.

knowledge building, or what others call virtue-signaling, rather than the real work of trying to move together into a future that allows for the survival of many and not just ourselves.

Why would we give ourselves with devotion to religious practice at all if we hold it as Shotwell notes, implicated, complicit, compromised, and ambivalent? Ambivalence about our own certainty, the value of a practice, and humility about human wisdom is also a longstanding value of the Christian tradition. The demand for practice to be effective, to scale up, to save the church and stop the hemorrhaging of members is more of the capitalist side of "best practices," and some of the literature on spiritual practice tends towards that conclusion, at least in its popular usage. The insistence that Christian practice is somehow pure and above reproach because of its focus on God is an inheritance of the legacy of colonial white supremacy.

Theologian Alex Mikulich, in the wake of the killing of Michael Brown, Jr., in Ferguson, wrote about the insistence of white and Christian innocence in the face of our own histories of genocide and systemic racism:

> White denial of responsibility, including how we are socialized into a racist society, is rooted in the American myth that we as a white nation are an exception and exceptional. This myth, of course, whitewashes history, forgetting a history of genocide of first American peoples and how our capitalist system is built on slavery and racism .... The story of innocence we tell ourselves renders the most basic questioning of white privilege and systemic racism invisible for critical reflection. It is not only that whites tend to live by the myth of American innocence, but we also live by a fantasy of Christian innocence.[70]

That fantasy of Christian innocence feels a part of the discourse of Christian practice that focuses solely on its virtue and does not reckon with the histories of domination that also are baked into Christian practice. To imagine that we could somehow form a habitus that keeps our mind in alignment with God's will, and then invite others into that divine positionality through imitating our practice draws on the cultural knowledge that replicates the histories of evangelism that lifted whiteness as civilizing and offering salvation to those perceived as savage without it. Conceiving religious practice as primarily a way of transmitting virtue backed by God's action on our side pairs too neatly

---

70   Alex Mikulich, "Whites Live a Fantasy of Innocence," *National Catholic Reporter*, November 7, 2014, sec. Arts and Opinion.

with the legacy of white supremacy and colonialism that is a part of white Western Christianity.

The reality of embodied practice is that it is at best ambiguous or ambivalent, serving dominant cultural interests within the church as well as potentially creating a way of life that brings us closer to God. As Elaine Graham notes, transforming practice allows for the transformation of doxa,[71] but we must always engage practice with the awareness that we might be transmitting domination as well as virtue with it, despite strong theological claims to the contrary in the discourse advocating Christian practice. We enter practice with the sure knowledge that we may be learning dominance as well as virtue, as in the words of Christine Pohl: "Recovering a rich and life-giving practice requires attention to good stories, wise mentors, and hard questions."[72] These hard questions include whether or not this historic form of the church that has participated through its practices in cultural genocide, the alienation of humans from their given habitat, justification for slavery and the oppression of women and sexual minorities, creating a culture with great economic disparity, is something our scholarly efforts should be serving to maintain or enliven.

---

[71] Graham, *Transforming Practice*, 99.
[72] Pohl, *Making Room*, 14.

CHAPTER 3

Questioning Education

A belief in education is one of the hallmarks of the historic white mainline Protestant denominations to which I have belonged and in whose seminaries I have worked.[1] In addition to their commitments to an educated clergy, they also had a history of starting Sunday schools, an effort to create basic literacy in children who had to work in factories and mines rather than attend schools during the rest of the week. Small denominational colleges cropped up across the United States in the nineteenth century, in many cases a missional effort to make higher education more broadly accessible to those outside the elite classes. The belief that education was close to salvation, both economic and religious, came to be one of the tenets of mainline white Christians.[2] While anti-intellectualism is now a notable part of white evangelical culture, historically many institutions of higher education in the United States, including the one where I work, were started to educate clergy to serve in regions that white people were settling.

While I share a vocation and an ongoing commitment to education, learning the history of Christianity in the colonial period, particularly the pairing of colonial expansion and imperial rule by European nations with the development of modern understandings of Christian education, has chastened my belief in education as a positive or neutral tool. Education, specifically Christian education backed by missional theologies, served as a tool of white supremacy that played a central role in the devastation of millions of human lives through the colonial era of Western expansion. This story is not how I generally frame the discipline in which I claim expertise, and yet I assert that these histories must be a part of how we teach and practice religious education. As a white person who is committed to liberative practices of education, giving an adequate account of the historical reality that Christian education paired with white supremacy and colonial imperatives in often seamless ways, leading to cultural devastation and genocide, is an important ethical reminder

---

1 A version of this chapter was originally published as Katherine Turpin, "Christian Education, White Supremacy, and Humility in Formational Agendas," *Religious Education* 112, no. 4 (July 2017): 407–17.
2 For a fascinating treatment of the history of the association of education with salvation, see Hannah Adams Ingram, *The Myth of the Saving Power of Education* (Pickwick, 2021).

of the potential dangers of educational forms learned in the process of white settlement.

Exploring this history helps raise questions about why and how we teach, and it might help us identify where the legacy of white supremacy and imperial domination live on in our daily practices of Christian faith formation and religious education. Traces of these habits of cultural imperialism and non-mutual pedagogies continue to be present in current religious educational practice in white Christianity. A commitment to ethical Christian educational practice requires humble acknowledgement of this history and its legacy and ongoing work to disrupt its rhythms in our own practice. While any educational venture requires authority and is an act of power, humility is an essential partnering virtue for educators who do not wish to faithfully replicate this history of domination and colonizing practice.

For many generations, liberal Protestantism associated education with the salvific work of Christianity. Practical theologian Hannah Adams Ingram demonstrates how both the historical development of the US public education system and ongoing educational policy statements in speeches such as the State of the Union regularly linked the practice of education with the language of salvation.[3] Churches promoted literacy through schooling so that everyone could read the Bible and gain access to salvation through receiving the gospel. As the Bible became the preferred religious authority, education was necessary to inform the priesthood of all believers.

But more subtly, education offered salvation in other ways. In the face of ongoing systemic structures of poverty, "getting an education" became a way to ensure more favorable outcomes for individuals and their offspring. Education in the Western imagination provides an individual solution for systemic poverty. This individualized solution places the onus of escaping social structures of economic oppression on full participation in the opportunities provided by a public education system, despite the reality of inequalities built into that system documented by study after study. If people are still poor, the blame for their economic struggles can be placed on their not having the character and determination to work hard in school to make a better life for themselves. In these and many other ways, a belief in the power of education to save has been a strong part of white Christianity.

The pairing of religious education with colonization happened with theological warrants from the Christian tradition, not entirely outside of the Christian tradition. In case we are tempted to link this history with the sinful part

---

3 Ingram, *Myth of the Saving Power of Education*, 1–19.

of human nature, perhaps saying that everything we do as humans is tainted with the mark of imperfection, I want us to consider how the Christian tradition helped shape the cultural logics that led to the use of religious education as a tool of subjugation without apology. As theologian Willie Jennings argues, "This imperialist form drew life from Christianity's lifeblood, from its missionary mandate and its mission reflexes," leading arguably to an even more virulent form of ethnocentrism than possible without the theological underpinnings.[4] After reckoning with that history briefly, links to current Christian educational practice bring into question the pedagogical habits and practices learned during the colonial era that continue to frame how we engage in education today, particularly amongst white Christian educators and their communities of practice.

1 Teaching as Universal Mandate for Conversion

> Matthew 28:18–20 [8]And Jesus came and said to them, "All authority in heaven and on earth has been given to me. [19]Go therefore and make disciples of all nations, baptizing them in the name of the Father and of the Son and of the Holy Spirit, [20]and teaching them to obey everything that I have commanded you. And remember, I am with you always, to the end of the age." (NRSV)

This text provides the grounding for the mission of the church as understood by my denomination, the United Methodist Church: "The mission of the Church is to make disciples of Jesus Christ for the transformation of the world."[5] Sometimes called "The Great Commission" and linked with practices of mission and evangelism, this text is fundamentally about teaching and learning. Authority has been given to Jesus and by extension to his followers to go and make *mathetes*, the Koine Greek term for "students" or "learners," of all nations and teach them to obey Jesus' commandments. While many contemporary denominations have divorced the notion of "discipling" from a process of education and turned it into something more akin to spiritual formation, the roots of the word are in education.

---

4 Willie James Jennings, *The Christian Imagination: Theology and the Origins of Race* (Yale University Press, 2011), 112.
5 *The Book of Discipline of the United Methodist Church*. Nashville, United Methodist Publishing House, 2012. Paragraph 120.

Unfortunately, this text that has been held in high esteem by white Protestants and that has been foundational to the colonizing practice of forced conversion defines education in a fundamentally non-mutual way. Postcolonial biblical scholar Musa Dube takes on this text and the havoc it created in colonial contexts, noting how it was interpreted and operationalized in an invasive manner:

> The command not only instructs Christian readers to travel to all nations but also contains a 'pedagogical imperative'—'to *make disciples of all nations*.' Does such an imperative consider the consequences of trespassing? Does it make room for Christian travelers to be discipled by all nations, or is the discipling in question conceived solely in terms of a one-way traffic?[6]

Dube argues that because the text fails to suggest that Christian disciples also must learn from other nations, it creates an unequal relationship between the disciples and those they encountered. She notes, "Consequently, if all nations are to be entered and 'discipled' by Christian teachers without any sort of reciprocal stance or attitude on the latter's part, do we not then find in the gospel an operative model of outsiders as infants to be 'uplifted'?"[7] Dube goes on to argue that formal education served as a primary "structural instrument with which to wrench and wean individuals away from their so-called pagan culture, backward state, and primitive beliefs. Put differently, formal education became a powerful tool of colonization and ultimately its own form of imperialism."[8] This cultural genocide was performed simultaneously to achieve religious salvation for people that European Christians perceived as lesser than themselves and to create docile socialized subjects for participation in the labor necessary for colonial projects that stole the labor and resources from the worlds they invaded. Justification for this stripping of natural and human resources came from uplift and salvific narratives which claimed that slaves and other subjugated workers were left better off by their Christianization and the "civilizing" influence of white Eurowestern cultures. Religious education, because of its dual socializing and converting roles, was often the initial tool of economic and cultural decimation in this scheme.

---

6 Musa Dube, "Go Therefore and Make Disciples of All Nations" in Fernando F. Segovia and Mary Ann Tolbert, *Teaching the Bible: The Discourses and Politics of Biblical Pedagogy* (Fortress Press, 2011), 224.
7 Dube, "Go Therefore and Make Disciples of All Nations," 224.
8 Dube, "Go Therefore and Make Disciples of All Nations," 226.

The Christian education that was practiced not only labeled cultural practices central to the social order of indigenous persons as demonic and barbaric, but also those who implemented it understood the people they invaded as of lesser intelligence and incapable of apprehending reality correctly. Dube notes of this cultural denigration, "As such, the coming of Christianity was accompanied by a structural process of pauperization, whereby our perceptions of reality and beauty were denied, and abetted by a variety of disciplines and practices."[9] She argues that by imposing a local standard on a universal scale, Christian teachers failed to meet their learners as "an equal subject, with dialogue and free exchange as a result."[10] Learners were considered children on a developmental scale in which European civilizations were understood to be the epitome of maturity. However, those immature persons were not considered precious or innocent, but instead were subjected to indescribable violence in the name of teaching them what it meant to be properly civilized.

The process that Dube critiques from her own African context has also been well documented in the Christian educational work with indigenous persons on the North American continent. As educational theorists K. Tsianina Lamawaima and Teresa McCarty describe, "The 'civilized' nation assumed that its right to dispossess Native nations went hand in hand with a responsibility to 'uplift' them, and mission and federal 'Indian schools' were established as laboratories for a grand experiment in cultural cleansing, Christian conversion, and assimilation of laborers and domestic workers into the workforce."[11] The partnering of Christian denominational bodies and the US government needed to engage this cultural cleansing project is well-documented in the work of scholar of American Indian traditions George "Tink" Tinker in his book, *Missionary Conquest*.[12]

Recent discoveries of thousands of children's bodies buried in unmarked graves in Canadian and US boarding schools run by Christian denominations in partnership with the government as part of the strategy of settlement have troubled the image of these schools as a part of a program of "educational uplift." The first report from the U.S. Department of the Interior documenting the deaths of children at these sites came out in May of 2022 under the leadership of Secretary Deb Haaland, the first indigenous person to run that

---

9   Dube, "Go Therefore and Make Disciples of All Nations," 228.
10 Dube, "Go Therefore and Make Disciples of All Nations," 233.
11 K. Tsianina Lomawaima and Teresa L. McCarty, *"To Remain an Indian": Lessons in Democracy from a Century of Native American Education* (Teachers College Press, 2006), 4.
12 George E. Tinker, *Missionary Conquest: The Gospel and Native American Cultural Genocide* (Fortress Press, 1993).

department. Initially the report documents over 500 deaths of children at 19 schools, but people involved in the investigation believe that this number will move to the tens of thousands, even in government documentation. Because so many of the graves are unmarked, have been moved, and the children were often farmed out to families where their deaths from overwork or disease were not officially reported, that full number may never be known.

However, the deaths of children are not the only elements of trauma represented in the practices of Indian removal to boarding schools. In press releases related to the report, Haaland noted, "The consequences of federal Indian boarding school policies—including the intergenerational trauma caused by the family separation and cultural eradication inflicted upon generations of children as young as 4 years old—are heartbreaking and undeniable."[13] The stated mission of the investigation involves "to comprehensively address the facts and consequences of its federal Indian boarding school policies—implemented for more than a century and a half—resulting in the twin goals of cultural assimilation and territorial dispossession of Indigenous peoples through the forced removal and relocation of their children."[14] Education for cultural assimilation is its own violent process, named by Andrea Smith as a practice of cultural genocide and one of the three pillars of white supremacy.[15]

Secretary Haaland and Assistant Secretary Newland, the primary identified author of the report, both note the incredible breadth of this educational strategy, including approximately 500 boarding schools and "over 1,000 other Federal and non-Federal institutions, including Indian day schools, sanitariums, asylums, orphanages, and stand-alone dormitories."[16] The language of militarized violence is evident in the description of pedagogies in this federal report:

> The investigation found that the federal Indian boarding school system deployed systematic militarized and identity-alteration methodologies in an attempt to assimilate American Indian, Alaska Native, and

---

13   https://www.doi.gov/pressreleases/department-interior-releases-investigative-report-outlines-next-steps-federal-indian.
14   https://www.doi.gov/pressreleases/department-interior-releases-investigative-report-outlines-next-steps-federal-indian.
15   Andrea Smith, "Heteropatriarchy and the Three Pillars of White Supremacy: Rethinking Women of Color Organizing" in INCITE! Women of Color Against Violence, ed. *Color of Violence: The INCITE! Anthology*, Reprint edition (Duke University Press Books, 2016), 66–73.
16   Federal Indian Boarding School Initiative Report, Volume 1, May 2022, US Dept of the Interior, Assistant Secretary-Indian Affairs, Bryan Newland, p. 82.

Native Hawaiian children through education, including but not limited to renaming Indian children from Indian to English names; cutting the hair of Indian children; discouraging or preventing the use of American Indian, Alaska Native, and Native Hawaiian languages, religions and cultural practices; and organizing Indian and Native Hawaiian children into units to perform military drills.[17]

The goal of this education was to eradicate the worldviews and cultural practices of indigenous persons and to replace them with white European cultural perspectives about land, labor, embodiment, and Christian religion. The strategies included kidnapping of children and removal from their families and communities, brutal physical retraining through bodily presentation and corporal punishment, suppression of language and therefore communication and connection amongst the children, and militarized training into conformity with the educational program.

The long memories and records of native American communities in the United States documenting the number of children who went missing from these schools point to the near-genocidal carelessness with which the children who went to these schools were treated. While Colonel Henry Pratt's injunction to "Kill the Indian in him, and save the man" through education (delivered in a speech in 1892 during the National Conference of Charities and Correction, in my hometown of Denver, Colorado) was taken as marching orders for founding places like the Carlisle School, in fact the schools in practice all too often killed *both* culture *and* student. The acknowledged scope of the number of children killed through this educational process is no doubt going to increase, even in the governmental accounting which will no doubt be undersized because of the potential economic liabilities marked by this acknowledgment. For example, Canadian and Australian governments have paid limited restitution to descendants of those removed to boarding schools, but these designations of which schools officially "count" as Federal and so on will no doubt limit access to any reparations to survivors. The report itself notes limitations to their ability to research due to inadequate funding and appropriations, incomplete reporting of deaths to the federal agencies, and ownership of sites by non-Federal entities or federal entities outside of the

---

17   "Department of the Interior Releases Investigative Report, Outlines Next Steps in Federal Indian Boarding School Initiative," May 11, 2022. https://www.doi.gov/pressreleases/department-interior-releases-investigative-report-outlines-next-steps-federal-indian.

Department of the Interior.[18] In these schools Christian discipleship, as envisioned in the colonial period of imperial expansion, joined a form of white supremacy with Christian evangelism and economic exploitation, with religious education as a primary tool of structural domination.

Theologian Willie James Jennings uses the life of José de Acosta, a young Jesuit priest and theologian who came to Peru in 1572, to further explore this link between Christian pedagogy and colonialism. He argues that Acosta "fashioned a theological vision for the New World that drew its life from Christian orthodoxy and its power from conquest"[19] Jennings argues that this impulse is not just an outgrowth of colonial power, "but it also reveals in a very stark way the future of theology in the New World, that is, a strongly traditioned Christian intellectual posture made to function wholly within a colonialist logic."[20] Acosta demonstrates how Christians evaluated the native population with a "white theological gaze," deeming them barbarians through assessing their "rituals, idolatries, behaviors, language, and practice."[21]

A member of the Jesuit order, Acosta brought the educational sensibilities of that order, a tradition of evaluation "to form Christian character through the humanist vision of *Bildung* in anyone so willing to be shaped."[22] However, the assessment of the original inhabitants of the land as ignorant and demonic leads to an important translation, in which Biblical narratives of "resistance to the gospel" get overlaid onto whole cultures that seemed alien to the colonizers and were made into enemies of the gospel if they were not willing to lay down their own cultural practices, belief systems, and self-governance. This set a new trajectory for traditioned Christian faith that linked it entirely with the colonial project. Jennings notes, "What comes into effect is a new form of ecclesial habitus in which the performance of theology—in teaching, preaching, writing and other ministry—becomes the articulation of processes of colonialist evaluation."[23] This expanded pedagogical evaluation linked with colonial force, the need to subjugate whole peoples to form workers merged with "the operation of forming theological subject," turning Christian formation into a hegemonic, unidirectional process, with, as Dube asserts, biblical

---

18 US Department of the Interior, "Department of the Interior Releases Investigative Report, Outlines Next Steps in Federal Indian Boarding School Initiative," May 11, 2022, 85. https://www.doi.gov/pressreleases/department-interior-releases-investigative-report-outlines-next-steps-federal-indian.
19 Jennings, *The Christian Imagination*, 83.
20 Jennings, *The Christian Imagination*, 83.
21 Jennings, *The Christian Imagination*, 103.
22 Jennings, *The Christian Imagination*, 104.
23 Jennings, *The Christian Imagination*, 105.

warrant in "making disciples of all nations" in non-mutual, unjust ways in the name of the gospel.

2 Education, Civilization, and Imperial Force

In contemporary times, this blend of Christian education, white supremacy and colonial "uplift" and "civilizing" attitudes continues directly in Christian mission efforts and US governmental economic development efforts in the Southern hemisphere. For example, many white evangelical groups sponsor missions to achieve gospel conversion in other parts of the world, often travelling to places where the indigenous population has already been converted to Roman Catholicism in previous centuries. Now they are in need of conversion to "real" Christianity in the eyes of modern missionary efforts. More subtle forms of the blend of social conversion and rebuilding are present in mission trips of white Christians going to non-white places to serve the local population and improve their economic situation in the name of Jesus. In each of these scenarios, an underlying assumption is that the missionaries and servant workers have something essential to teach or share with those they encounter, often without much attention to the mutual learning that should occur in the exchange. These efforts have and must continue to be critiqued for the way they continue to perpetuate the histories of imperialistic Christian education begun in the colonial period.

Religious aspects continue to be a part of the educational mission, even when what is purportedly being shared is secular American-style democracy. Historian of religious education Dennis Gunn traces the link of education and imperialism by analyzing the rhetoric of one of the founders of the Religious Education Association, William Rainey Harper. Gunn analyzes the support for the "ideological framework of American imperialism" coexisted with a vision for peace in the construction of the REA:[24]

> This vision for religious education was rooted in his overarching educational aspiration for the United States. He believed that the United States, critically informed and democratically inspired by the Bible, could be the 'deliverer of the world,' as its prophet of democracy. Such a vision

---

[24] Dennis Gunn, "William Rainey Harper's Founding Vision for the REA and the Rhetoric of American Imperialism," *Religious Education* 117:2, 2022, 125. DOI: 10.1080/00344087.2022.2045785.

reflects the quintessential early twentieth century progressive spirit, with its abiding faith in American democracy and in the power of education to change the world.[25]

For Harper, not only does religious education work for the uplift of those in need of salvation within the United States, it can be exported to invite other cultures into the superior status of the United States, prophetically inviting them into the salvific understanding of social organization that we believe will benefit them. This belief in education relies on a sense of the supremacy of white Christian culture that would be shared through the practice of education, bringing others into the light of Western democracy.

The links between religious education and international policy in this imperial project articulated by William Rainey Harper continue in the current century in US foreign policy. For example, Pulitzer Prize winning New York Times journalist Nicholas Kristof called for education as the best way to combat declared enemies in 2008: "Military force is essential in Afghanistan to combat the Taliban. But over time, in Pakistan and Afghanistan alike, the best tonic against militant fundamentalism will be education and economic opportunity."[26] The belief that education rather than military intervention could best bring about the end of terrorism from the Taliban was behind the support of author Greg Mortenson and his book *Three Cups of Tea*.[27] Not only did Mortenson's book gain the attention of the book clubs of many well-meaning white liberals and create a young readers version of his memoir that was taught in many public schools, his educational mission to build schools through the Central Asia Institute (CAI) received incredible financial support. As popular nonfiction author Jon Krakauer puts it after writing an entire book to debunk Mortenson's inflated claims of success and the basic veracity of his story:

> His invented tales of derring-do turned Mortenson into a celebrity and generated $80 million in donations to CAI. But they also distorted the reality of life in the remote areas of Pakistan and Afghanistan where most of the CAI schools have been built, smeared the reputations of colleagues and villagers who assisted him, and promulgated ugly cultural

---

25   Gunn, "William Rainey Harper's Founding Vision for the REA,"125.
26   Nicholas Kristof, "It Takes a School, Not Missiles," *New York Times*, July 13, 2008.
27   Greg Mortenson, *Three Cups of Tea: One Man's Mission to Promote Peace—One School at a Time* (Penguin Books, 2007).

clichés about the violent nature and religious fanaticism of the tribal communities he purported to help.[28]

The fraudulent claims of Greg Mortenson of his own status as a white savior able to save these regions from the influence of the Taliban through building a large number of schools was met with the eager belief of Americans that education could be salvific. In describing what he calls the "Girl Effect," Mortenson claims in multiple places: "When a girl gets an education to at least a fifth-grade level, three important things happen: Infant mortality drops significantly, population explosion is curbed, and the basic quality of health improves dramatically."[29] The desire of Americans to use education to bring about democracy in the land of what was considered a national enemy after 9/11 was seemingly insatiable, even as the veracity of Mortenson's own story and the claims of his effectiveness were entirely debunked, his co-author took his own life by suicide, and Mortenson was forced to return over a million dollars to the CAI that he had fraudulently used for his own purposes.

Feminist scholar Rafia Zakaria further documents how these white supremacist beliefs about the need to save women in other parts of the world through education and moral improvement developed in the colonial period continue to be used to leverage support for neoliberalist military strategies. "Just as imperial feminists during the British colonial era had convinced themselves of their own benevolence in improving the lives of native women, so too did secure-feminists believe that they were 'saving' Afghanis and Iraqis from themselves."[30] Again, note the language of salvation that creeps into the notions of education and assimilation that underlie these practices. Zakaria points to the ways in which the "history of racial privilege that made white women so comfortable in claiming moral authority and in exercising power over Brown men" was not considered in claims of the War on Terror being about saving women's dignity and advocating for women's rights. The focus on saving women through educational uplift was used as cover for intensely violent military campaigns in public relations efforts related to the war:

---

28   Jon Krakauer, "Greg Mortenson, Disgraced Author of 'Three Cups of Tea,' Believes He Will Have the Last Laugh." *Galleys* (blog), May 4, 2022. https://medium.com/galleys/greg-mortenson-disgraced-author-of-three-cups-of-tea-believes-he-will-have-the-last-laugh-760949b1f964.
29   https://www.goodreads.com/interviews/show/408.Greg_Mortenson.
30   Rafia Zakaria, *Against White Feminism: Notes on Disruption* (W.W. Norton & Company, 2021), 86.

The effort to eradicate terror (read: *Islamic* terror, not white nationalist terror, despite the latter's considerably larger tally of dead Americans) was one of providing schools and health clinics and even beauty parlors, assisting in legal reform and the development of domestic-violence shelters, drafting progressive constitutions. The small matter of devastating bombings that left thousands dead and more disabled, forever splintered families, and wrecked livelihoods was a necessary means to that shining feminist end (emphasis original).[31]

Zakaria tracks how the emphasis on education and economic development offered in discussions and legitimizations of the war was used to mask the violent force that was also being used in the region, linking militarized invasion and educational efforts in an all-too-familiar pattern.

Practical theologian Christine Hong also traces the use of education as a civilizing project that violently forces assimilation into the interests of the dominant culture while erasing "everyone and everything in its way."[32] She notes:

Civilization for many racially and religiously minoritized folx means that there is always a dichotomy of dominance and subjugation, a struggle and striving for assimilation to dominance, and when one fails to assimilate, death and erasure. Civilization is violent in the way colonial and religious powers, such as that of Euro-American Christianity, have historically exercised it.[33]

What is perceived as a "softer" form of development, the use of education and economic development rather than military decimation, also hides a violence towards nondominant persons in its assimilationist agendas. Becoming civilized, or advancing civil society through education and development, sounds like a positive and peaceful development. However, it requires assent to the cultural norms and forms of the dominant group. Hong goes on to call for a focus on "the *uncivilization* of spaces and places, of teaching and learning" as a practice of resistance to this colonial legacy of calls for civilizing others.[34] She describes such educational spaces: "Uncivilizing spaces of teaching and

---

31   Zakaria, *Against White Feminism*, 82.
32   Christine J. Hong, *Decolonial Futures: Intercultural and Interreligious Intelligence for Theological Education* (Lexington Books, 2021), 80.
33   Hong, *Decolonial Futures*, 80.
34   Hong, *Decolonial Futures*, 82.

learning often means leaning into wilderness and imagination, something that Native scholars in their work of imagining decolonial futures and anticolonial practice, call indigeneity."[35] Calls for civil discourse in academic classrooms often mask the forced assimilation to white norms of behavior and belief rather than actual dialogical conversation that would allow for deep conflict or challenge of those norms.

3 Pedagogical Eternalities and the Education of Children

Traces of these impulses towards cultural superiority and what Jennings' calls the "white theological gaze" are still built into the discipline of Christian education. To attend to them, let us consider the pedagogical and theological logics lying beneath the colonial educational practices that may still persist in contemporary Christian educational projects. To describe what was going on in Acosta and his Jesuit contemporaries, Jennings turns to Augustine's concept of *faith seeking understanding*, noting that in the colonizers' assessment of the natives, we see instead *faith judging intelligence*.[36] Because Acosta and others mistrusted the capacity for intelligence among those they worked with, they shifted instead to the constant formation of habit as the primary educative method:

> Put bluntly, these disciplinary realities for Acosta transform the New World into one large, ever-expanding classroom with no beginning or ending period, an unrelenting pedagogical eternality .... This is the ground upon which the ideologies of white supremacy will grow: a theologically inverted pedagogical habitus that engenders a colonialist evaluative form that is disseminated through a network of relationships, which together reveal the deep sinews of knowledge and power.[37]

The posturing of educator to educated learned in these historic forms of Christian education continue to a lesser degree in contemporary Christian educational practice.

As one example, I want to look at the way the educational task of nurturing faith in the next generation may perpetuate some of these colonizing

---

35 Hong, *Decolonial Futures*, 96.
36 Jennings, *Christian Imagination*, 108.
37 Jennings, *Christian Imagination*, 109.

impulses. Traditions that attend most carefully and energetically to Christian formation, to educating the next generation into the faith, are often the most likely to attempt to create the kind of "pedagogical eternalities" learned from the colonial period. A biblical text from Deuteronomy 11:18–19 (NRSV) justifies formation in all areas of life: "You shall put these words of mine in your heart and soul, and you shall bind them as a sign on your hand, and fix them as an emblem on your forehead. Teach them to your children, talking about them when you are at home and when you are away, when you lie down and when you rise." That imperialist tendency, the desire to declare a better way that the next generation should live into, gets played out on children and youth, who also tend to be imagined by their adult teachers as unknowing, susceptible to the corrupting influences of the world, and primarily people to be formed by bodily habit towards the Christian faith in totalizing environments so as to not "lose" them from the church as adolescents or young adults.

This kind of colonizing formation of the next generation can be witnessed most clearly in segregationist white evangelical Protestant communities in the United States. These communities sponsor private Christian schools that are closely linked to church and home formation so that children experience the kind of totalizing formational environment that does not allow for interaction with secular culture, which is seen as potentially corrupting and destructive to faith. Not coincidently, many of these private evangelical Christian schools tend to have been founded at the historical moment of racial integration in public schooling as well.[38] While the stated mission of the school is to provide an education strong in character, in which Christian belief in the authority of the Bible or patriarchal notions of family and gender are not challenged, the timing and emergence of these Christian day schools in the South point to a deeper kind of formation that they are trying to preserve ... formation into whiteness. These communities, while using a desire for Christian formation as the rationale, also achieved continued racial segregation in the name of protecting their children from corrupting influences and providing an excellent education in private schools, not available in the public schools now "corrupted" by the entrance of non-white students.[39]

This effort continues through the process of trying to control the narrative of textbooks related to US history, including the fight over whether public

---

38   R. Andrews, *The Dynamics Involved in the Introduction of Cultural Diversity into the Mission of the Evangelical Christian School.* Dissertation. ProQuest Dissertation Publishing, 2002.

39   https://southerneducation.org/publications/history-of-private-schools-and-race-in-the-american-south/.

education should cultivate critical awareness of historic oppression for non-white persons and immigrants in those stories. Often this fight is framed as the desire for parents to extend the character-building restrictive environment of the family home rather than expose children to awareness of histories of racism and alternative sexualities. The reluctance to teach these histories is also advocated as a desire to cultivate a love for God and country, a patriotic character seen as essential for faithfulness to God. Public education is seen as the appropriate venue to cultivate support for a white Christian nationalist movement as evidence of building character. Taking many fronts, this conflict also emerges through the desire to use public funds for Christian and other private educational institutions, through voucher programs and a constant attack on the imagined "indoctrination" of vulnerable children through public education and higher education.[40]

In the late part of the 20th century, homeschooling networks emerged that further isolated children, ensuring that the home was the primary socializing environment, and that parents could have sole control over the intellectual and faith development of their children.[41] These networks share Christian-based academic curriculum with an emphasis on character formation.[42] The home becomes a seamless pedagogical environment in which they must teach their children to love the Lord, protecting them from other cultural forces that would lead them astray. This contemporary example of a totalizing "pedagogical eternality" creates a situation in which the entire environment a young person interacts with must contribute to forming Christian habits and character, without any sense that there is a faith seeking understanding in the child that could withstand or benefit from exposure to cultural difference, to non-Christian friendships or teaching relationships, or to other authoritative discourses of human meaning-making such as the scientific method.

---

[40] For an example of this kind of legislation in the state of Tennessee in 2024, see https://www.chalkbeat.org/tennessee/2024/03/25/private-school-voucher-esa-history-timeline-tennessee-bill-lee/.

[41] The top three reasons for homeschooling children in the United States in those families that homeschool are listed as "a concern about school environment, such as drugs, safety, or negative peer pressure; a desire to provide moral instruction; emphasis on family life together." A desire to provide religious instruction is also in the top five reasons. See https://nces.ed.gov/programs/coe/indicator/tgk/homeschooled-children.

[42] In the United States about 75% of homeschooling families are Christian, and as Wilhelm and Firmin note, "concern for the control and direction of character development among the home school children (religious or otherwise) seems to be a common thread among many families." Gretchen M. Wilhelm and Michael W. Firmin, "Historical and Contemporary Developments in Home School Education," *Journal of Research on Christian Education* 18, no. 3 (September 2009): 304.

Lest more mainline Protestants and moderate Catholics believe they are out of the woods in these forms of imperial education, these traditions also have a series of religious educational texts concerned about the potential loss of Christian belief in the next generation. A survey of the titles of some major texts cited and taught in Christian education include concerns about the need to evangelize the next generation: John Westerhoff's classic *Will Our Children Have Faith?*, Thomas Groome's *Will There Be Faith?*, Christian Smith's *Soul Searching* and Kenda Creasy Dean's *Almost Christian*.[43] Each of these books begins by declaring the next generation as being vulnerable to falling back into a non-Christian way of being, and therefore imagines them as key targets for Christian formation through comprehensive socialization and embodied practice in Christian communities. One of the classic ways to rally energy for religious education is by casting the next generation as potentially lost to their contaminated broader cultural environment, not unlike the way that Acosta and his cohort saw the inhabitants of the New World. Educators evaluate the next generation as hapless, out of the realm of the discipled ones, and in need of intervention through some serious intentional formational effort before the reach of the broader culture corrupts them out of the realm of salvation.

To be fair, the content of many of these texts contains much more nuance about the agency of children and adolescents, and the authors espouse the belief that the Holy Spirit is capable of working within the next generation independent of the salvific educational efforts of their communities.[44] The insights about socialization, formation, faithful friendships and mentoring relationships with adults, and engagement in embodied practice that they name are important additions to the field of Christian education. But the way these texts get titled and positioned in the market reinforces the motif of Christian education as colonizing uplift in a foreign and potentially corrupting environment. I am not condemning these texts, or even my own works that advocate for communal contexts of socializing practice, but I am drawing the connectional through-lines between these efforts and the white supremacist, colonizing logic that got merged with Christian formation in the

---

43   John H. Westerhoff, III, *Will Our Children Have Faith?* Third Revised Edition (Morehouse Publishing, 2012); Christian Smith and Melina Lundquist Denton. *Soul Searching: The Religious and Spiritual Lives of American Teenagers,* Reprint edition (Oxford University Press, 2009); Kenda Creasy Dean, *Almost Christian: What the Faith of Our Teenagers Is Telling the American Church* (Oxford University Press, 2010).

44   Smith's *Soul Searching* is a notable exception to this nuance, and he is the author without formal training in theology or Christian education in this group of texts.

colonial era. Approaching the next generation with desperation for their maintenance within the Christian community, with non-mutual forms of socialization and habit formation through immersive pedagogical environments for the strengthening and continuation of a particular form of Christianity, draws uncritically on the history of colonizing educational models for its habits of educational practice.

As discussed in the previous chapter, the intense focus on embodied Christian practice in community that emerged in the late twentieth century in white mainline and evangelical Protestantism in the US, just as these traditions were coming to terms with losing their place of cultural prominence in the culture, also points to this trajectory. When faced with declining numbers and decreasing cultural dominance, these traditions drew on what they have known best historically: shaping the next generation through embodied practices of the tradition and dominant socializing communities. This formation is considered life-giving, providing exposure to virtuous practices of faith that pass on traditional wisdom, but it also draws on the embodied practices of disciplining environments with a never-ending pedagogical reach. While the experience of many ex-vangelicals who have emerged from some of the communities who engaged in these vigorous forms of pedagogical eternalities point to the stifling and sometimes abusive nature of these environments, particularly if your embodiment or sexuality does not allow you to conform to expected gender performance, the claims of the adults in these communities is that they are concerned and working hard for the salvation and purity of their children's souls. There can be a thin line between what is considered vigorous formation and what is experienced as religious or spiritual abuse, a lack of freedom to challenge the education or perspectives that are offered without fear of rejection or punishment.

4   Education with Humility

So many of my graduate theological students want to teach, to bring other people into their enlightened understanding of social justice, of religious traditions, of spiritual practice. I have become suspicious of that impulse, even as I can honestly say that being a teacher is central to my identity. I am suspicious of this calling because teaching is an exercise of power. We undertake any project of teaching or education because we believe that where people currently are is not adequate to their situation and that they need some kind of change to improve their lives. Even when education is intentionally liberative, seeking to help students to gain the agency to "read the word and the world" as Brazilian educator Paulo Freire named it,[45] this is a change that is imposed through an exercise of authority on the part of the teacher.

When we claim the power and authority to teach, to go and make disciples, what are our ethical responsibilities to those we wish to educate? Taking seriously the history of white supremacy in Christian education in the Western world calls for attention to the reality that not all forms of education are necessarily beneficial for students. Attending to the legacy of colonial domination and white supremacy highlights how these practices embody the belief that we know better than those we teach and assume our own better state and the need to bring others into it. As Dube notes,

> At issue here is the fact that we are all inscribed, given its global reach and impact, within the historical experience of imperialism. Therefore, unless our critical practice takes deliberate measures to understand the mechanisms of past and present imperialisms—to understand the marriage of imperialism with issues of gender, race, class, religion, and sexual orientation—even the most liberationist of discourses will end up reinscribing the structures of violence and exploitation.[46]

We are the bearers of a legacy habit of understanding Christian education as a nonmutual, unidirectional project. While this form of educational practice has been roundly critiqued and resisted even as it is replicated, particularly in adult and liberationist religious educational literature, it still persists as part of the background of many Christian educational ventures.

When education was practiced by European colonizers, like Christianity, it became entwined with a project of white racial domination. That enmeshment does not mean that education is a wholly doomed project, but it does mean that we must reckon with this history before we engage in educating in the name of Christ. We must check ourselves. Why are we so desperate to impart our ways of being to the next generation? What part of that is desire for their well-being, and a generous act of sharing inherited wisdom? What part of that desire is an inherent sense of confident supremacy that we have learned from our history as part of Christianity interpreted in the colonial period? What part of it has a history in the colonizing impulse to bring others into our fold, to be able to control them and their resources through subjecting

---

[45] Paulo Freire and Donaldo Macedo, *Pedagogy of the Oppressed: 50th Anniversary Edition*, 4th edition (Bloomsbury Academic, 2018, 193.

[46] Musa Dube, "Go and Make Disciples," 243.

disciplined bodies to a regime of pedagogical force, to "civilize" them? Knowing that religious education has been used as a thoroughly white supremacist strategy of imperial force historically, what does that mean for the interrogation of the current practices of the discipline? Dube suggests this requires an intentional choice "to counteract imperialist domination by embarking on a critical practice that seeks to understand, expose, undermine, and arrest the imperialist forces of oppression and exploitation."[47]

The history of Christian pedagogy that Dube, Jennings, Tinker and others relate has demonstrated that practices of religious education couple very nicely with white supremacy and cultural imperialism. When we educate because we believe that people's thinking or way of being in the world needs improvement and that there is wisdom from our cultural heritage that would lead to a better way of being in the world, we know from our history that this train of thought is closely related to the dangerous territory of supremacist thinking. The opposite impulse of supremacy is humility, and this virtue is essential for those who wish to educate in Christian faith. Humility as a virtue requires honest self-appraisal, a conversion to other persons who are quite different than us as equally valuable, and a proper understanding of the community's importance within the created order.

Humility in reckoning with the history of white supremacy in Christian education begins with honest self-appraisal that takes into account both the gifts and the horrors of our own tradition. Theologian Norman Wirzba describes humility as follows: "If we understand humility as beginning in a detailed and honest estimation of ourselves, as when Bernard of Clairvaux defined humility as 'the virtue by which a man recognizes his own unworthiness because he really knows himself,' how, given our propensity for either self-promotion or self-deprecation, are we to arrive at such honesty and clarity?"[48] A "detailed and honest estimation of ourselves" in religious education means being honest about our roots in the history of Christian imperialism, and seeking to understand how the habits learned in that process continue to impact contemporary practices of formation and education.

Attending to these roots can be disruptive to one's sense of identity and confidence in the value of one's cultural tradition. Theologian James Cone points to the reality that sharing these histories often makes the people who benefit from them uncomfortable. He notes, "Whites do not like to think of themselves as evil people or that their place in the world is due to the colonization

---

47 Dube, "Go and Make Disciples," 235–236.
48 Norman Wirzba, "The Touch of Humility: An Invitation to Creatureliness," *Modern Theology*, 24: 2, 2008, 231.

of Indians, the enslavement of Blacks and the exploitation of people of color here and around the world. Whites like to think of themselves as hard working, honorable, decent and fair-minded people."[49] In response to this struggle, embracing humility means being willing to tell these stories and accept the responsibility for their legacy. It means teaching these histories, accepting the charges of participation in cultural decimation, and honestly seeking to discover where we are still participating in this kind of educational venture. Rather than continuing to promote Christian formation as a primarily benevolent venture, we must be painfully honest in describing where it has gone wrong and continues to go wrong.

Within religious education, many contemporary scholars have worked hard to counteract this historical colonizing form of Christian education. One place to find this in the field is in the literature on religious education in multicultural settings. Many of these authors focus on humility as a critical virtue for educators when working with others who are different from them. For example, Kathleen Talvacchia codes this aspect of humility as "seeing clearly," and the process of coming to see clearly as one of conversion: "Seeing clearly depends on a conversion to the other, to understanding and awareness of both personal prejudice and social structural difference that affects the other in different ways, depending on their social location to the dominant culture."[50] Humility requires the honest assessment of both individual and collective histories of oppression in their fullest, and attention to how these affect our educational efforts as teachers. Seeing clearly requires the humility of understanding that one's own approach or experience does not apply to all persons universally, and it requires careful listening to the experiences of those unlike us. Humility does not always pair well with the authority required to teach, but the two do not have to be mutually exclusive.

This conversion to the other is also rooted in historical Christian resources such as the works of the desert fathers and mothers on humility. They did not understand humility as self-degradation or self-hatred: "Instead, humility meant to them a way of seeing other people as being as valuable in God's eyes as ourselves. It was for them [the ammas and abbas] a relational term having to do precisely with learning to value others, whoever they were."[51] This

---

49 James H. Cone, "Theology's Great Sin: Silence in the Face of White Supremacy," *Black Theology* 2:2. 2004, 146.
50 Kathleen T. Talvacchia, *Critical Minds and Discerning Hearts: A Spirituality of Multicultural Teaching* (Chalice Press, 2003), 67.
51 Roberta C. Bondi, *To Love as God Loves: Conversations with the Early Church* (Fortress Press, 1987), 18.

empathetic response to others subverts the kind of self-righteous judgmental gaze that is central to colonizing forms of education. Rather than judging those whom we wish to educate as deficient in some way that needs remedying, humility requires that we see potential students first as valuable in God's eyes and also as knowledgeable and intelligent in their own right. Whether or not what we desire to teach is valuable must be negotiated with the students' own experiences, cultural norms, and the values of their community.

This conversion to the other whom we hope to teach is also present in liberationist Brazilian educator Paulo Freire, who confessed how long it took for him to learn to humbly respect and be converted to the peasant farmworkers he was charged with teaching: "Coming back to my question, it took time for me to learn that the people with whom I was working already had lots of knowledge. The question for me was exclusively to understand what were their levels of knowledge and *how* did they know."[52] This approach to humbly recognizing the extant intelligence in communities in which we hope to educate is articulated beautifully in the "funds of knowledge" approach to teaching in public schools, which begins with the simple premise: "People are competent, they have knowledge, and their life experiences have given them that knowledge."[53] Primarily addressing the ways that working-class and poor communities are defined in terms of their deficiencies for the children who come from them, the approach taken by Gonzalez et al is "to view these households primarily in terms of their strengths and resources (or funds of knowledge) as their defining pedagogical characteristic."[54]

Humility as a virtue of the educator is particularly important in situations where education happens across differences of race, culture, sexuality, age, and social class. In their important work on multicultural spiritual formation, Elizabeth Conde-Frazer and S. Steve Kang talk extensively about the virtue of humility in educational efforts across the spectrum of human difference. In reaction to the supremacist tendencies that make themselves evident in these interactions, Kang notes the need to abandon the hierarchy of teacher as knower and students as "empty receptacles." Instead, he argues, "The teacher must utilize her authority appropriately to make it clear from the beginning that she is on the pilgrimage along with her students and is

---

52   Myles Horton and Paulo Freire, *We Make the Road by Walking: Conversations on Education and Social Change*, Eds. Brenda Bell, John Gaventa, and John Peters, reprint edition (Temple University Press, 1990), 65.

53   Norma Gonzalez, Luis C. Moll, and Cathy Amanti, eds. *Funds of Knowledge: Theorizing Practices in Households, Communities, and Classrooms* (Routledge, 2005), ix–x.

54   Gonzalez, Moll, and Amanti, *Funds of Knowledge*, x.

open and expecting to learn from them just as the students are expected to learn both from one another and the teacher. To achieve this, the teacher must consistently convey humility and openness in her interaction with students."[55] Conde-Frazier argues that humility comes from self-understanding that is balanced and accepting of one's true nature. She notes, "Those who exhibit humility do not see themselves as greater than others. Therefore, they do not usurp the place of others. This sense of self and neighbor allows us to relate to one another not according to the social and economic statuses of our cultures but according to our true human worth."[56] This movement beyond usurping the place of others is critical to education that resists cultural imperialism and paternalistic formative environments.

Conde-Frazier and Kang both come from cultural groups that have been on the receiving end of historic missionizing education during the colonial period which impacts their perspective on these approaches to education. Conde-Frazier has modeled a decolonial pedagogy through her work with Esperanza College and its broader cultural interventions in Philadelphia.[57] Conde-Frazier's influence on another generation of religious educational scholars working in a decolonial mode, notably Christine Hong, Anne Carter Walker and Patrick Reyes, all of whom are scholars of religious education with eyes wide open to the impact of white colonial Christianity on the field.

The attention to the agency of learners and respecting their cultural knowledges has been an important legacy of the work of Paulo Freire and others in the field of religious education. His work and connection with Latin American liberation theologians and the World Council of Churches meant that attention to liberative pedagogy was a part of late twentieth century scholars in the field, including Thomas Groome and Daniel Schipani.[58] On the one hand, such calls for educators to respect their students' intelligence and agency are commonplace in contemporary Christian educational literature in the white mainline. On the other hand, fears about the continuation of denominational

---

55 Elizabeth Conde-Frazier, S. Steve Kang, and Gary A. Parrett, *A Many Colored Kingdom: Multicultural Dynamics for Spiritual Formation* (Baker Academic, 2004), 155.
56 Conde-Frazier, Kang, and Parrett, *A Many Colored Kingdom*, 195.
57 For more about the mission of Esperanza, see https://www.esperanza.us/about-the-agency/our-impact/. For her description of her own work in that setting, see Elizabeth Conde-Frazier, "Religious Education for Generating Hope," *Religious Education* 112:3, 2017, 225–230.
58 Daniel Schipani, *Religious Education Encounters Liberation Theology* (Religious Education Press, 1998); Thomas H. Groome, *Sharing Faith: A Comprehensive Approach to Religious Education and Pastoral Ministry* (HarperSanFrancisco, 1991).

structures, the practice of Christianity into the next generation, and the influence of cultural noise often leads educators to revert to strategies of casting the next generation as endangered by their cultural context and in need of strong embodied formation. Biblical scholar Walter Brueggemann imagines that the covenantal tradition of the gospel can help us move from self-enhancement and preservation to walking humbly with our God: "It depends rather on self-abandoning companionship along the way, for it is the act of companionship (and not self-celebration) that gives staying power, self-respecting dignity, and eventually wellbeing."[59] This includes cultivating and invoking respect for those we have been culturally formed to regard as less intelligent than us, including children and adolescents, those we would wish to evangelize, and those who belong to other religious traditions. As a counter to historical habits of colonizing white supremacy in Christian education, careful cultivation of the capacity for "self-abandoning companionship" as educators is a challenging but essential formational task.

---

59 Walter Brueggemann, "Walk Humbly with Your God: Micah 6:8," *Journal for Preachers* 2010 33:4, 19.

CHAPTER 4

Questioning Intervention

Some years ago I was sharing a draft chapter with faculty colleagues on how difficult it is to describe what is currently happening in a given context for those engaged in practical theological reflection.[1] The many layers and levels of ideational and material forces impacting any given situation, from the intrapsychic to the cultural/ideological to institutional structures and governmental policies, mean that no description of "what is going on" will ever be complete. I had ended the chapter suggesting that the unending layers of complexity in description might be contained for the moment by what interventions were being considered by the practical theologian engaged in the descriptive reflections, by the possibilities of the answers to the question of "what then, shall we do?" in a reflective process.

A colleague on my faculty, trained at the University of Chicago in an anthropological approach to studying religion, protested at the notion of allowing intended intervention to delimit the scope of the descriptive task. "You broke the prime directive!" he said, with a nod to the prohibition of interference with civilizations that are less developed as expressed in the Star Trek fictional universe, a saying used in his own training as a cultural anthropologist. "In the process of studying what is going on, you can't intervene! That changes things!" At the time, I (somewhat) calmly explained that the purpose of practical theological reflection was entwined with the praxis of ministry and leadership. This moment of descriptive work was part of a larger action/reflection model in which a leader of a community was trying to make wise decisions about what they should do in their role as leader. In light of this purpose, intervention in situations was a given, the question was how well that intervention aligned with the contextual realities and adherence to faithful response in dialogue with the norms of the tradition in which they were leaders.

The connection of theory and practice, the formation of students as leaders who have a sense of capacity and responsibility to engage in artful ministry, and the ability to respond to the dilemmas presented by daily life in the work that students find themselves are absolutely at the heart of my vocation as a

---

[1] For a finished version of this chapter see Katherine Turpin, "The Complexity of Local Knowledge" in Joyce Ann Mercer and Bonnie Miller-McLemore, eds., *Conundrums in Practical Theology* (Brill, 2016), 250–275.

teacher. And yet, these notions of influence, shaping, and the logic of transformation are closely aligned with a desire to be in control of situations that is grounded in the logics of white supremacy and colonization. Intervention by a leader requires a sense that one's own insertion and effort in a given situation will lead to an improvement in the conditions of that situation, or at least will result in less harm and more life-giving rather than death-dealing conditions. Intervention is the assumed practice of those accustomed to being in control and whose agency is rarely limited in social situations.

In this chapter, I am questioning my own declaration that intervention is an assumed appropriate response from ministerial leaders and practical theologians that should be habituated through educational formation. I am not joining my colleague in naming the appropriate role of the practical theologian as distanced observer, who can somehow research and understand without affecting the community about which she wishes to learn. That myth of objective observer or resesarcher has been thoroughly debunked elsewhere as a colonial project, a task I won't replicate here. I am calling into question the easy habit of intervening, of deciding what should be done, of taking professional control and responsibility, and underneath this habit the white logics of progress, transformation, and "fixing stuff" that are built into notions of intervention in the work of practical theology. I am thinking of the seminary students who appear in my classes because, ultimately, they want to "change the world," a stance that is valorized and encouraged in their undergraduate university formation. Their assumed position of intervention is linked with the culture of whiteness, particularly linked to the temptations of white saviorhood and the myth of progress and mastery.

1   The Role of Intervention in Practical Theological Reflection

In her book *Places of Redemption*, theologian Mary McClintock Fulkerson names the relationship of intervention to the work of practical theology in healing the wounds that we encounter in our work: "Equally important is the way reading this situation as a wound implicitly assumes an emancipatory interest and demands a response of change. Thus, practical theology is also a particular way of attending to the structure of a situation; *it is an inquiry shaped by a logic of transformation* (emphasis original)."[2] Practical theologians

---

2 Mary McClintock Fulkerson, *Places of Redemption: Theology for a Worldly Church* (Oxford University Press, 2010), 22.

engage in reflection upon the theological dilemmas of particular communities with the assumption of the responsible role of one who will intervene in those dilemmas. In intervening, they hope that their praxis will do no harm and will bring about healing, transformation, salvation, or change for the better. Paying attention to the wounds and the dilemmas experienced by communities allows for inquiry that results in more faithful response to these challenges, often in collaboration with the members of the communities experiencing those challenges. Or, as Bonnie Miller-McLemore puts it: "Practical theologians understand method as a means to ecclesial and social change. In fact, a distinctively practical theological objective of method is to have a transforming influence on religious faith in congregations and society."[3] Intervention and transformation are the currency of the purposes of the discipline and the work of its scholars.

In his introductory text to the field, Richard Osmer named this the "pragmatic" task of practical theology, the answer to "How shall we respond?," which he defines elsewhere: "Forming an action plan and undertaking specific responses that seek to shape the episode, situation, or context in desirable directions."[4] Those "desirable directions" are meant to be in conversation with the normative task of consultation with the voices of the Christian tradition to seek something akin to living in alignment with God's desire for the situation, ascertained through the earlier reflective questions of "what is going on" and "what should be going on?" While both Osmer and religious educator Thomas Groome in his model of shared Christian praxis acknowledge that this reflective task is best engaged dialogically in the faith community with the help of the triune God, both recognize a clear role for the practical theologian or religious educator in leadership of the process.[5] While Groome describes a more collaborative action/reflection model rooted in liberationist educational commitments and facilitated by a capable educator, Osmer expresses more of a professional leadership model by academics and clergy that is accountable to the community but not necessarily collaborative within it. When Osmer describes the pragmatic leadership required, he notes that the practical theologian acts first and later reflects with the responses of the community to that

---

3 Bonnie J. Miller-McLemore, "Contributions," in ed. Bonnie J. Miller-McLemore, *The Wiley-Blackwell Companion to Practical Theology*, Vol. 72, Wiley-Blackwell Companions to Religion (Wiley-Blackwell, 2011), 11.

4 Richard Osmer, "Practical theology: A current international perspective," HTS *Teologiese Studies / Theological Studies* [Online], Volume 67 Number 2 (16 November 2011).

5 Thomas H. Groome, *Sharing Faith: A Comprehensive Approach to Religious Education and Pastoral Ministry: The Way of Shared Praxis* (HarperSanFrancisco, 1991).

action: "determining strategies of actions that will influence situations in ways that are desirable and entering into a reflective conversation with the 'talk back' emerging when they are enacted."[6] In this model, the practical theologian acts on behalf of the community, and the community provides feedback after the fact to shape the future interventions of the leader.

Don Browning named this initiating work of the leader as the "strategic" nature of practical theology, the idea that this form of theological reflection is an engagement with intent to affect the outcomes of a community in a particular direction. Even before he published his classic work *Fundamental Practical Theology*, it was clear that Browning had received pushback about the interventionist nature of the work of the practical theologian as he described it. He notes in that book:

> Some of my colleagues have objected to the military or political sound of the term *strategic*. It suggests to them images of ground, air, or naval maneuvers in the midst of battle. Even worse, it suggests complicated models of anticipation, calculation, and retaliation of the kind associated with the elaborate nuclear strategies of the Cold War era.[7]

That tension about calculated control or strategy as a colonizing or militaristic orientation to a community or situation is what I am also questioning in this chapter. Browning indicates that strategic intervention involves good pastoral leadership and the accountability of the practical theologian to the communities about which she reflects rather than calculating or militaristic intervention. But the calculating and conquering resonances of the word "strategic" may echo the colonial past of the word in ways that Browning was not discerning. Browning goes on to a conversation about the move between practice and theory and to reflect on the importance of "practical wisdom" grounded in Aristotelian notions of *phronesis* in the work of practical theology. In the end, he muses, the overall purpose of practical reason is "the reconstruction of experience. When inherited interpretations and practices seem to be breaking down, practical reason tries to reconstruct both its picture of the world and its more concrete practices."[8] This "broad-scale interpretive and reinterpretive process" sounds perfectly reasonable, and yet underneath this work might lurk the remnants of a set of world-building and reconstructing assumptions of colonialist logics in a hermeneutical package.

---

6   Richard Robert Osmer, *Practical Theology: An Introduction* (Eerdmans, 2008), 4.
7   Don Browning, *Fundamental Practical Theology*, revised edition (Fortress Press, 1995), 8.
8   Browing, *Fundamental Practical Theology*, 10.

In their introductory text Gordon Mikoski and Kathleen Cahalan name "Interventionist and Critically Constructive" as one of their key features of practical theology: "Practical theologians are unapologetic change agents. Much of our work aims at critically assessing what is destructive and diminishing of our lives and what can be changed in order that individuals, communities, or societies can strive toward a more just common good."[9] This notion of being an "unapologetic change agent" is part of what makes "practical" theology practical. The purpose of the work of the field is to improve situations, to lead towards more faithful and life-giving outcomes, or in their language "a more just common good." One concern is the easy assumption that imagined interventions will result in more life-giving conditions, but it may also be true that the outcomes of intervention are aligned with maintaining power and that notions of the common good may or may not include the input of those who are not a part of an in-group or a dominant culture. Changes are not always equally beneficial for all who experience them, and discerning what is the "common good" and how it is brought about is a much more political and at times contested and incommensurate project than might be assumed.

2   Agency, Assumed Control, and the White Savior

One of the expressions of dominant culture is the assumption that one has the power to fix situations of injustice, sinful behavior, or the "wounds" of the world in McClintock Fulkerson's language, bringing them more into line with a desired ideal. The desire to make the world a better place, or to help the church live into its gospel mandate with more fidelity, often motivates the work of practical theology. This assumption that intervention will lead to progress is woven deep into the psyche of white Western Christianity. Somewhere in the combination of the scientific revolution of the Enlightenment, the colonial projects of civilizing and enlightening so-called "savages" around the world, and the society-shaping projects of the Social Gospel movement, the heady mix of "bringing forth the Kingdom of God" and "progress towards a better life" became intertwined in powerful ways. Perhaps the "Kingdom of God" language itself bears the roots of political desires of co-opting and deploying hierarchical power for the good from its early origins. The notion that one can intervene

---

9   Kathleen A. Cahalan and Gordon S. Mikoski, "Introduction" in Kathleen A. Cahalan and Gordon S. Mikoski eds., *Opening the Field of Practical Theology: An Introduction* (Rowman & Littlefield Publishers, 2014), 6.

in a situation and bring about healing or salvation requires a sense of efficacious power that is linked through whiteness to an image of the white master or heroic charismatic individual. In its worst forms it becomes the imagination of a white savior capable of swooping in and ending the oppression of persons of color (that, for the record, other colonial interventions generated for the purpose of increasing civilization).

World-changing transformations have often had devastating results for those whose situation is being transformed. In the colonial era, the work of civilizing uplift was often paired with a removal of resources and wealth towards the colonizing nation. This violent removal of resources and resulting impoverishment of the colonized was often a hidden reality. Postcolonial practical theologian HyeRan Kim-Cragg says it this way: "Many postcolonial scholars have demonstrated how the very identity of Europe is shaped by the need for Europe's colonized Others, and yet this need must be defended, if not denied."[10] She draws on the work of postcolonial scholar Gayatri Chakravorty Spivak, who notes: "as the North continues ostensibly to 'aid' the South—as formerly imperialism 'civilized' the New World—the South's crucial assistance to the North in keeping up its resource-hungry lifestyles is forever *foreclosed*."[11] The white savior offers aid, development, education, civilization, and technology while simultaneously requiring raw materials, labor, destruction of environmental integrity, and migration to maintain its position of dominance. What is mythologized as salvation, development, and uplift is rightfully understood as deep economic interdependence masked by unequal power relations and exploitation.

The critique of the myth of the white savior has been developed through criticism of particular tropes within very popular and award-winning films in the United States where white characters are centered to tell the stories of the suffering of communities of color who need those heroic characters to lift them out of their difficult realities. White savior movies such as *To Kill A Mockingbird, Lawrence of Arabia, Mississippi Burning, Dangerous Minds, Freedom Writers, Amistad, Green Book, The Help, Blind Side*, and many others demonstrate their cultural currency in their popularity at the box office and with dominant culture-centered Oscar voters, even as their message has been roundly critiqued by the communities purported to be saved, the families whose stories were told in these narratives (as in *Green Book*), and those whose

---

10 HyeRan Kim-Cragg, *Interdependence: A Postcolonial Feminist Practical Theology* (Pickwick Publications, 2018), 12.
11 Kim-Cragg, Interdependence, 12.

stories are minimized in favor of the white main character. The repeated retelling and subsequent awarding of this genre of story points to their deep cultural resonance, codifying meaningful narratives that capture the desires and worldviews of their majority white audiences. A liberal enlightened form of racist trope, the white savior myth positions people of color (or their stand-ins, such as alien races in *Avatar*) as being hapless and in need of motivation, wisdom, salvation, or heroic inspirational intervention in order to be rescued from the horrible conditions of their existence. As sociologist Matthew Hughey notes:

> Many of these films are what critics call "Magical Negro" or "White Savior" films—cinema in which implicit and explicit racial stereotypes are employed to structure the inter-racial interactions where one character labors to redeem another. In comparing these two genres, this article provides an overview for how both cinematic forms reproduce racist messages by naturalizing the supposed cerebral rationality, work ethic, and paternalistic morality of select White characters while normalizing Black characters as primordially connected with nature, spiritually connected to the carnal, and possessive of exotic and magical powers. Together, these films subversively reaffirm the social order and relations of racial domination by reproducing centuries' old understandings of racial difference.[12]

Missing in these narratives are often the histories of racist social engineering, exploitation of labor, extractive colonizing, and cultural oppression that generated the oppressive conditions from which communities of color must be "rescued" in the first place. Schools do not just become underfunded and underresourced, nor neighborhoods created where the majority of people in them have little to no access to the means of thriving, without direct intervention and misdirection of resources by the dominant group for the profit of shareholders or in the name of economic development. In the educational versions of these films, those conditions are naturalized as places needing uplift from white saviors because of the unredeemed suffering and backwardness of the people living within them without an analysis of how the situation came to be.

---

12   Matthew W. Hughey, "Racializing Redemption, Reproducing Racism: The Odyssey of Magical Negroes and White Saviors," *Sociology Compass* 6, no. 9 (2012), 751.

Many years ago, I interviewed my faculty colleague and scholar of American Indian religious traditions George E. "Tink" Tinker about his work in teaching in our Justice and Peace program.[13] He reflected on the largely white and middle-class students that he had taught, noting: "White people have an inordinate need to want to fix things." He describes his experience as the term progressed in a class focused on social justice, students begin to despair at the depth of the wounds they encountered and wanted to know what they could do to eradicate the injustice about which they were learning: "I tell them there are no quick fixes, no easy answers. If we institute a government policy, there are always ramifications that generate more problems and injustice." Another colleague, ethicist Miguel De La Torre, in this same round of interviews, reminded me that it is an expression of the deep connection with structures of power to assume that you can "fix" injustice. The recognition that injustice is embedded in deep structures to which people are ideologically committed brings at first a sort of shock when privileged students discover that they are individually powerless to change the structures and may, in fact, be deeply invested in their maintenance. De La Torre notes, "They learn for the first time what many people of color have always already known—how hopeless it really is. Once they lose their idealism, they realize that they are going against the very power structure that gives them power. The goal then is to help them realize the frustration inherent in working for justice, but to still not give up. This is an important part of the learning." This idea of embracing hopelessness as a form of solidarity with those who have long had to endure under resilient oppression has been further developed in De La Torre's more recent works.[14]

The educational goal in the face of this temptation of white saviorhood is to move from assumed agency because of a station of privilege to a more modest or chastened form of agency that recognizes the depth and seeming intractability of injustice as well as one's complicity in creating it. This movement is difficult because as dominant culture persons, individual power and agency are our assumed reality, a part of our worldview about the value of a human life. Ethicist Sharon Welch, in her work with the nuclear disarmament movement, learned that the white ethic of control with its dreams of enacting progress often discouraged white people from engaging with issues where they could not predict or control the outcome, such as the complex

---

13   These interviews are recounted more fully in Katherine Turpin, "Disrupting the Luxury of Despair: Justice and Peace Education in Contexts of Relative Privilege," *Teaching Theology and Religion*, 2008, vol. 11 no. 3, 141–152.
14   Miguel A. De La Torre, *Embracing Hopelessness* (Fortress Press, 2017).

issues of ending the possession and potential deployment of nuclear armaments at the international or global level. Welch works to offer a model of power for people who have it and want to use it well: "A key dimension to this view of power is a nondualistic understanding of good and evil and, correspondingly, images of hope that can counter cynicism and despair without relying on utopian expectations or millennial dreams of inexorable progress and long-lasting social change."[15] She sought to define an ethic of risk where professional control was de-emphasized on behalf of engaging with justice issues even if their outcomes were not going to change in one's lifetime. As De La Torre noted above, white people must develop the strength to work for justice without hopeful imaginings that they are able to control the outcome in their favor.

Such an ethic of risk runs against white norms of professional behavior, where being responsible and in control of situations is paramount. It runs against white notions of leadership, where having the power to individually enact change as a strong person who can influence others is considered desirable. And finally, it runs against the myth of the white savior, the narrative trope where an individual white person of principle manages to lead people of color to overcome the racist barriers that have hither fore oppressed them. As I mentioned before, the white savior narrative is a deeply favored storyline in US cinema, but it is also a covert part of the narrative of almost every youth mission trip taken by churches across racial and class boundaries. This deeply and tenderly beloved myth is a part of the vision of many clergy who are church planting in urban neighborhoods or MDiv students who start their education seeking to change the world. The idea that a committed and principled [white] leader can come into a situation and effect change where communities [of color] have been struggling for years to survive and navigate the challenges before them unsuccessfully can underlie the call to ministry for many good-hearted white Christians. However, it also re-enacts a colonial vision for transformation based in the civilizing control of whiteness.

In her very helpful book about activism in compromised times, ethicist Alexis Shotwell notes that the need to be right, to work from a point of personal purity, is problematic notion of control rather than working to face challenges. She notes:

> The point is to *change the world, this* world, and so the point is complicated, compromised, and impossible to conceptualize, let alone achieve

---

15   Sharon D. Welch, *A Feminist Ethic of Risk*, revised edition (Fortress Press, 2000), xi.

alone. People doing movement work usually get lots of things wrong, which might not be such a problem—if the purpose of the work isn't to be right. Instead, our purpose is to contingently make it be that something that *deserves a future* has one.[16]

Part of living in complex systems that are failing to address issues like climate change is that there is no point outside of the complex systems from which to be entirely right, nor is it possible to individually fix situations through intervention. Instead, we work together in the compromised and compromising ways that are available so that other species and those most vulnerable to situations of injustice have the possibility of a future.

3   Intervention as Religious Meaning-Making

Intervention by leaders takes a different form for those who engage in the more neoorthodox forms of practical theology, where intervention is not about social engineering or communal progress, but rather the hermeneutical project of learning to speak the languages of faith to make meaningful connections and engage in more rigorous faithful embodied practice. Intervention in this stream of practical theology means bringing people into true and faithful understanding of how God is at work in the world, offering practices that help us take on the habitus of Jesus Christ, or learning to see the world as God would have us understand it. Intervention in this hermeneutical work imposes Christian meaning upon the struggles of daily life, the chaotic and delightful course of living as a human in the world, in order to bring about a sense of goodness, beauty, and purpose. We intervene so that others may interpret the world in a faithful way, that they might find Christocentric meaning in the rhythms of their existence, and through that give witness to the providence of God and the working out of salvation in the details of one's individual and communal walk with God. This deep belief in meaning-making as a powerful human activity may also become linked with notions of progress and managing narratives in order to bring about increased Christian faithfulness.

The work of Robert Orsi has helped me come to terms with the ways that the practice of meaning-making itself is a kind of intervention in the Western imagination, a layering of a narrative structure of faith over situations that

---

16   Alexis Shotwell, *Against Purity: Living Ethically in Compromised Times* (University of Minnesota Press, 2016), 196.

may not ultimately redeem those situations but may instead play out tragic resonances of relationship to stories and figures that are inherited in the tradition while perpetuating them. In his explorations about the interpretation of persons with disabilities by the Roman Catholic church of his childhood and other particular case studies, Orsi questions whether meaning-making is a life-giving or a controlling practice of the church. For example, Orsi reflects upon the ways that sacred figures such as saints in the Roman Catholic tradition mediate the holy in ways both life-giving and death-dealing. One of the stories he shares is the relationship of his grandmother to St. Gemma Galgani. Galgani's story, marked by her intense suffering and lifted as a model to many mid-Twentieth century Catholics, provided a "narrative conjuncture of these two lives":

> Born in the same time and place, Gemma and Giulia were both early and profoundly shaped by grief and absence that made them both raw and vulnerable to the prospect and the threat of withdrawal and separation. Both were ensnared in bitter domestic entanglements with close relatives who were cruel to them, exploiting their weaknesses, sorrows, and needs, according to the stories.[17]

Orsi indicates that bringing the two lives together involved both pain and love, interpreted through the stories told of the saint in American Catholic publications of the era.[18] For Orsi, the intense difficulty of these stories and the reality "that at the heart of the telling of them there remains a core of uncertainty and even distress that narrative can only circle but never resolve" calls into question "whether or not 'meaning-making' is the best way of thinking about religions."[19]

Orsi reflects on the ambivalent nature of religious practice and meaning-making that was available to his grandmother through her relationship with this saint:

> At the very least we can say that if meaning is being made here out of pain and blood, the movement between life and meaning—the social, psychological, domestic processes of meaning making—can be terrible

---

17 Robert Orsi, *Between Heaven and Earht: The Religious Worlds People Make and the Scholars Who Study Them* (Princeton University Press, 2006), 139.
18 Orsi, *Between Heaven and Earth*, 136.
19 Orsi, *Between Heaven and Earth*, 111–112.

and destructive and that the meanings made, the lives made, with religious media can be dreadful and painful. It is also the case that Gemma and Giulia were born into religious stories that existed before them and that there was a narrative waiting for them that had little to do with their agency or intentionality. What I see when I look at both lives is confusion, cruelty, disorientation, and sorrow; *meaning* is not the first word that comes to mind.[20]

In contrast to the common belief that sense-making leads to a sense of purpose, healing, or salvation during difficult times, Orsi resists the idea that the hermeneutical practices of religious meaning-making always bring comfort, purpose, and sustenance to those who engage in them. In fact, they may be the source of cruelty, violence, and destructive control of bodies and dismissal of experiences even as they offer the stories and tropes that interpret those same experiences: "The very same religious idioms do tremendous violence in society and culture and bring pain to individuals and families all the while that they ground and shape the self, structure kinship bonds, serve as sources for alternate imaginings of the social world, and so on."[21]

Orsi finds a deep productivity in the layering of religious meaning with the experiences of daily struggle that his family members experienced, but he questions whether this intervention, this resonance with divine figures that makes sense of experiences of suffering and tragedy in light of the Christian tradition, is actually a good thing. Instead, Orsi argues:

> Another way of thinking about this is to say that the movement between life and meaning or between sacred and profane is not a straightforward one and that the meeting of the two often enough deepens pain, becomes the occasion for cruelty, catches persons and communities in stories that are made against them (or that are supremely oblivious of them in their own particularities), that may alienate them from their own lives, and that bear within them the power to undermine them and make them and the people around them miserable and confused.[22]

Here the process of sense-making co-opts the difficult experience of suffering and sanctifies it, de-legitimizing its tragic impact and declaring it all right

---

20 Orsi, *Between Heaven and Earth*, 143–144.
21 Orsi, *Between Heaven and Earth*, 171.
22 Orsi, *Between Heaven and Earth*, 144.

because of its resonances with suffering in the religious tradition. This may not actually help the person who is making Christian interpretations of their experiences grounded in connections with the stories that the tradition offers, but may in fact lead to death-dealing interpretations rather than sustenance or hope.

Orsi, following Talal Asad, posits that "meaning making" is a "distinctly modern, Western preoccupation and a distinctly post-Enlightenment and intellectualist approach to religion."[23] He is also speaking against a reductionist understanding of religious practice in the sociology of religion as an opiate of the masses, or as a rational choice that supports one's own well-being. Instead, the project of meaning-making might lead to this tragic story of dreadful resonance. Meaning-making, or the hermeneutical task of connecting religious tradition with the stuff of daily life, becomes for Orsi not a heroic practice of finding meaning but rather a form of media that entangles the religious believer with meanings that may work against him or her: "This leads to a more chastened view of culture generally and of religion in particular, one that steers clear of words like *empowerment, agency* (simply), and *transcendence* and instead moves in the register of the tragic, of the limited and constrained, or what I would think of as the real."[24]

This focus on the tragic, or the real world of limits and constraints without a need to fix them or interpret them through the Christian narrative as somehow exemplary or redemptive, has been an important insight offered from disability theologians as well. The biblical narratives of healing from disability have at times been problematic in creating an expectation that illness or disability should be something that gets fixed by faith. Theological tropes of redemptive suffering have positioned people with disabilities as needing to serve as exemplary figures who are content with their suffering as a way to demonstrate their faithfulness and trust in God. In light of these historically problematic approaches to dealing with limitations, disability theologians have also named the problematic nature of engaging disability as only an exceptional human experience requiring healing and fixing. Theologian Deborah Creamer reflects on how the experience of human disability reorients us to the experience of embodied limits. She notes, "This proposal suggests that limits, rather than being an array of unfortunate alternatives to omnipotence, are an unsurprising characteristic of human nature."[25] Creamer indicates that philosophy and

---

23 Orsi, *Between Heaven and Earth*, 144.
24 Orsi, *Between Heaven and Earth*, 170.
25 Creamer, Deborah Beth. *Disability and Christian Theology Embodied Limits and Constructive Possibilities* (Oxford University Press, 2009), 94.

theology have struggled with the reality that "bodies are leaky, messy things" and have "repeatedly struggled with what it means to have limits—including the ultimate limit, death."[26] She calls on the presence of limitation as a normal human experience rather than an exceptional one, describing the ways that most humans will experience increasing limits as their bodies age and all will die. Not acknowledging these limits with theological honesty is problematic on many levels: "In these denials, we live a lie, a lie that harms other people (those on whom we project and reject these limits), the environment (when we pretend that it also has no limits), and even ourselves."[27] Meaning-making narratives that attempt to redeem or deny these experiences of limitation, suffering, and loss do not resolve their reality, and indeed can be a source of harm to the people they are meant to help.

One of the problems of belief in intervention, being the white savior, and the myth of progress without limits is that these habitual ways of meaning-making often fail to account for the reality of the limited and the tragic in human existence. The desire to be helpful and to fix things can be particularly harmful in situations where issues are complex, interests are competing, and there is no immediate solution. This might take the form of a hospital chaplain called in to "fix" the grief of someone experiencing the sudden tragic death of a loved one in the Emergency Room so that medical professionals don't have to deal with it. Belief in individual intervention lies behind the state legislature calling for better performance from schoolteachers and social workers to overcome the layers of economic oppression and resource starvation experienced in hard-living communities and somehow rescue individuals without elected leadership addressing the structures that generate brutal conditions of existence for many families. Ministers are asked to overcome urbanization, declining birthrates, and other demographic churches face to somehow fill pews with people and offering plates with dollars. The belief that leaders and professionals can individually intervene in order to fix (or at least mitigate) complex realities can lead to never actually addressing the depth of those quandaries or imagining a different way forward within the limitations that actual life on earth together imposes. In these complex realities the logic of transformation can lead to interventions that are experienced as paternalism, embodiments of denial, culturally inappropriate, placing band-aids on deep wounds, and colonizing cultural invasions.

Where the Christian religious tradition might invite us into moments of lament in the face of suffering or confession and repentance in the face of

---

26 Creamer, *Disability and Christian Theology*, 116.
27 Creamer, *Disability and Christian Theology*, 119.

wrongdoing, the sense of needing to "do something," to be a person of action who gets stuff done, can lead to superficial engagement with personal struggles and social programs rather than addressing the complex depths that only groups of people working together over time might address. It can lead to only awarding grants and funding programs to established groups that have a track record of success and that can demonstrate measurable progress on sometimes meaningless measures (developing "grit" for instance). That "can-do attitude" can blame individuals for not being able to overcome the conditions of their existence, whether tragic or systemically arranged to be death-dealing. "Fixing stuff" can deny the realities of ambiguous grief or complex PTSD, refuse to recognize the ongoing impact of generational trauma, shifting the blame of complex systemic oppression onto individual responsibility. In other words, intervention in this mode can simply make bad situations worse by seeking positive transformation without fully reckoning with the depth and intractability of suffering and injustice built into the very structures of social existence.

4   The Myth of Progress and Salvation as Whiteness

Lying just underneath the commitment to intervention is a myth that history is bending itself towards better outcomes for human life through the march of progress, and that intervening will lead to a better outcome as history moves towards its fulfillment. As theologian Gordon Oyer notes, "The idea of progress has shaped Western culture's worldview since it emerged from the Enlightenment era. This idea asserts that advances in science and technology, along with modern political structures and expanding overall wealth, are destined to perpetually improve human experience."[28] Leaders are those persons who enable that progress by leveraging advances in technologies of production and social organization to bring about that imagined civilized future that will be an improvement to the difficult and problematic situation in which we find ourselves. A difficulty arises in that each new era seems to present humans with new challenges to their survival and flourishing, with the limitations, implications, and consequences of the choices of their ancestors, and with the realities of what it means to be creature rather than creator showing the lie in the myth of progress. In a little essay on the myth of progress, economist

---

28   Gordon Oyer, "Confronting the Myth of Human Progress: Thomas Merton and the Illusion of Privilege," *The Merton Annual* 28 (2015), 149.

and scholar of European thought John Gray wryly notes, "But no new technology can abolish scarcity, do away with the necessity of choice, or alter the fact of human mortality."[29] He acknowledges the way that this myth links up with the desire for control to produce a fantasy that fuels notions of the possibility of unlimited economic growth and utopian hopes for a beautiful future:

> The dream that technology serves for us is a dream of complete control. It's a dream with ancient sources in Western traditions. It's the dream that we can cease to be mortal, earth-bound creatures subject to fate and chance. It's a product not so much of science as of magic. The project of using technology to re-make the world according to our will captures the fantasy by which we have been ruled during much of the 20th century. It was a fantasy of progress without instability.[30]

Rather than a religious studies appreciative sense of myth as story that bears forth deep values and truths that a culture wishes to share from generation to generation, Gray, an economist, uses "myth" here as a substitution for "fantasy, dream, or magical thinking," an impossible or improbable imaginative story decoupled from the boundaries of reality.

Theologian Willie Jennings is again helpful in tracing the ways that the "ancient sources in Western traditions" that Gray names more generally are a mix of the ideologies of discovery and conquest that are a part of the colonial project forged together with notions of new life in Christ:

> From the beginning of colonialism, salvation and the transformation of land and peoples have been coupled together, and that coupling turned Christianity's creative powers against itself. Christian faith is about new life in Christ and forming life inside that newness. The new situation of colonial power enfolded the newness that is Christian faith within the newness of transforming land, people, earth, and animal.[31]

Jennings goes on to note that the desire for transformation is not inherently evil, but coupling it with the practices of cultural erasure that often go along with it in colonialist logic, bringing about destruction and submersion of those who are led rather than inviting them into life together, was destructive.[32] For

---

29 John Gray, "The Myth of Progress," *New Statesman* 4/9/1999, 28.
30 Gray, "The Myth of Progress," 28.
31 Willie James Jennings, "Whiteness Isn't Progress: How the Missionary Project Went Horrifically Wrong," *The Christian Century* 135, no. 23 (November 7, 2018): 28–31.
32 Jennings, "Whiteness Isn't Progress," 29.

Jennings, there is a qualitative difference in gathering people together, allowing the realities of difference that one encounters to permeate one's own vision for transformation, and bringing oneself into alignment with those differences as they acknowledge their depth and wisdom. This is a call for communion rather than fixing. However, Jennings notes, the "site of hope for Christian settlers" was to appropriate these situations for their own purposes and to also make them into the way they thought the world ought to be.[33] That simultaneous combination of transformation and extraction for one's own benefit was a destructive legacy of whiteness.

Questioning the myth of progress, or the idea that we can encounter suffering or woundedness in the world without immediately seeking to fix it feels problematic. Are we just to settle into living with injustice? Embrace oppression? Not bind up the wounds of the brokenhearted? In questioning white supremacy and colonial logics, we may feel that we are abandoning all hope of healing or transformation, Jennings notes, because we think this is the only viable route to change. In fact, we defend the damage done in the name of progress because we can't imagine other ways that people might work together outside of the worldview of extraction and commodification: "Some argue that everything good produced through modern economics outweighs its collateral damage—the denial of indigenous ways, the reductionism inherent in scientific investigation, and the commodification, fragmentation, and reassembling of life into products for exchange."[34] As an example, we might consider recent public arguments by United States Representative Tom Cotton in a NYTimes opinion piece that the founding fathers understood "slavery as a necessary evil" for the eventual economic and political wellbeing of the nation, arguing against school curriculum based on the 1619 Project that acknowledged the horrors of chattel slavery and its legacy for African-descended persons.[35] The elimination and curtailing of hundreds of thousands of human lives, the taking away of their dignity and freedom, and the theft of labor and destruction of social and cultural ties can all be justified because without that beginning, the US economy and democratic system would not be as developed as it is now. The current progress justifies the oppression and horrors that allowed for the consolidation and extraction of wealth in the hands of the economic elite.

Practical theologian Kathleen Cahalan senses the collapse of intervention into theological arrogance and calls for a clarification of the relationship between the work of ministry and the idea of progress: "Clarifying the relationship between the reign of God and ministry is very important, since far

---

33 Jennings, "Whiteness Isn't Progress," 31.
34 Jennings, "Whiteness Isn't Progress," 31.
35 https://www.bbc.com/news/world-us-canada-53550882.

too often Christians confuse ministry with bringing about the reign of God. This sentiment is most clearly seen in language that describes Christians as 'building' or 'bringing about' the kingdom through efforts to create a world of peace and justice."[36] Cahalan makes a strong argument that God's reign is "sheer gift, both in its present and final reality, and no one, not even here knows the hour or day (Mark 13:32)."[37] She notes, "It is certainly not something we can bring about by working harder and we cannot manipulate God into bringing it about; we can ask for its coming—'your kingdom come'—and for readiness, but God's graced presence is a reality and gift that God grants freely and lovingly."[38] At the same time, she argues that living as disciples requires the recognition and response to this gift of God's presence, that "our efforts at neighbor love, reconciliation, prophetic words, deeds of justice, and stewardship of the earth is a response to the call of God to love what God loves and to live lives that reflect God's reigning presence in them."[39] This notion of discerning responsiveness to God's work in the world is quite different than the language of strategic intervention or transformation as the language of ministry. In many ways, this is an old fight in in Christian theologies of vocation about what humans have the power to do in terms of participation in divine Providence and what is an inappropriate taking on of the role of God. A serious self-check on the notion that white people are somehow responsible for salvation in the end and can bring it about through intervention seems important in not replicating the notion of intervention as fixing.

5 From Intervention to Design for Collective Flourishing

What might intervention look like without embracing the strategies of fixing, white saviordom, and progress that arise from the legacy of whiteness? In his book *The Purpose Gap*, practical theologian Patrick Reyes takes up the importance of the work of design, working with the principles laid out by Sasha Costanza-Chock. Reyes is still focused on world-building, and certainly believes in intentional design work for challenging the matrix of domination. He reflects, "Good design is taking responsibility for changing the conditions of one's material world."[40] But Reyes also provisions for intentional questioning that places front and center "the flourishing of the community" rather

---

36 Kathleen Cahalan, *Introducing the Practice of Ministry* (Liturgical Press, 2010), 60.
37 Cahalan, *Introducing the Practice of Ministry*, 60.
38 Cahalan, *Introducing the Practice of Ministry*, 60.
39 Cahalan, *Introducing the Practice of Ministry*, 61.
40 Patrick B. Reyes, *The Purpose Gap: Empowering Communities of Color to Find Meaning and Thrive* (Westminster John Knox Press, 2021), 58.

than the intervention of the designer by asking question such as: "Does the design reflect the needs of all its members, not just a chosen few? Does the design lead to the liberation of the least of these? Does the design reflect the freedom people are trying to achieve for themselves?"[41] In addition to these questions about who interventions benefit and whether they designed for liberation or collective freedom, Reyes is asking about how to "build worlds that reflect a regenerative future for us collectively—worlds that create more life than they destroy?"[42] This acknowledges that any intervention has the capacity to be both life-limiting and live-giving. While asking important questions about who designs interventions, who carries them out, and what aims they serve, Reyes maintains a belief in intervention, but calls for ethical practices of design that take seriously the weight of world building and its implications for all who are impacted by it. The questions of ongoing sustainability, the challenges to unequal and unacknowledged interdependence, and the focus on the whole community rather than leader mark the work of design as imagined by Reyes as something qualitatively different than strategic intervention by an individual leader.

Instead of progress, control, saviorship, change-agents, and intervention, our work as practical theologians may also be to encourage the move to endure, accompany, belong, or be in communion with situations of struggle and suffering.[43] Practical theology is best understood not as an outcomes-based science. As a warning, this may also mean that practical theological reflection may therefore not be a form of leadership or ministry particularly valued in a productivity-oriented late capitalistic cultural setting. Challenging the habit cultivated by whiteness to take heroic individual action to fix stuff or to intervene to make things better, practical theologians may need to sit with ambiguity, struggle, incompleteness, human limitation, and mortality. Design may require the collective engagement of generations in imagining and creating a sustainable future. This slow imagining and design for a different future where survival is meant for all violates the link of being a professional in white culture with notions of mastery and an easy assumption of agency as someone who gets stuff done.

---

41 Reyes, *Purpose Gap*, 58.
42 Reyes, *Purpose Gap*, 59.
43 While I am questioning easily assumed white agency to intervene and its connection to the myth of progess and the white savior narrative, I also humbly acknowledge the important work of scholars like Valerie Miles-Tribble, who is asking for urgent action and intervention from black churches related to justice issues. See Valerie A. Miles-Tribble, *Change-Agent Church in Black Lives Matter Times: Urgency for Action* (Fortress Academic, 2021). There is a qualitative difference in arguing for intervention from a womanist communitarian perspective than from a narrative of individual mastery.

Within the demands for efficacy in ministerial roles, capitalist notions of productivity through intervention find their way into the work of practical theology. For example, hospital chaplains are asked to engage in caregiving practices that are outcomes-based with research-driven evidence of their efficacy. While one might have sympathy for wanting to eliminate evangelistic practices of conversion in the midst of physical vulnerability or offering meaning-making platitudes or prayers that do not acknowledge the depth of suffering in chaplaincy work, the notion that accompanying those who suffer in hospital will somehow demonstrate efficacy in health outcomes can feel like a violation of the practice itself. Discerning where to accommodate demands of demonstrated success in intervention and where to insist that perhaps the work of ministry and spiritual accompaniment doesn't produce immediate results can put chaplains and faith-based grant funded agencies in a difficult position. The bottom-line thinking operative in white corporate culture will ask, why should we invest money in you, why should you be here if we can't measure the change, the transformation you have wrought? Why waste time and money investing in people, communities, projects, or relationships if you can't prove that they are beneficial through the demonstrated outcomes? That unmitigated belief in progress and transformation can violate the realities of struggle and suffering, the tragic real that Orsi reminds us of.

I return to the helpful proposal of ethicist Alexis Shotwell here as she argues for what it means to live ethically in compromised times. She calls for staying with the trouble and working to future survival in the midst of the calamity of climate crisis despite knowing that our interventions are always compromised and limited:

> We cannot predict what might emerge from individual and collective practices of staying with the trouble, except that it holds the possibility of another world, still imperfect and impure, and another one after that. The possibility of other worlds, hospitable to hosting many worlds, might be beyond our capacity to imagine. Still, such a possibility can only arise because of our imperfect attempts to make it so.[44]

The hard reality is that ministry does not mean assuming you have something to contribute and should be able to control the outcome in an ongoing line of progress towards the kingdom of God by assimilating others into your project of civilization and progress. Unlearning whiteness means recognizing that our

---

44   Shotwell, *Against Purity*, 204.

desires to intervene for transformation, for saving the world, may actually not be of God. Important questions for practical theology may be how, in that capitalistic notion of productivity, do we focus instead on the sense of communion with others and the whole of creation that Jennings asks for? How do we advocate for vulnerability and permeability of leaders rather than skilled intervention that leads to measurable wins? How do we live in the real, as Orsi names it, that realm of limitation and circumscribed possibility that may mean our work provides resonance within the tragic? How do we trust a fragmentary stitching together of the pieces that allows us to hold all that is, honestly and nonproductively, even as we work to imagine a future where interdependence is acknowledged and the survival and flourishing of all is sought? The next chapter takes on what it means to be a leader in such a world where the efficacy of individual intervention is chastened.

CHAPTER 5

Questioning Leadership

The formation of leaders has been a significant focus in theological education in the United States in the first two decades of the twenty-first century. As "perhaps the youngest and least developed subdiscipline within practical theology,"[1] practical theological scholars publishing and teaching on leadership formed the Academy of Religious Leadership in the late 1990s, though certainly this form of reflection built upon earlier work in church administration and claims ties to examples of leadership all the way back to the biblical record. Despite its relatively recent emergence as a subdiscipline, through the language of granting and accrediting agencies, denominational desires for reversing the trends of decline, and curricular revisions responsive to these pressures, leadership has been a key orienting metaphor for the work of practical theology in its re-emergence as an academic discipline as well. Bonnie Miller-McLemore names attention to leadership as an important contribution of the field of practical theology: "A significant part of the field deals with congregational, organizational, and leadership development."[2] For example, Osmer relates leadership, in particular servant-leadership, to the pragmatic task of practical theology, writing an entire chapter on it in his introductory practical theological text. The Lilly Endowment, Inc., has focused deeply on pastoral leadership and cultivating vocation in order to encourage leadership in younger people, particularly through entering the ministry as a first career, through its funding of the now-mostly defunct programs on theological exploration of vocation in young people and leadership development programs like the Forum for Theological Exploration (FTE).

Despite the generally shared assumption of the importance of leadership in practical theology and theological education, the task of forming leaders is worth interrogating so that those we train as practical theologians do not take on the mantle of leadership quite so comfortably, particularly when what is sought is individual hierarchical leadership in the forms shaped by white colonialist logics. The concern that underlies the presumed agential intervention

---

[1] Michael Jinkins, "Religious Leadership" in ed. Bonnie J. Miller-McLemore, *The Wiley-Blackwell Companion to Practical Theology*, Vol. 72, Wiley-Blackwell Companions to Religion (Wiley-Blackwell, 2011), 309.

[2] Miller-McLemore, "Contributions," in *Wiley-Blackwell Companion to Practical Theology*, 14.

of the practical theologian discussed in the prior chapter and its easy alignment with dominant culture notions of white saviors and the myth of progress is worth pursuing a bit further here. Those interventionist tendencies align with forms of white supremacy that understand leadership in terms of dominating or charismatic power performed by an individual within a hierarchy, particularly a white male individual who commands the labor of other bodies, in order to bring about outcomes that are pre-determined by dominant culture as benevolent or beneficial. It is this form of leadership that I question in this chapter.

In her book *Introducing the Practice of Ministry*, Kathleen Cahalan uses the following definition of leadership as one that is commonly articulated in the field: "people who persuade and influence others to carry out a common purpose, who are given the authority to direct people and resources, who are called upon to give vision and meaning to a collective effort."[3] Three tasks related to the exercise of power are evident in this definition: power to persuade and influence, authority to allot resources, and power to cast a vision on behalf of a group's experience. In each of these tasks, Cahalan is careful to note their accountability to common purposes and collective effort, echoing Osmer's claim that leadership is on behalf of the community as a form of service, not for self-advantage, but performed to build up the community.[4]

An underlying ambivalence has often been present in practical theological work on leadership, particularly concern about religious leadership relying on models and approaches to leadership drawn from social sciences and corporate practice without much critical theological reflection on the corporate implications of those modes. Practical theologian Michael Jinkins does not move to link corporate forms of leadership with the extractive white values of capitalism or individualism, but the uneasiness of what it means for the church to align with notions of corporate management in its understanding of leadership is present. Jinkins notes that as early as 1956, H. Richard Niebuhr's work on the pastoral director model both "legitimized the administrative leadership of ordained ministry, even as he attempted to orient that leadership away from the image of a corporate executive or a 'big operator.'"[5] It seems that the notion of leadership so aligns with the idea of colonial or corporate executive that it is difficult to imagine forms of leadership that focus more wholistically on cultivating the life of the community rather than attending

---

3 Kathleen A. Cahalan, *Introducing the Practice of Ministry* (Liturgical Press, 2010), 57.
4 Cahalan, *Introducing the Practice of Ministry*, 57.
5 Jinkins, "Religious Leadership," in Miller-McLemore, ed., *Wiley-Blackwell Companion*, 313.

primarily to the person of the leader and their actions. The leadership theory text used most often among those practical theologians teaching leadership since 1985, Heifetz's *Leadership without Easy Answers* points to the role of leader as "equipping a group to negotiate and draw on its shared and competing values in meeting the changes of its environment" or leading "adaptive change."[6] These models begin to pay more attention to the interconnection of leaders and followers, but still highlight the individual capacity to facilitate that change and to negotiate differences.

Jinkins also points to two other models of leadership common in current literature in practical theology, one based in pastoral care Seward Hiltner's notion of shepherding/organizing and one based on the notion of spiritual direction or guidance, for example as developed by Christian Scharen.[7] These are interesting moves, attempting to reclaim historic and distinctive metaphors other than corporate leader from Christian ministry and eschewing those "categories derived from general leadership and management theory" in order to "segregate it from general human 'commerce.'"[8] The recent emergence of "political pastoral care" or "congregational care" as a way of thinking of the work of the pastoral leader or practical theologian rather than administrative leadership may also be a response to reframing the notion of leadership into something less indebted to colonial models of administration and more rooted in the care for the community or in notions of attending to the shared life of larger groups of people.

1   **On Leaders and Followers**

Once long ago in my work as a youth minister, I was facilitating a program on leadership and met with unexpected resistance from a middle schooler who was the youngest of three children and the child of the pastor of the congregation. "Not me. I am not a leader. I am a follower!" declared Sean,[9] emephasizing the word "follower" with great gusto to the laughter of the rest of the group. On the one hand, this young person did follow in the wake of his powerful older sisters in a way that made this moment of confession feel truthful. On the other hand, the idea that we would be forming young people, particularly a young white man, to be a follower was a laughable conclusion

---

6   Jinkins, "Religious Leadership," in Miller-McLemore, ed., *Wiley-Blackwell Companion*, 313.
7   Christian Scharen, *Faith as a Way of Life: A Vision for Pastoral Leadership* (Eerdmans, 2008).
8   Jinkins, "Religious Leadership," in Miller-McLemore, ed., *Wiley-Blackwell Companion*, 316.
9   A pseudonym.

within the group. Of course, it was absurd for him to aspire to merely be a follower, wasn't it?

Sean's disruptive intervention in my effort to form leaders has struck with me over the years in considering the implications of continuously forming leaders. Who was helping any of us to be good followers to all of the stellar leaders we were seeking to create amongst the people we teach? I wonder if perhaps we don't talk about forming followers much because leaders in a colonizing or dominant culture mode don't require followers, or people who willingly choose to contribute to the visions cast by leaders. In a colonial system, leaders need bodies to exploit to engage in the labor that makes their so-called "self-sufficient" progress a reality. They don't need followers, they need labor, an economic resource rather than an agential human person or discerning community. Colonizing leaders delegate tasks to others who must engage in the complex work to complete them.

My theological school once had a president whose image of colonizing leadership was captured in a protest he lodged when asked to engage in more than just idea-generation but also to be involved in designing the processes and pathways that would lead to the change he envisioned. He protested, "It's like this. If we were creating a new water system, I describe the beneficial outcomes of having new access to water and create the blueprints. It is your job to figure out how to dig the trenches and lay the pipe." In this case, he declared we would have an online degree program, and it was up to the rest of us to make that work in a short timeframe with the limited faculty and financial and technological resources that we had. He had cast the vision. We were required to make it happen on his behalf. In this story we see the classic model of the colonial leader as figurehead and envisioner of new worlds. In order for that "self-sufficient" white male leader to function, he needed the labor of other bodies to embody the transformation he declared to be at hand. He also needed designers and organizers and people to gather others together to engage in the real work needed by the community. This faulty model of heroic individual leadership leaves a burdened populace faced with the actual work of addressing the needs of the community. Ironically, this particular president claimed ethics and leadership as his two content knowledge areas on the faculty, and he did in fact receive credit from the Board of Trustees for being the one at the helm in a season we were quite innovative and moved our curriculum online. This declaration felt like a deep betrayal to the team of people who actually struggled to make that move a reality, a Cuban-American dean and two white women faculty, who put in the time and labor and creative energy of love to create a vital and sustainable online program, as well as the many faculty and students who struggled together in the early years to turn this experiment into a meaningful venture. This is the epitome of the white male colonizing leader, drawing on the expertise and labor of other nondominant people to accomplish what they in the end receive credit for.

Questioning leadership feels counter-intuitive in a professional education setting. Students come to us wanting to feel more competent and knowledgeable as leaders of faith communities, nonprofits, and other ministry settings. It is a temptation to meet them in that desire for agency and efficacy, to teach them methods of theological reflection that help them feel they will be able to have control over seemingly intractable situations of woundedness and injustice. We are morally persuaded to form them as leaders, and any number of granting agencies and denominational officials will support this outcome of theological education. But this kind of individual leader who relies on the delegation of labor of others to actually craft a viable response to the challenges that a community faces is steeped in colonial forms of administration and unequal power that must be dismantled.

2   From Corporate Rock Star to Interdependent Co-collaborators

The nature of white colonizing norms embedded in what is understood as good professional leadership is that the responsible role of leader requires control over a situation, the ability to lead effectively and to be recognized as competent in responding to crises and the tricky morasses of regular institutional life. It is, as theologian Willie Jennings teaches us, education into leadership understood as the self-sufficient white man, with control, possession, and mastery as the key outcomes of knowledge:

> A vision of the self-sufficient man—one who is self-directed, never apologizing for his strength or ability of knowledge, one who recognizes his own power and uses it wisely, one bound in courage, moral vision, singularity of purpose and not given to extremes of desire or anger—is a compellingly attractive goal for education and moral formation. The power of this vision is that it binds a man to a task, a job, a vocation, or a philosophy that ironically takes the focus off the man, thereby drawing him to a work and a world greater than himself but inextricable from him and his power.[10]

---

10   Willie James Jennings, *After Whiteness: An Education in Belonging* (Eerdmans, 2020), 31.

This is education into being the master, a "marriage of ancient forms of Christian formation with modern colonialist logics, combining a civilizing impulse with a soteriological sensibility."[11] Racialized and gendered others become civilized into full humanity by becoming leaders in the form of the master, a white self-sufficient male with a vision of salvation for others. If they are not recognized as leaders, their fate is to have their bodies exploited in the relentless grind of "digging the ditches and laying the pipe" for a water system that the leader receives the credit for creating.

One of the fascinating developments of the past five years has been artist and activist Tricia Hersey's work as the Bishop of the Nap Ministry in advocating rest as resistance to imperial forms of domination and rest as reparations amongst black bodies in particular and people of color more generally. Hersey declares that rest is not something one has to work to earn. Refusing non-stop hustling, submission to the grind demanded by one in late capitalism, is a deeply disruptive practice: "Don't let anyone tell you it's easy to disrupt grind culture via rest. It is a lifelong meticulous practice that starts with a slow deprogramming, collective thinking, radical care and refusal. Poverty is real & systematic demonic traps also real. It's not just lay down and vibe."[12] This ministry is a profoundly decolonizing response to the demands of white supremacy in late capitalism that white people lead and other bodies "dig the trenches and lay the pipe."

By declaring the right to rest as a divine right that need not be earned, Hersey and others who have picked up the themes of her work are engaged in an ongoing liberative practice to deprogram from the idea: "We exist in a culture that supports sleep-deprivation; we have been brainwashed by capitalism to work at a machine-level pace, and to equate our worth with how much we can produce."[13] While Hersey credits the source of her ideas in black liberation theology, she also echoes theologies that acknowledge the political nature of sabbath, including biblical commandments that declare that even slaves have a need for rest, and the ecological notion of letting the earth lie fallow for a season and not be relentlessly extractive of it. By questioning the grind culture demanded of followers, this disrupts a notion of white supremacist leadership as well. Refusal to supply leaders with the endless supply of labor they need to enact their schemes disrupts a concept of leadership as exploitative individual

---

11   Jennings, *After Whiteness*, 107.
12   @TheNapMinistry, Instagram post, 2/16/22.
13   Tricia Hersey, "Playboy Symposium: Rest is a Divine Right," Feb. 8, 2021. A book-length exploration of her work is now available in Tricia Hersey, *Rest Is Resistance: A Manifesto* (Little, Brown Spark, 2022).

practice and raises the question of what a different form of leadership might look like.

Philosopher and social change activist adrienne maree brown is helpful in imagining the importance of interdependence in thinking about shared forms of leadership that do not call for singular leaders and delegated laborers who make things happen. In fact, she has a healthy suspicion of individual leaders, asking, "In an interdependent movement, with decentralized innovation and leadership—how do we respond to the gift and curse of the charismatic leader?"[14] While she is willing to note that the individual leader can bring some gifts, she also notes: "The work of promoting and protecting one personality is as different form the work of organizing as holding one's breath in is from an exhale."[15] In imagining what leadership looks like in a movement that has many people bringing gifts, she speaks of the importance of avoiding getting isolated from those whole hold you accountable, advising: "If you are in a leadership position, make sure you have a circle of people who can tell you the truth, and to whom you can speak the truth. Bring others into shared leadership with you, and/or collaborate with other formations so you don't get too enamored of your singular vision."[16] That trait of vision, so often valued in colonialist versions of leadership, here has the risk of seducing the leader into failing to collaborate with others. Seeking to form circles of truth telling others, who share in the work of leading the community with their own gifts, is essential to avoiding the allure of promoting and protecting oneself as the heroic one who directs the movement or brings about the organizing.

Unfortunately, circles of leaders or shared models of leadership are not a form of organization that is deeply recognized by important outside groups. In the world of nonprofit and grassroots organizing, networks of powerful individual leaders, often expressed through the importance of creating relationships over time, receive many of the funding opportunities and influential promotion through official recognition by governmental entities at all levels. brown discounts the importance of these preferences, noting that what actually moves groups forward are the many people involved in carrying out their missions:

> Whether a leader is great or not, funders have traditionally preferred the narrative of a rock star leader, and have invested in individuals more than missions. The people of an organization make or break the work, and the

---

14   adrienne maree brown, *Emergent Strategy: Shaping Change, Changing Worlds*, reprint edition (AK Press, 2017), 98.
15   brown, *Emergent Strategy*, 99.
16   brown, *Emergent Strategy*, 100.

best mission will not be realized without the right people behind it. The shiny stars are rarely the ones actually getting the work done, or even doing the most exciting thinking in the organization.[17]

While paying lip service to the many people that are necessary to make anything happen, something about whiteness wants to elevate the single figure, the extraordinary individuals who are leading the charge. In contrast to this individual model, the work of movements and successful organizations require practices of interdependence in which participants can lean on each other and "meet each other's needs in a variety of ways." Rather than valorizing the extraordinary vision, charisma, and commitment of individual leaders, says brown, "we have to decentralize our idea of where solutions and decisions happen, where ideas come from."[18] It is difficult for historically white institutions and funding agencies to recognize the value of collective genius, the ecologies of wisdom that allow for such interdependent movements and organizations. The habitual practice of valorizing of CEOs and extraordinary and heroic individuals trains our eyes to ignore that something different might be going on.

3 The Paradox of Servant Leadership

As the purpose and vision statement of my seminary was being re-written, a list of what we prepared our students to become was generated: "Iliffians are activists, servant-leaders, and innovators in diverse religious, secular, and academic communities." The language of servant-leader does not crop up accidentally among alumni of seminaries trained in the latter part of the twentieth century, the group of people who introduced this term into this communal statement. As Michael Jinkins notes:

> Arguably the most influential concept of leadership among religious leaders and theological educators that has emerged in the past 50 years comes from management researcher Robert Greenleaf, whose 1969 essay "The Servant as Leader" later became the opening chapter of his book," and focused on "value-rich" or "principle-centered leadership.[19]

---

17   brown, *Emergent Strategy*, 101.
18   brown, *Emergent Strategy*, 87.
19   Michael Jinkins, "Religious Leadership" in Miller-McLemore, ed., *Wiley-Blackwell Companion*, 308.

While the term "servant-leader" may have been an appropriate corrective to the narcissistic, individual heroic leader of white men in corporate America in the late 1970s that was considered problematic, it assumes a kind of kenotic choice to give up the power one already possesses in order to become a servant to the people. For those who have never had that automatically-granted power in a given role, and who in fact struggle to have their authority and skill set noticed because of their embodiment in terms of race, gender, ability, sexuality and so on, claiming that title is deeply problematic. If everyone expects you to be a servant already, to act like their self-sacrifical mother because of their gender, or to be attentive to your needs before your own because of their race, the idea of servant-leadership can be an invitation to lean into your own oppression. The act of giving up one's power to become a servant or slave assumes an initial position of dominating power, even divine power, given its links to the person of Jesus Christ giving up equality with God to become a servant. The metaphor of servant-leadership is a form of leadership aligned powerfully with the lived experience of individual white males who are more likely to be instinctively granted authority when placed in roles with power in a hierarchy rather than treated with suspicion.

In his chapter on the pragmatic task of practical theology, which he equates with servant leadership, Richard Osmer begins by naming the stark decline in the historically white mainline denominations and argues for the importance of the "pragmatic task of *leading change* (emphasis original)" in light of those trends.[20] He notes, "The leaders of mainline congregations face not only the external challenge of a changing social context, but also the internal challenge of helping their congregations rework their identity and mission beyond the era when they were at the center of cultural influence and power."[21] In this moment, I think Osmer correctly identifies the genesis of such a strong emphasis on leadership in theological education and in denominational continuing education of their pastors within the mainline. The fear of decline, the loss of being at the center of power, and changing demographics towards a more racially and religiously diverse population (including the rise of the "nones") led to a belief that better leadership from pastors could somehow reverse these changes, which were framed as "decline." Being decentered from a dominant position and losing resources in the form of money and members has been deeply painful for white mainline churches, and by extension, for the theological schools that are dependent upon them for students and monetary support. And yet, there is something suspect in naming this as "decline."

---

20 Richard Robert Osmer, *Practical Theology: An Introduction* (Eerdmans, 2008), 176.
21 Osmer, *Practical Theology*, 176.

It harkens to the decline of civilizations, the decline of decency, something linked to the lament of loss of dominance and a desire to regain the upper hand in influence and power.

Additionally, demanding better leadership from individual pastors in light of this decline feels like an unhelpful and damaging strategy based in a deep belief in the power of the individual to enact social change through leverage the labor of many unnamed others. To suggest that broad social trends in terms of declining birth rates among the white population, urbanization and the loss of economic opportunity in rural areas where many churches are closing, increased immigration, and greater racial and religious diversity that are causing this "decline" could somehow be overcome by the improved and more charismatic professional work of individuals in ministry is both an expression of the extreme individualism of whiteness and an affirmation of the deep cultural belief within whiteness that social change can be effected by individual effort. It ignores the deep analysis and goes for a strategy that doesn't address the depth of change being experienced.

That point aside, Osmer's notes that there are three kinds of leadership needed in this moment: task competence (the ability to perform the tasks of ministry well), transactional leadership (social influence to achieve goals through trade-offs), and transformational leadership (the ability to enact deep change in the identity, mission, and practices of a congregation).[22] Then he goes on to focus most explicitly on the deep and messy work of transformational leadership. He notes the difficulty of such work, saying: "Such times often are filled with conflict, failures, and dissatisfaction, as well as new vitality and experimentation. During such periods, transformational leaders must remain committed to their internal vision, even as they empower others to reshape their vision."[23] Note here the way that the leader is poised as the one with a special vision that is internal and independent of the vision of others whom they are meant to empower. The leader here is set up as somehow set apart from the congregation, needing powerful internal resources to stay the course and get others onboard with the direction of change they envision and propose.

Osmer engages in an extended theological argument for the spirituality of servant-leadership, including reflection on kings in Israel, Deutero-Isaiah, and Paul's use of these images in the letter to the Philippians.[24] He sums this up in the following:

---

22 Osmer, *Practical Theology*, 178.
23 Osmer, *Practical Theology*, 178.
24 Osmer, *Practical Theology*, 183–192.

> Paul's use of the Servant Songs of Isaiah to portray Christ's royal rule represents nothing less than a reversal of the way power is conventionally understood. Power is not a matter of resources, might, or status. Nor is it a matter of wielding influence for one's own advantage. Rather, power pre-eminently is self-giving love in which the needs of others and the community take precedence. It is a matter of love that is willing to suffer with and for others.[25]

He then goes on to explain how this change in power provides an ethical norm for the behavior of congregational members with one another, which is an interesting shift from the work of the leader that he has been naming before. Indeed, his eventual definition of servant-leadership explains the shift in exactly who should be thinking of power differently:

> *Servant leadership is leadership that influences the congregation to change in ways that more fully embody the servanthood of Christ* (emphasis original). It is not primarily a matter of personality traits, like being self-effacing, mild-mannered, or overly responsible. To the contrary, leading a congregation to change in ways that more nearly approximate its mission as a contrast society and social catalyst will take courage, resolve, and the ability to empower others.[26]

So, servant-leadership is about getting the *congregation* to embody the servanthood of Christ while the leader must have courage and ability to empower others. While acting for deep change may ruffle feathers among the center of the congregation, Osmer reassures leaders that "You will gain power by empowering others."[27] There is a reassurance here that this moment of giving away power will end with re-exaltation and the regaining of power, as in the Christ hymn, where in the end, every knee bows and every tongue confesses the lordship of Christ. The danger of using Christ as the model of servant-leadership in a tradition that also in the end proclaims the Lordship of Christ may be creeping into your mind at this point. The notion of servant leadership problematically embodies assumption of the leadership of individual white male embodiment that begins and ends with holding power.

To take this a bit further, as indicated in Osmer's work the notion of servant-leader combines the idea of the capacity for power necessary for leadership

---

25 Osmer, *Practical Theology*, 189.
26 Osmer, *Practical Theology*, 192.
27 Osmer, *Practical Theology*, 197.

named early in this chapter—power to persuade and influence, authority to allot resources, and power to cast a vision on behalf of a group's experience—with the notion of giving up that power to become as a servant. This combination of terms does something powerful to a mind steeped in Christian scripture as it evokes the language of the hymn calling believers to imitate Christ from the second chapter of Philippians (here the CEB translation, which translates the Greek word *doulos* as "slave" which is often translated as "servant," making its paradox even more evident):

> 5 Adopt the attitude that was in Christ Jesus:
> 6 Though he was in the form of God,
>   he did not consider being equal with God something to exploit.
> 7 But he emptied himself
>   by taking the form of a slave
>   and by becoming like human beings.

While the kenotic act of "emptying oneself" is here valorized as being Christ-like, it leads to another dangerous alignment. The first notion is that one is initially "equal with God" and therefore needs to humble oneself or empty oneself to become like the mere mortals. The notion of servant-leadership captures in it first the idea of an original state of mastery or even divine power, which is then graciously handed over to become like a mortal. To imitate Christ is a long-historic spiritual practice, and yet, that alignment between self and God can be dangerous if you are in a community that aligns salvation with whiteness. And then, in the end, the payoff is being exalted again like Jesus's lordship is re-established in the end. Humbling oneself to be exalted maintains the position of the leader with divine power as the initial state and back in alignment with God as the end state, with the strategic choice of releasing power a temporary moment. In this way, even a model of leadership that is meant to treat power differently in the end reinforces the maintenance of power in the hands of those who already have it.

4 Decolonizing and Liberating Leadership

I have begun to wonder if "leadership" or the word "leader" is so wrapped up in notions of white, male, patriarchal, supremacist framing that it isn't redeemable. Does it so regularly tap into individualist notions of white saviorhood and control described in the last chapter that we perhaps should stop using it at all as a framing for the work of ministry in practical theology?

I once asked this question of Monique Moultrie, a womanist ethicist currently working on a project describing the unique models of collaborative leadership amongst black lesbian women in movements for social change, and her answer was very wise indeed. She said that to stop using the term "leader" for people who are able to effectively gather the energies of a community in order for it to work together for its own purposes and dignity is to cede the word over to white supremacist understandings of individual colonial mastery so that they will continue to persist culturally without resistance. And so, the question is not whether or not to use the term leader, but how to decolonize and liberate notions of leadership so that they can point to the more complex skills of gathering and organizing intricate and polyvocal communities without silencing difference, eliminating dissidence, or erasing divergent wisdoms.

Even as we reclaim the notion of leader, Jennings' work is a reminder that seeking control, possession, and mastery is a death-dealing practice of leadership that is ultimately a failed project of salvation encoded as embracing whiteness. But he also advocates that persons involved in religious leadership can develop skill in gathering a crowd of diverse persons and in allowing their cultural knowledges, perspectives, and approaches to life to permeate one's own rather than engaging in the silencing and eradication of those wisdoms as in the colonial project. It is hard at times, in reading Jennings' book, to keep an eye on the belonging he ultimately seeks, since he is so powerful in describing the distortion of seeking mastery that has caused isolation and division. When he defines the notion of belonging as communion, it feels both elusive and powerful: "By communion, I mean the deepest sense of God-drenched life attuned to life together, not with people in general but with the people that comprise the place of one's concrete living and the places (the landscapes, the animals, and the built environments) that constitute the actual condition of one's life."[28] Shifting the notion of "good leader" from one who demonstrates possession, control, and mastery or one who saves or fixes other people into what one imagines they should be, Jennings advocates for formation of those who can gather people together to experience genuine communion in connection with the broader scope of creation.

Discussions of leadership in practical theology have begun to similarly name a different form of leadership that lays down the self-sufficient master for a more permeable and vulnerable figure. As an example, Graham Stanton argues that because the church is not a capitalistic venture with customers and products, drawing on leadership literature from the corporate world to

---

28   Jennings, *After Whiteness*, 14.

form leaders can lead to the uncritical participation in notions of consumerist leadership.[29] We might add to this concern participation in colonizing leadership or exploitative leadership. He notes, "Some recent discussions of the theology of ministry have either made no mention of ambiguity and vulnerability as features of Christian leadership (such as Esau 2017), or do so but continue to advocate traditional leadership practices grounded in assumptions of predictability and control (Wimberly 2010; Rahberg 2017; Lingenfelter 2018)."[30] Stanton draws on the work of organizational theorist Ralph D. Stacey to focus on five areas other than managerial effectiveness with assumptions of predictability and control: the quality of participation, the quality of conversational life, the quality of anxiety and how it is lived with, the quality of diversity, and unpredictability and paradox. He notes that taking the complexity of relationships that make up the church into account "will particularly promote a participative ecclesiology with a focus on genuine dialogue among all members of the church community. Or in other words, complexity theory encourages us to recognise the social form of the church as conversations all the way down."[31] The action of leadership that Stanton calls for is "curating dialogical spaces,"[32] a notion not unlike Jennings' notion of gathering the crowd and allowing it to permeate one's own sense of belonging in an act of deep communion.

Dialogical spaces that include a diversity of peoples and perspectives, and that take into account relationship with the natural world and all of its species, will include conflict and ambiguity if they are truly spaces where many voices can be heard. This leads me to my favorite definition of community from Parker Palmer:

> In true community we will not choose our companions, for our choices are so often limited by self-serving motives. Instead, our companions will be given to us by grace. Often, they will be persons who will upset our settled view of self and world. In fact, we might define true community as that place where the person you least want to live with lives.[33]

---

29 Graham D. Stanton, "A Theology of Complexity for Christian Leadership in an Uncertain Future," *Practical Theology* 12, no. 2 (May 2019), 151.
30 Stanton, "A Theology of Complexity," 147.
31 Stanton, "A Theology of Complexity," 153.
32 Stanton, "A Theology of Complexity," 154.
33 Parker J. Palmer, *The Company of Strangers: Christians and the Renewal of America's Public Life* (Crossroad, 1981).

Community, particularly community with genuine diversity of experience and background, is conflictual, difficult, tenuous, and requires constant maintenance and tending. It demands a lot of background time devoted to coming to know one another without strategy, extractive motivation, and without particular aims or purposes to create the generative milieu in which it works together as an ecology of difference. Such dialogical and permeative existence across difference may bring forth anxiety and uncertainty rather than mastery and control in the long-term work of leadership, particularly for those formed in dominant culture. Whereas Stanton finds this complexity neatly countered by trust in a providential God and working with a strong vision of shalom as peaceful coexistence, I have less confidence that the presence of God takes away the anxiety and complexity and at times fruitlessness of dialogue or moments of conflict of purpose and direction. Leadership, in my experience, always involves wading into the messy complications of "conversation all the way down" if it refuses to slide into assimilating all of those voices into a singular vision owned by the master. It involves deep self-doubt and willingness to experience conversion to the other. It involves sleepless nights and grief at the failures and harms that are perpetuated within the community. Leadership is never glorious or full of good feelings, it more regularly involves a vulnerability and deep questioning of one's role and legitimacy when viewed through the lens of professional mastery.

The willingness to lay down an individual sense of mastery, control, or even competence in leadership may also have much more positive impact on the emerging strengths of the community than the formation of colonialism may allow whitewashed imaginations to anticipate. My colleague and practical theological scholar of leadership Kristina Lizardy-Hajbi notes in her work on postcolonial leadership that such a move makes important space for other strengths to emerge in a community of faith:

> As examples, churches that make space (material/physical space, symbolic space, relational space, and theological/religious space) for eruption of subjugated, indigenous knowledges actively invite and empower people on the fringes of their communities to have an equalized role in shaping and leading in various areas of ministry, thus creating openings for new perspectives, practices, and rituals that transform the faith of the whole. Acknowledging and living into the reality that those who are designated as positional leaders or trained clergy are not the only ones with religious knowledge and authority—moreover, that everyone in the community possesses profound wisdom, experiences, and knowledges equally and in multiple forms beyond rational, intellectual knowledge—

breaks open previously closed structures and systems surrounding worship, preaching, governance, and formation and discipleship, among other areas.[34]

Lizardy-Hajbi recognizes that what we sometimes read as disruptive insights or divergent knowledges in fact may open up important new wisdom and vision to draw upon in charting the life of the community together into the future. It may disrupt closed habits and practices that are hindering the life of the community, if "embraced with openness, curiosity, and humility (rather than reticence, disregard, and arrogance/condescension)."[35] To put it bluntly, no one person is self-sufficient and able to cast a vision for a diverse community, and no one community or cultural orientation is able to fully critically reflect on its own perspective without engagement with subjected knowledges discarded in the formation of their life together.

These reflections lead Lizardy-Hajbi into advocating that we should not use the singular word "leadership" but instead the non-existing English word "leaderships" to describe the multiple modes in which activities to gather communities to address their challenges can exist. Like Moultrie, Lizardy-Hajbi is not ready to give up on the use of the term "leader," noting that during this time of global pandemic and a reckoning of economic and social inequalities, "pastoral leaders and communities who can nurture and restore relationships, cocreate life-affirming structures and resources, and seek wholeness and justice individually, communally, and systemically are needed now more than ever."[36] However, Lizardy-Hajbi calls for serious attention to the colonial roots of our current notions of leaderships and the need for them to be reframed in terms of healing and communal justice:

> Fantastical ideas of pastoral leaders as conforming to coloniality's default notions of pastor as CEO, lead authority figure and knowledge bearer, singular head of staff, or white, male, heterosexual, and able-bodied (usually leading a large, white, suburban Protestant congregation) are reimagined in ways that contribute to the re-existence and resilience of the whole community, not to prescribed commitments to order, success, and competition endemic within eurowestern worlds.[37]

---

34   Kristina Isabel Lizardy-Hajbi, "Frameworks Toward Post/Decolonial Pastoral Leaderships," *Journal of Religious Leadership* 19, no. 2 (2020), 122.
35   Lizardy-Hajbi, "Frameworks Toward Post/Decolonial Pastoral Leaderships," 122.
36   Lizardy-Hajbi, "Frameworks Toward Post/Decolonial Pastoral Leaderships," 130.
37   Lizardy-Hajbi, "Frameworks Toward Post/Decolonial Pastoral Leaderships," 127–28.

Lizardy-Hajbi makes the connection between this singular notion of leadership and the default categories that fit into it best: white cishet male, upper-class, able-bodied, and likely on the younger end of middle-aged. Others who try to take on this role do not have the whiteness magic that allows them to take on the mantle of leadership, to be the one who take credit for the labor of others in a way that only increases their individual standing.

Practical theologian James Nieman uses the metaphor of dancing to think about how we engage the local wisdom of congregations. He has several pragmatic pieces of advice that he learned over time as a leader of congregations about the disposition of humility needed to listen to nondominant voices that embody its deep wisdom: "Whenever we encounter something in a congregation (or really any group) that makes no sense to us, it's easy to conclude it makes no sense at all. Far more difficult is to retain an open posture toward such practices, to await an alternate rationality that may be driving the strange thing we have only newly encountered."[38] Like dancing, attunement to the congregation when its vision is strikingly different from one's own needs attention to the rhythms and movements that are present and the patience to discern what it signifies, what wisdom it captures.

In trying to capture the powerful shift from leadership as mastery to something qualitatively and substantively different, Stephen Lewis, Matthew Wesley Williams, and Dori Baker reflect the need to dismantle this notion of what they call the "Lone Ranger" leader, focusing instead on a non-heroic form of leadership: "Heroes rescue folks in danger and fix what's broken; healers help living systems reconnect to their wholeness."[39] By shifting to a notion of leader as healer, they imagine a form of liberating leadership that "seeks to dismantle the dominant forms of living and leading that reinforce the oppressive norms of empire. It helps to create alternative ways of being that open new, expansive possibilities for communities to flourish."[40] Liberating leaders work "within and beyond current structures of reality to explore and enact life-giving alternatives to the death-dealing systems of empire" by "cocreating the conditions for the community to discover its power and address its complex challenges."[41] These authors point out the dangers that heroic leaders face in trying to gain

---

38   James R. Nieman, "Dancing," in Dorothy C. Bass, Kathleen A. Cahalan, Bonnie J. Miller-McLemore, Christian Batalden Scharen, and James R. Nieman, *Christian Practical Wisdom: What It Is, Why It Matters* (Wm. B. Eerdmans Publishing Co., 2016), 98.
39   Stephen Lewis, Matthew Wesley Williams, and Dori Baker, *Another Way: Living and Leading Change on Purpose* (Chalice Press, 2020), 128.
40   Lewis, Williams, and Baker, *Another Way*, 129.
41   Lewis, Williams, and Baker, *Another Way*, 129.

achievable wins, namely that they rarely attempt to address complex problems that are embedded in self-renewing systems and well-developed institutions and policies that require strategic and systemic work by groups of people to generate movement or change.[42] The heroic individual leader is focused on leaving an identifiable specific legacy, rather than recognizing that healing leadership ends with the recognition that the community itself gathered its strength to address the struggles that it faced.

As an alternative, Lewis, Williams, and Baker lift up the work of civil rights leader Ella Baker, who was an organizer for the NAACP and one of the elders who helped young people come together to form SNCC and begin to coordinate what were episodic and disconnected moments of resistance into a movement for change. They note: "She urged freedom-seeking folk to move meaning-making into strategic organized activity, building communities that together pursue questions, experiment with answers, analyze situations, and use iterative collective action as a resource from which to learn over time."[43] Ella Baker's genius was in bringing people together and designing processes for them to listen to one another and to strategize how they could draw on their collective energies to address the challenges at hand. Here, the movement of leadership is from personal possession to leaderful communal practice that engages the wisdom embedded in all participants in a movement through attention to process, the quality of how a community lives into its life together as a marker of greatness:

> Attention to process—*how* we listen, *how* we engage in dialogue, *how* we organize time, *how* we receive and integrate feedback, *how* we convene and connect people, *how we* manage organizations, *how* we build leadership in others, *how* we design organizational experience, *how* we motivate and mobilize collective action, *how* we tend our inner lives— all this reveals key markers of liberating leadership.[44]

In embracing this leader-full, process-oriented model of organization in order to draw out the wisdom of the community for collective action, Lewis, Williams, and Baker upend the notion of leader as vision-caster and authority bearer, instead moving to leader as someone who enables a community to find many capable people with the wisdom to collectively address challenges

---

42 Lewis, Williams, and Baker, *Another Way*, 136.
43 Lewis, Williams, and Baker, *Another Way*, 134.
44 Lewis, Williams, and Baker, *Another Way*, 140.

that matter to them in the deepest ways, rather than a single professional who meets the metrics of his achievable goals.

Ella Baker did not receive the kind of recognition and public acclaim that the Rev. Martin Luther King, Jr., did for her stunning contributions to the Southern Freedom Movement during what we now call the Civil Rights Era. She has no federal holiday named after her. But to those involved in the movement, her skill and commitment in organizing and her ability to bring out the leadership in people from across the class spectrum in the movement was genius. Baker worried that charismatic leaders actually disempowered the depth of leadership in the movement and weakened it, specifically in making those without King's educational and class status disaffected by the strong focus on him as the face of the movement. Her powerful biographer, Civil Rights historian Barbara Ransby notes what Baker said about altering the concept of leadership: "Instead of the leader as a person who was supposed to be a magic man, you could develop individuals who were bound together by a concept that benefited the larger number of individuals and provided an opportunity for them to grow into being responsible for carrying out a program."[45] Baker was one of the historical figures that young black leaders in the Black Lives Matter movement reclaimed as essential to building a strong movement that was leaderful. Knowing that no single leader would be enough to be the face of the movement, and that instead a depth of strong people building together was essential to reach the long-term goals of the movement, they turned to Baker's notions of leadership through collective action. Baker dismissed the importance of charismatic leaders, instead wishing to connect and build networks of concerted effort. Ransby continues to describe Baker's understanding:

> "Strong people don't need strong leaders," she argued. In Baker's view, oppressed people did not need a messiah to deliver them from oppression; all they needed was themselves, one another, and the will to persevere. The clerical leaders of SCLC, King included, held a very different notion of leadership. As Baker put it, they saw themselves as the new "saviors."[46]

As Ransby notes, it was partially due to King's own sexism that Baker was relegated at times to supportive roles, such as promoting his book sales, that

---

45   Barbara Ransby, *Ella Baker and the Black Freedom Movement: A Radical Democratic Vision* (University of North Carolina Press, 2003), 188.
46   Ransby, *Ella Baker and the Black Freedom Movement*, 188.

no doubt also contributed to her frustration with him as a public figure. It was his close advisors, such as Bayard Rustin, who continued to amplify her efforts and suggest that she be put in charge of organizing efforts that could not fail if the movement was to succeed. Her form of leadership should be deeply instructive to how we understand what actually brings about change over time. It is not a magically superhuman wise and visionary leader but rather persons leveraging their collective effort into strategic action.

The first time I taught this book by Lewis, Williams, and Baker my students began to wonder if "leadership" was even the term for this work of gathering people, for the cultivation of a communal ethos that would allow a diverse community to discover its own strengths and work together to respond to the struggles it faces and discover the beauty in its existence. After watching the authors of the book do their strong work in redefining leadership in an anti-imperial, decolonial fashion they wondered if the framing of "leader" itself contain within it the toxic colonizing conception of the individual hero such that it could not be redeemed? After all, as a great deal of management and psychological literature has demonstrated, the line between the qualities of someone with narcissistic personality disorder and someone identified as a charismatic leader are often permeable or nonexistent. As leadership theorists Rosenthal and Pittinsky claim: "Narcissism—a personality trait encompassing grandiosity, arrogance, self-absorption, entitlement, fragile self-esteem, and hostility—is an attribute of many powerful leaders."[47] Or, to use Jennings' terminology, is leadership inevitably connected with toxic notions of self-sufficient mastery? While the authors continue to want to use the term leader, the primary movement in their book describes more of a communal form of discernment, cultivation of purpose, and leverage of relational power for flourishing.

A pointed article by psychologists Nicklas Steffans and S. Alexander Haslam explores the connection between those most interested in leadership theories and the psychological trait of narcissism. They note that while one might assume that since leadership is largely defined in the field as "the process of motivating people to contribute to the achievement of group (or organizational) goals,"[48] that the literature on leadership might reflect noble goals of reaching for a common good. Instead, they cite numerous studies that point to the way that leadership theories primarily serve to exalt the concerns of and justify the rewards given to an elite few leaders.[49] Steffens and Haslam sought

---

47 S.A. Rosenthal and T.L. Pittinsky, "Narcissistic leadership," *The Leadership Quarterly*, 17(6) (2006), 617.
48 Niklas K. Steffens and S. Alexander Haslam, "The Narcissistic Appeal of Leadership Theories," *American Psychologist* 77, no. 2 (2002), 234.
49 Steffens and Haslam, "The Narcissistic Appeal of Leadership Theories," 234.

to study whether leadership theory appealed more to narcissistic leaders and even asked if becoming a leader framed in the way leadership theory is written might promote increased narcissism in leaders.[50] Their study demonstrated that the more narcissistic people are, the more drawn they are to leadership theory, particularly leadership theory focused on the individual leader:

> [T]he associations between narcissism and endorsement of leadership theories were strongest for leadership theories that revolve primarily around the individual leader (e.g., directive, leader–member-exchange, trait, and charismatic approaches to leadership). On the other hand, the associations were weaker for group and other-oriented forms of leadership (e.g., participative, identity, authentic, and servant ap- proaches to leadership). Nevertheless, it is worth noting that even among this latter cluster of theories, all associations were still positive.[51]

The significance statement by the authors about their research sums it up poignantly: "These results suggest that people's engagement with leadership research is motivated more by a personal concern for the self than by a social concern for the greater good."[52] One of the directions that the authors suggest for leadership theory in order to promote collective ends rather than narcissistic tendencies is for theories to "pay much more attention to followers and to the broader social context in which leaders operate" through "the generation of *integrative analyses of leadership and followership* (emphasis original)."[53]

Fortunately, in the field of practical theology this attention to the life of the whole community, leaders and followers together, is something that is being developed, often by the very people at places like the Forum for Theological Exploration who are called upon to develop the next generation of theological leaders. For example, Patrick Reyes reflects on the need to "design and build more equitable institutions and society" not by trying to find individual stars who can survive in the current inhospitable conditions and hopefully shine bright enough to inspire change. He notes, "If, instead, we slowed down and looked for inspiration, we would see that we can bear witness to the constellation of knowledge, power, and wisdom that exists in our community."[54]

---

50   Steffens and Haslam, "The Narcissistic Appeal of Leadership Theories," 237.
51   Steffens and Haslam, "The Narcissistic Appeal of Leadership Theories," 242.
52   Steffens and Haslam, "The Narcissistic Appeal of Leadership Theories," 234.
53   Steffens and Haslam, "The Narcissistic Appeal of Leadership Theories," 243.
54   Patrick B. Reyes, *The Purpose Gap: Empowering Communities of Color to Find Meaning and Thrive* (Westminster John Knox Press, 2021), 93.

Looking at constellations rather than stars calls into question the notions of single skilled leaders in hierarchical systems as being worthy of emulation, as mentoring individuals in the next generation with similar skills and traits. Instead, what is called for is people who nurture conditions for whole communities to be able to leverage their varied wisdoms and to work together to address situational challenges and nurture the potential of the members in all of its varied glory. He later goes on to note, "Excellence is no longer defined by single leaders but by the health and thriving of the whole."[55] The continued focus on skills for individual leadership with integrity does not allow for movement towards the complex world-changing desires for liberation that are being expressed by many communities.

5 Fragment Workers and Poetic Imagination

Willie James Jennings chooses a different metaphor than leaders for this practice of gathering diverse communities of belonging: "fragment workers." In a lecture I attended he talked about the possibility of theological educators learning from skilled African-American quilters taking up one fragment from their bag and stitching it together with another as a practice of creating something useful and beautiful. Rather than the image of a self-sufficent masterful leader, he notes that this image "conceals from us where our true work in education begins—that is, in working in the fragments."[56] In our work of theological education we only have fragments left to work with, much like a skilled quilter has the scraps left in their bag to piece together:

> There are the fragments of faith, the creaturely pieces of memories and ideas and practices that we work with to attune our senses to the presence of God. Then there are the colonial fragments that have shattered our worlds and which we are constantly trying to unfold and piece together. And then there is the commodity fragment that we struggle against that organizes our processes of exchange and deeply penetrates our visions of relationality.[57]

In the wake of the tragic history of colonization and the commodification of late capitalism, there are some scraps of faith left to begin to piece together

---

55 Reyes, *Purpose Gap*, 93.
56 Jennings, *After Whiteness*, 32.
57 Jennings, *After Whiteness*, 17.

even as we have imaginations shaped by these other destructive forces and fragments that demand to be included. We don't inhabit traditions, says Jennings, in some grand theological or intellectual home that we must possess, control, and pass on as wisdom to the next generation. Instead, he notes, "We are fragment workers aiming at patterns of belonging."[58] The demands of "a soul-killing performativity aimed at the exhibition of mastery, possession, and control with the tacit assumption that this ongoing work of exhibition illumines talent and the capacity for leadership"[59] drives us into isolation and being the master rather than imagining that other peoples are also able and in fact deeply skilled to "gather" people.

In her naming of "fractured times," including the decline of Christendom, patriarchy and colonialism, and "ecological, religious and political fracturing," feminist practical theologian Nicola Slee talks about the problematic desire to fix and to intervene and the need for theology to engage in a different way. Within the fragmentation of human knowledge and systems, Nicola Slee calls for practical theologians to avoid reinstatement of "a grand, meta-narrative upon the disorder. This is essentially a response of denial, frequently motivated by fear and a refusal to give up the iron grip of control."[60] But she also wonders about a response in which "those who have been most disadvantaged by the religiously endorsed grand narrative rejoice in its breakdown and revel in the fissures of the broken system, seeking not to reconcile the contradictions but to exploit and enlarge them."[61] Her advice is to avoid either of these responses, seeking total control through denial of the realities of fragmentation or seeking to dismantle everything without attention to the damage such nihilistic destruction might entail.[62] Slee continues, "This is a theological approach that is modest yet visionary: attentive to the diversity and particularity of things. It seeks to hold each fragment up to the light for critical scrutiny but also for appreciation, finding joy in the small, fragile thing. It analyzes and responds to brokenness with realism and hopefulness, not looking to fix things so much as to hold and bear them."[63] Being attentive to the realities

---

58 Jennings, *After Whiteness*, 17.
59 Jennings, *After Whiteness*, 18.
60 Nicola Slee, *Fragments for Fractured Times: What Feminist Practical Theology Brings to the Table* (SCM Press, 2020), 12.
61 Slee, *Fragments for Fractured Times*, 12.
62 Even as I write this section, I do wonder about the advice not to burn it all down to those who have been most disadvantaged by the system from Slee. I am here hearing avoidance of a wanton, exploitative nihilism while also holding the possibility of a political strategy that seeks to exploit distortions and enlarge the failures of dominant systems as a part of dismantling them purposefully in seeking a more just communion.
63 Slee, *Fragments for Fractured Times*, 13.

of life together in seeking to live together "with realism and hopefulness" is a form of leadership that eschews intervention for a holding together of the fragments over time.

Not surprisingly, both Jennings and Slee often work in poetic form, both in their published writing and by their own description in their journals and personal sense-making of the world. As opposed to the argument driven logic of academic prose, the genre of poetry has the gift of holding together fragments of insight without resolution in a way that gives form and even perhaps beauty to thought, but does not force dissonant experiences or insights to cohere seamlessly.[64] Unlike a thesis-driven argument that musters evidence to support one small point in a form of linear rationality, or unlike a grant report that documents measurable outcomes through the demonstration of actual changes that can be attributed to a leader, poetry makes meaning in a more open-ended and evocative way. Evocative and open-ended are key words for allowing imagination for a different future in a community to function. What Jennings and Slee are beginning to describe is how a community can experience its own reality in a focused way attentive to beauty and life, but not in a resolved or task-oriented/productive way as it lives into a different future together.

Lewis, Williams and Baker name this cultivation of possibility as a key feature of leadership: "The primary task of liberating leadership is to create alternative spaces for a different future to emerge. Liberating leadership cultivates conditions in which people may actually experience another way. In this other way, the Eternal incarnates a holy alternative to the stifling status quo."[65] Cultivating conditions that are different from the current realities requires the work of shared imagination rather than an individual leader providing vision on behalf of the community that everyone else must be coaxed into seeing and embracing as well. Emergent theorist adrienne maree brown names the ways that the capacity for imagination was a victim of the disempowering conditions of colonialism: "Imagination is one of the spoils of colonization, which in many ways is claiming who gets to imagine the future for a given geography. Losing our imagination is a symptom of trauma. Reclaiming the right to dream the future, strengthening the muscle to imagine together as Black people, is a revolutionary decolonizing activity."[66] brown lifts afrofuturism and

---

64 I am indebted to the work of poet and practical theologian Shawn Fawson for the insight about why poetic form matters in holding together human experiences of trauma and complex suffering with resolving the contradictions that they entail. Her dissertation, *Sustaining Lamentation in Traumatic Grief Through the Contemporary Elegy: A Practical Theology of the Poetics of Testimony* explores this more fully.
65 Lewis, Williams, and Baker, *Another Way*, 146.
66 brown, *Emergent Strategy*, 164.

science fiction, particularly that of Octavia Butler, as among the places where people begin to imagine and practice a different future together: "The future is not an escapist place to occupy. All of it is the inevitable result of what we do today, and the more we take it in our hands, imagine it as a place of justice and pleasure, the more the future knows we want it, and that we aren't letting go."[67] In the work of collective imagination we encounter not a leader casting a vision for a community, but a community dreaming together and practicing their way into the future through small moves that enact justice and pleasure, bit by bit, together.

For years as someone in religious education, I was all about building up the community, drawing on the wisdom of all participants, building capacity intergenerationally, peer-to-peer learning and models that rotated moments of giving leadership. The idea of focusing on the qualities of a single leader did not matter much to me, and I was left rather cold by the discussions of leadership that drew on corporate and capitalist endeavors for theoretical bases. And then, I worked in an organization with a narcissistic and destructive leader for nearly seven years. The structures of power did not want to have another failed president, and so they continued to allow this toxic leader to continue holding the leadership role, while the organization found many workarounds, assigned minders to thwart or blunt the worst of his public actions, and coalesced power in other areas of the institution to resist the destructive patterns of communication and relating of this particular leader. Again and again we were told the story that the failure of this leader would be the failure of the institution, and so we had to prop up his leadership for our community's survival, even as strengths and decisions were emerging from everywhere else in the institution that were creative and resourceful.

Throughout that experience (and in its extended aftermath), I became a believer in the importance of good leaders. As long as institutions were structured with hierarchical role-based decision-making systems (i.e. presidents, vice-presidents, deans, department chairs), the qualities and skills of the people occupying those roles mattered tremendously. The next job description for president at my institution after our particularly narcissistic and colonizing leader included the word "humility" as a key virtue of the person who would take the position. At the same time, that season of my professional life also highlighted the ways that strong communities have leaders and persons who can generate and wield power in many aspects of their life together without holding the assigned role of leader. I learned that not looking to hierarchical structures to expect good decisions but instead building channels of

---

67   brown, *Emergent Strategy*, 164.

communication and smaller networks of good work practicing together into a differently imagined future can delegitimate the belief in the heroic single leader and actually remove power from this structural model of hierarchical leadership. In other words, I experienced a community that was leaderful and mutually-supportive in seeing the world in new ways, despite our official narcissistic leader, and through that shared work we dismantled trust in that form of leadership as our way to salvation.

Whether as poets, fragment workers, healers, or constellations, intentional guidance and engagement with communities as they find their own wisdom and strengths to respond to what comes their way through processes of connection, discernment, and collaboration is critical. How to nurture the skills of designing those processes without falling into white supremacist notions of leaderships that favor hierarchies of power with those visioning a salvation like unto themselves on the top and those whose bodies and labor are exploited in the name of bringing about those visions on the underside is an ongoing piece of dismantling the legacy of white supremacy.

CHAPTER 6

Questioning Congregations

For a period of about five years, I did not teach an introductory class in religious education despite my faculty appointment being solely defined in that area.[1] Teaching the introductory class introduced a basic clash of realities that I could not resolve well in a ten-week term. Namely, the majority of the U.S. literature about religious education presumes participation in a congregational setting that has some relevance to the formation of identity and commitments. European literature about religious education presumes a schooling setting with required religious education classes, even though a shared community of religious belief is not assumed. Neither situation was relevant to well over half of the students in any given introductory class in my teaching context in a school of theology.

Many of the students in my classes were planning to work as chaplains in hospital or hospice settings where they would not be a part of a formative religious community since they would be working short-term with more crisis-oriented populations. Others were planning to work in religiously based non-profits with a highly mobile client base and small professional staffs who engaged the work for a variety of reasons, not all of them religious. Even those who were working in parishes knew that they would only see the bulk of their parishioners once a month for two hours or less, given church attendance statistics in the Western part of the United States. While I can help these students make connections between their non-congregational vocational contexts and the literature of congregationally-based religious education, this massive translation project ends up being a different topic entirely than what is presumed by the academic literature in religious education in the United States, where an imagined vital congregation serves as a significant community of shared identity and practice. So, I avoided trying to introduce the topic of religious education as an academic subject until I could figure out how to approach it in a way that made sense to my students in the current context.

Many students had deeper issues with institutional religion and their experience growing up in high commitment congregations and often white evangelical Christian schools associated with nondenominational congregations. They had experienced robust institutions that attempted to create the kind

---

1 A version of this chapter first appeared as Katherine Turpin, "Religious Education beyond Congregational Settings," *Religions* 9, no. 11 (November 2018): 1–8.

of seamless formational environments that I described as a part of the legacy of colonial Christianity earlier, meant to keep them from the sinful influences of the world and particularly those communities with different worldviews or religious commitments than their parents. And those institutions had often been traumatic, often along the lines of policing gender and sexuality, but also sometimes related to the distorted accounts of US and Christian histories, scientific suspicion, and racial exclusivity that was taught within them. The judgment and shunning that many of our students had experienced from their white religious communities, and by extension often their families once they left those churches and schools, meant that they had deep suspicions about the congregation as a positive formational environment. Why would they intentionally recreate the pedagogic violence they had experienced in such communities by attending so carefully to the formation offered in the curriculum of the whole life of the church? What I saw as a benign or benevolent attempt to create a robust formative environment in the literature of congregational education and spiritual formation my students consistently read as a potentially abusive one.

This experience in finding my field largely irrelevant to my students raised the major question: what does religious education or spiritual formation look like in the United States without the presumption of belonging to an established community of faith? While many scholars are positioning themselves as working within a post-secular environment and struggling with the realities of religious nonafilliation, I see the continued influence of religious and spiritual discourse and practice in the United States. Institutions are built to endure, and some forms of institutionalized Christian community will endure in the United States for a long while. However, I do not believe that congregations will have the same central location of social and formative importance that they had in the nineteenth and twentieth centuries in the United States. Some may rightfully argue that they never had this kind of importance, and that harkening back to a time when churches had more cultural influence is nostalgia, plain and simple. But the stack of basketball trophies from the mid-twentieth century in the basement of my Denver mainline protestant congregation indicates something different. For social interaction, athletics, life cycle and significant ritual occasions, and community gatherings, the church was the only game in town in many communities for a long time. This is no longer the case, and the strategy of voluntary weekly religious schooling or socialization into institutional Christian communities similarly no longer holds as a strongly viable approach to religious education.

This diminished location of Christian institutions in the social structures of U.S. white middle class Christianity is often expressed in concerns from clergy and church employees about the failure to protect Sunday mornings for congregational participation as once was the cultural norm. Even for those who might feel more positively towards shared congregational life, the pace of late capitalism can make regularly setting aside a weekend morning difficult. Given the rush of schedules created by households in which all adults must work outside of the home for pay, other family activities and household tasks end up crammed into weekend hours. Participation in congregational events gets put onto an even playing field with sports participation, trying to get groceries and put the home in order, finishing school and work tasks, and taking time to rest.

For others, the congregation is a service provider and not a community of faith that one would join. Some years back as a volunteer Sunday school teacher I had a family who declared that this year, they had made a commitment to "do Sunday school" for their 4 and 6-year-old daughters. It was clear that this was a choice among many enrichment activities for their children, and after one academic year commitment, they chose something different to do on Sunday mornings the next year. At first, it was hard to wrap my head around the idea that someone would treat the faith community as the same as any other enrichment opportunity for their child, important enough in some ways to make a one-year commitment, but largely interchangeable among many other important commitments to their growth and development. When we talked with the parents about the life of the whole community being essential to their own growth in faith through worship, service, and community relationships, they seemed puzzled by this, as if we had asked them to commit themselves fully as a family to the personal development offered by the soccer boosters' organization. The church just was not that important to them, even though they sought some cultural familiarity with the Christian tradition and perhaps moral formation for their children through their participation in religious education classes for the year. But being a member of a congregation? Not important.

When I speak to committed Christians of the grandparent generation about their adult children, they often express sadness that their children are not involved in a community of faith. They took their children to church regularly, and they tried to emulate Christian values in their home, and yet their children have no interest in belonging to the institutional church. They often feel ashamed that they have failed to pass on the Christian faith to the next generation. However, if you ask these same parents about their adult children: Do you believe they are good people living lives indicative of the values in which you raised them? They will provide a litany of how proud they are of their children, how their work reflects concern for those who have experienced injustice, how their children have taught their grandchildren to be compassionate and wise in ways that they never felt they managed with their own children at that age. When I think of the dozens of conversations I have had like this over the past decade, I ask two questions. First, have these parents truly failed to pass on their faith when they admire the deepest values that their children have taken from their upbringing? If they admire the way that their children are living their lives and have a sense of integrity about their practices and commitments, should there be concern about whether or not they are members of a congregation? Second, why is membership in a formal Christian community the most obvious marker for whether or not they have successfully taught the next generation the Christian faith? In some cases, the next generation has also jettisoned any notion of God, Christian belief, or other markers of Christian identity. In other cases, many of these identity-bearing beliefs are present, just not a felt need to participate in a formal Christian community.

The commitment of the field of practical theology to support the church makes even asking the question of whether Christian religious education or spiritual formation can happen without participation in a formal Christian community feel like a professional betrayal. My academic fields of religious education and practical theology count the support and upbuilding of the church as one of the reasons for their existence. So, to ask the question of how important a community of faith is to the task of religious education or practical theology is almost unthinkable. The religious education texts that I used to teach as basic to the field, such as Maria Harris' *Fashion Me a People*, Anne Wimberly's *Soul Stories*, Charles Foster's *Educating Congregations*, and Thomas Groome's *Christian Religious Education* all presume the existence of a community of faith that has identity bearing weight and some level of moral authority for its participants (or at least a Catholic schooling setting where the church tradition is authoritative).[2] If communities of faith did not engage in religious education in the United States, who would? Does the notion of spiritual formation make any sense at all without embedding that learning in formal participation in congregations? Does practical theology with its roots in a single normative Christian tradition have any place in public, religiously-plural settings?

---

2   Maria Harris, *Fashion Me a People: Curriculum in the Church* (Westminster John Knox Press, 1989); Anne E. Streaty Wimberly, *Soul Stories: African American Christian Education*, revised edition (Abingdon Press, 2005); Charles R. Foster, *Educating Congregations: The Future of Christian Education* (Abingdon Press, 1994); Thomas H. Groome, *Christian Religious Education: Sharing Our Story and Vision* (Jossey-Bass, 1999).

1 The Prominence of the Congregation in White Christianity

Participation in a Christian community offers some things that are hard to imagine being a Christian without, such as access to communal worship and sacramental life. For example, John Wesley, one of the founders of the movement that led to the development of my own denomination, grew worried when the class meetings he had invented were taking off in popularity and people ceased to attend daily or weekly Eucharist in Anglican parishes. He feared for the health of the souls of parishioners who did not experience these means of grace on a regular basis. For many expressions of Christian discipleship, gathering with the faithful for worship is an essential element of formation, and congregations are the presumed context for that experience.

Additionally, we know that in moral development theory that one of the major predictors of how people within that community will believe and live is the way that their primary community lives and believes. As creatures who have evolved through social cooperation, the people around us are still essential to how we think about the world and what is good within it. The constitution of these communities has evolved and perhaps become distorted in an age of social media and diminished institutional belonging, but our evolutionary heritage continues to mean that the influence of those around us matters in the formation of our commitments and worldviews. Communities remain essential to human identity formation, even though communities are less stable, more networked, and more episodic than in prior generations.[3]

Additionally, in the educational theories of John Dewey and Paulo Freire that have undergirded a great deal of theoretical work in Christian religious education in the past half century, the role of the community is essential to the construction of knowledge.[4] Through communal processes of shared exploration, discovery, and work participants reconstruct knowledge suitable to contemporary contexts, which is the occasion for true learning, as opposed to indoctrination or forced assimilation into social norms. These theoretical underpinnings reinforce a sense of the need for cooperative community for adequate learning to occur.

However, in many non-Christian contexts outside the United States, voluntary congregations are not considered necessary for the formation of religious belief. Studies of immigrant groups have noted that coming into the US forced

---

3 Jeffrey H. Mahan, *Church as Network: Christian Life and Connection in Digital Culture* (Rowman & Littlefield Publishers, 2021).
4 John Dewey, *Experience And Education*, reprint edition (Free Press, 1997); Paulo Freire, *Pedagogy of the Oppressed: 50th Anniversary Edition*, fourth edition (Bloomsbury Academic, 2018).

other religious groups into a voluntary congregational structure even when this is atypical in the country of origin. For example, building local mosques became a necessity for Muslim immigrants: "Lay involvement in mosque activities becomes important for preserving both religious and ethnic identities, a challenge not found in their Muslim countries."[5] A key element of establishing a congregation was providing religious education for members in forms recognizable in US culture: "Immigrant congregations are also incorporating Christian ways of imparting religious education by offering Sunday school classes for children and adults. For example, some Buddhists hold sutra study classes for the youth as well as adults; the Zoroastrians have Gatha classes, modeled on Protestant Bible study groups."[6] The congregational setting and the schooling model of religious education were seen by incoming groups as essential to form and preserve both ethnic and religious identity in a US setting by new immigrant groups. In this way participation in a local community of faith became a marker of religious identity in a manner that would not have been normal in their country of origin.

A recent study by sociologist of religion Nancy Ammerman and colleagues indicated the continued importance of communities of faith in religious formation in the US context. Having set out to document everyday spiritual practices in a time of declining institutional affiliation, she notes a surprising finding: "One of the most striking results of this research has been the degree to which participation in organized religion matters."[7] The researchers found in many arenas that they examined that attending services frequently made a difference in the frequency of the participant's spiritual practice, that participation in a site of interaction where religious or spiritual language was the common language led to adoption of increased spiritual elements into their lives. She notes, "So when we ask about the sites in which spiritual discourse is produced, congregations and other organized spiritual groups are both obvious places to look and surprisingly downplayed in a culture and a discipline that have glorified the life of the individual spiritual seeker."[8] Ammerman certainly found other practices based in individual home life that were considered deeply spiritual by her participants, such as interaction with pets and

---

5 Helen Rose Ebaugh and Janet Saltzman Chafetz, "Structural Adaptations in Immigrant Congregations," *Sociology of Religion* 61 (2000), 137–138.
6 Fenggang Yang and Helen Rose Ebaugh, "Transformations in New Immigrant Religions and their Global Implications," *American Sociological Review* 66 (2001), 8.
7 Nancy Tatom Ammerman, *Sacred Stories, Spiritual Tribes Finding Religion in Everyday Life* (Oxford University Press, 2013), 301.
8 Ammerman, *Sacred Stories, Spiritual Tribes*, 301.

the natural world. But for most, the regular occurrence of spiritual practices increased along with participation in communities of faith.

Given this deep assumption about the importance of the congregation to the formation of religious belief, and indeed the impact that participation in a congregation can have on spiritual development, the primary response by many denominations over the past decades to the decline in membership and regular attendance in their congregations is to attempt to reverse the trend by reviving congregations as communities of vital practice. Imagining that religious education or transmission of the tradition to the next generation is impossible without membership in a local community, white mainline denominations such as my own, the United Methodist Church, have poured energy and resources into church growth, into improving clergy efficacy and leadership skills, and into evangelism and marketing efforts to attempt to reverse the decline of its congregations. The expansion of the denomination into every community in the United States had been such a historic marker of its cultural success, much like a franchising expansion in a fast-food restaurant chain, the decline in affiliation and the closing of many smaller communities and the shrinking of others felt like a failure in the mission of the church.

Of course, a cynical read on these efforts might be that the diminishment in budgets, collective power, and cultural status that comes along with declining institutional affiliation motivated these efforts at evangelism and church growth. Certainly there was a great deal of hand-wringing in mainline white Christian denominations at their membership decline as the white nondenominational and evangelical congregations appeared to be holding steady and even growing. A great deal of ink was spilled over the failure of the less heavy-handed and conforming theologies of these groups that were clearly not able to inspire the next generation to join, with calls for clearer doctrine and better formational efforts with embodied practice to revive the congregations. Sociologists of religion would name that these declines and maintenances of population had more to do with birthrates and urbanization than with the kind of theology proclaimed, a claim that has played out as white Southern Baptist, evangelical, and nondenominational congregations have experienced declines as well in recent generations.

In the literature of Christian religious education, recent works by Boyung Lee and Charles Foster have continued to emphasize the importance of institutional community in congregational education. In the work of Charles Foster, the loss of a "catechetical culture of formation in congregations" has been a major factor in the collapse of faith formation.[9] The loss of intergenera-

---

9   Charles R. Foster, *From Generation to Generation: The Adaptive Challenge of Mainline Protestant Education in Forming Fait* (Wipf & Stock Pub, 2012).

tional mentoring and a compelling narrative of God in the congregational space leads to the need to rebuild the catechetical community as an adaptive change necessary for the transmission of faith from generation to generation. He believes this challenge "requires a lively and ecclesially grounded educational imagination" that challenges and reframes the technological orientation and marketing strategies that are dominating conversations about educational work in congregations.[10] The primary context for that educational work remains established Christian congregations.

Religious educator Boyung Lee's concerns about the importance of congregations also stem from her sense that vibrant community is sparse in the individualistic white context of the United States. Although she understands the congregation as an important base for educational work, she joins Foster in not assuming that congregations already have the kind of community that is necessary for religious education: "Thus helping congregation members to be connected to one another will be an important role for a leader to play: creating safe leaning environments and sound relationships among members is integral to both personal and communal transformation."[11] She also speaks of the need for the church to "not wait for people to come to educational programs, but bring your religious education to where people are and where community is and can be created."[12] This admonition shares this sensibility of the community that educates as somewhat distinct from the institutional church. Her approach of the Traveling Bible Study, an effort that met over lunch and in relationship to the workplaces of the adult participants, where they could wrestle with how notions of evil and temptation played out in their daily lives, is an interesting compromise between a desire for communal interaction and educational events presented in a time and place related to the ongoing lives of participants. Her attention to how improved administrative structures in congregations can support good educational work belies her belief that congregations are still an essential community for this work, but her proposals indicate deep listening to the context where institutional life can be burdensome to maintain and may interrupt the formation of community.

Mai-Anh Le Tran asks a harder question, namely, whether we are deceiving ourselves in thinking about preserving something "pure and precious" at the core of congregational life, and whether instead, congregations might them-

---

10   Foster, *From Generation to Generation*, 120.
11   Boyung Lee, *Transforming Congregations through Community: Faith Formation from the Seminary to the Church* (Westminster John Knox Press, 2013), 69.
12   Lee, *Transforming Congregations*, 69.

selves be part of the problem. She notes the inefficacy of response to changing cultural conditions: "Put differently, responses to tectonic structural shifts in mainline Protestant churches seem to range somewhere between fearful paralysis and entrepreneurial fits. At either end of the spectrum, the obsession is still centripetal—inwardly focused, myopically spiraling."[13] She ponders the erasure of memory, habitus of *dis*imagination, fractured sanctuary, use of the Bible as a weapon of mass destruction, and banking curricula of mainstream congregations and asks seriously about the violent nature of religious education in these congregational settings.[14] However, she speaks hopefully about "faithful individuals and congregations engaged in valiant action against the public pedagogies of *dis*imagination."[15] But her vision of the church is a community in transit, organically improvisational, an "enabling community of practice" that is able to be "responsive to specific situations, contexts, and needs," rather than a settled and powerful institution.[16] This community is imagined by Tran primarily in moments of protest and witness and resistance, a "kind of protested faith for Christian communities—a faith that is tested and testing, protested and protesting in the midst of contemporary social disease."[17]

2   Congregations as Institutions of Whiteness

The establishment of congregations and the building of church buildings was a strategy of civilizing and colonizing the North American continent. A church building, like a school and a post office, was a marker that a white settlement had moved from outpost in the wilderness to a "real" town that could be trusted for others to inhabit. Historically white denominations partnered with the Federal government of the United States, carving up the continent amongst themselves to start these congregations as a joint missionizing and occupying strategy in order to claim the continent for its white settlers.[18] One

---

13   Mai-Anh Le Tran, *Reset the Heart: Unlearning Violence, Relearning Hope* (Abingdon Press, 2017), 56.
14   Tran, *Reset the Heart*, 57.
15   Tran, *Reset the Heart*, 75.
16   Tran, *Reset the Heart*, 147.
17   Tran, *Reset the Heart*, 129.
18   George E. Tinker, *Missionary Conquest: The Gospel and Native American Cultural Genocide* (Fortress Press, 1993).

can see the legacy of this policy where I live in rural Wyoming, where each small town has a single Episcopalian church, often in a log building, as its only mainline Protestant presence. Why are all of these churches Episcopalian? This was the territory giving to the Episcopal church to create congregations and boarding schools, while other territories were given to other groups, such as the Lutherans in Alaska or the Methodists in South Dakota.

Even by the mid-twentieth century, as patterns of habitation and work had changed, many of these rural congregations lost the support in terms of people and resources that they needed to survive. As among the initial institutions established to anchor white civilization in these lands once occupied by American Indians, their social and cultural function no longer were needed as mass communication and modes of transportation were available that effectively shared white culture across great distances. For example, my grandfather was a lay Methodist-Episcopal Church South pastor in Western North Carolina in the 1960s to an eight-point charge. Once served on a circuit by an ordained Methodist minister, each hollow in the mountainous terrain had a small church that served the couple of extended families that were within riding distance by horse and wagon in what had been Cherokee territory until the mid-nineteenth century. Once cars and paved roads were present, those many small outposts of white religion were no longer really needed. A high school teacher during the weekdays, my grandfather served these churches, two-a- Sunday, for over a decade. Each one had a membership of between five and twenty people, and now all but two are closed entirely except for the family cemeteries that are located near them. The decline of the mainline Protestant church in the latter twentieth century includes the closing of many congregations like these that had outlived their "civilizing" function on the frontiers of white settlement. Did they once have earnest Christian disciples who cared for one another and strove to love God and neighbor as they were commanded? I think it is very likely. Were they also used to consolidate white power in communities and on lands that once belonged to indigenous persons who had been removed in the few years before and around their founding through governmental investment? Also, yes. That socializing function of Christian congregations that is advocated in religious education also has a history in colonizing and invading lands and cultures that once belonged to others. Like many other institutions built on US soil such as courts, schools, and businesses, churches were utilized to solidify the social and economic structures that belonged to white colonizers even as they were also an expression of piety and sincere Christian devotion.

Institutional religion has gotten a terrible reputation in the past few decades. Between clergy sex abuse scandals, instances of financial fraud and ostentatious accumulation of wealth in mega-churches, the alignment of Christian communities with far-right politics to wield powerful policy influence, and other more mundane examples of pettiness and relational betrayal experienced by persons within congregations, many people do not want to be associated with religious institutions or to affiliate with them. There is a sense that with consolidated power and bureaucratic structures comes abuse of that power, manipulation, insincerity, and greed. Many want to claim that they are spiritual people or that they have sincere belief in God but do not want to align with congregations or even with the identity label "Christian." However, despite an ongoing popular culture resistance against government and other big institutions, there are also a thousand ways in which those same institutions continue to serve white folks best. The church is concerned because big institutions with a lot of power and influence are a marker of success in whiteness, and the process of challenge of cultural authority and belonging is a sign of decline. The center of white culture in much of the United States has moved from the church to other powerful institutions, leaving a sense of loss and failure for white religious institutions. The power for social engineering and control in leveraging strong institutions seems desirable and like an expression of God's providence and blessing on the project of missionizing. But if we know that part of that leveraging also involved exclusion, cultural homogenizing, and displacement of others, how do we measure that as former success or glory? What if part of ending white supremacy within the church also means giving up what were once considered markers of success, such as increasing institutional membership and wealth?

Just after the first wave of the pandemic, when the vaccines were becoming widely available and social contexts were starting to open up again in the United States, a blog post by the Rev. Paul Baudhuin circulated heavily amongst my former students now serving as clergy. In the post Baudhuin speaks of his own burnout as a clergy person, evident before the COVID-19 pandemic but accelerated through it. One of the reasons he gives for the depth of burnout is that the location of the US church in late capitalism means that counting "noses and nickels" becomes the primary way that effectiveness in ministry is measured, and he believes that despite efforts to also share stories of transformation or accounts of discipleship, this is the only way it can go. "Because our entire system is not actually built on 'going' and walking with people in nurturing a Jesus shaped spirituality driven by acts of worship, devotion, compassion, and justice; but it is, quite frankly, built on convincing people to show up at our buildings and give us money. In exchange for that, there is a lot of good and honest spirituality offered out there, but that's just it: It's an exchange. It's a business. We have been consumed by consumerism."[19] Baudhuin ends the blog declaring that he is done growing the church and will seek smaller, more sustainable ways to engage in ministry, defined as "Nothing super attractive beyond authentic, intimate community trying to live Jesus-shaped lives in the world." He recognizes that this calls into question the ability to be supported financially, with health benefits and future renewal leaves and all that the successful growth industry of church makes possible.

That last bit is what serves whiteness so well in building orderly systems like institutions. They preserve and protect the gains that whiteness acquired for those that benefit from them. Always such a good worker with a metaphor, in response to a question about church decline at a retreat with clergy I was a part of, preacher and professor of religions Barbara Brown Taylor asked, what if this isn't a decline, but rather the numbers getting smaller are like a fever finally going down? Put another way, what if a sign of dismantling the fever-dream that is whiteness in late capitalism is the de-stabilization of congregations as institutions, and the need for rebirth of communal connections that are more organic and less well-funded? This imagination joins a conversation from the late twentieth century about the end of the mix of empire and church called "the Constantinian church" or the end of "Christendom" with some hopefulness that the divorcing of the two might lead to more authentic Christianity. That conversation was still deeply desirous of a different kind of outpost Christianity with communities that formed different moral people.[20]

Those markers of success related to capitalism are also not easy to relinquish. What if the diminishment of religious and educational institutions simply means that global corporations have more power and there are no sites of contestation for their cutthroat competitive consolidation of resources? But this kind of arms race for power puts the church with the state and the corporation, and that is not perhaps the kind of Christian community or human community that is needed. Whiteness finds it hard to create those institutions without getting coopted into the whole corporate capitalist project.

The defense against decline has also historically led to congregations and denominations feeling a need to defend the church against critique. The support of religious institutions as an extension of support of God has often been named by people in power in response to claims of sexual abuse, misogyny, or other abuses of power protected within the institutions. As hospital chaplain

---

19   https://shorturl.at/VR9FI, downloaded 2/21/22.
20   Stanley Hauerwas and William H. Willimon, *Resident Aliens: A Provocative Christian Assessment of Culture and Ministry for People Who Know That Something Is Wrong* (Abingdon Press, 1989).

and cultural critic J.S. Park noted on social media posts: "Christians, please consider that when somebody is wounded by the church, your impulse to 'defend the church' needs to be last priority. The priority is tending to the wounded people. The people ARE the church. The institution doesn't need your defense. The people do." Part of unlearning whiteness and decolonizing notions of the church requires rethinking what religious community looks like without seeking or defending institutional power to control.

3 Decolonizing Community and Moving beyond Congregations

In my own work as a religious educator I now recognize that I too-easily collapse the idea of an educational community with the idea of an institutional structure or an established congregation. I have recently begun to wonder if this understanding of community as most commonly embedded in institutional forms may be a particularly dominant culture trait associated with whiteness. The assumed control over formative environments expressed in the belief that congregation should continue to be the center of the social life of human communities, serving as the dominant religious environment that will shape the next generation, may be an expression of white mainstream Christian privilege. The longing for powerful religious institutions comes from a racial memory of having been in charge of them for a long time.

Communities without this privilege often generated much more robust versions of religious education because they assumed that as a minority population they would have to work hard to pass on the wisdom of the tradition to the next generation. This has been true for, say, the highly committed religious educational efforts of the Church of Latter-Day Saints. Their invention of before-school seminary and school release time religious education came from the concern that their nondominant tradition would not survive without careful attention to education. Historically, the work of Catholic and Jewish parochial schools in the era of Protestant-dominated public education in the United States has also been an example of this phenomenon. In fact, the decline of the cultural prominence of mainline protestant denominations might be a boon to the practices of religious education and spiritual formation through other communal means.

Letting go of the presumed congregational context also raises significant concerns for the practice of religious education. Stable institutional life has allowed for paid full-time, educated clergy to be supported in their work in many white mainline congregations. If education is to happen in more provisional communities that are not institutionally- based, the question of where teachers and mentors will come from with the time to craft educational experiences arises. Of course, a problem already exists in recruiting and training volunteer teachers and mentors in many congregations, as well as having voluntary learning participants, and having the economic means to support fulltime professional clergy. But this experience is shared with nondominant communities, where clergy and religious leaders have often been bivocational, unpaid, and in some cases, without the benefit of theological education or other professional preparation for their work.

If we take seriously that formal religious institutions or congregational contexts do not seem a relevant context for even those pursuing theological education, we have to begin thinking differently about the future of religious education and spiritual formation in relation to congregations. What allowed me to resume teaching an introductory religious education class was the recent work of many colleagues in the field of religious education who do not presume the context of the congregation as a primary context for religious education. These authors have struggled to articulate the importance of religious education in response to violence in particular, and almost none of them rely on an institutionally based community of faith as a reliable socializing or educating community. And yet, they simultaneously witness to the importance of a gathered community for the role of support of vocation, experiences of revelation, and resisting the violence and injustice of US culture in the name of Christian commitment. These are scholars for whom community is essential, but the institutionalized congregation is negotiable or even undesirable as a context for religious education. As Mai-Anh Le Tran expresses her doubts about congregations: "In what ways are Christian faith communities plagued by enduring violence, perpetuated explicitly and implicitly through forms of religious educational malpractice?"[21] These colleagues are paying attention to conditions on the ground, and they have heard, particularly from younger generations, concerns about the viability of formal religious institutions in addressing the deepest hurts and needs for education experienced by their communities.

One example of this is the work of Leah Gunning Francis describing the work of religious education in the wake of the death of Michael Brown in Ferguson, Missouri. In her interviews with a number of religious leaders and activists who were part of the ongoing response to this extrajudicial killing, Francis describes disconnects between younger and older generations, particularly the distance between the faith leaders in established religious communities and the young activists organizing the nightly protests. This work gives

---

21 Tran, *Reset the Heart*, 56.

witness to the need for leaders of established religious communities to put their bodies on the line and learn to follow in solidarity the lead of a new generation that is leading a different kind of religious transformation. She notes, "Often the clergy would follow the lead of the young people by listening to them, offering advice when warranted, and giving them space to find their own voices. They supported, affirmed, and prayed for the young activists."[22] Francis and Tran shared the experience of watching and participating firsthand in the dramatic public liturgies and protests in Ferguson, MO, that served as a provisional and powerful context for religious education within the Black Lives Matter movement.

Not coincidentally, these new explorations come primarily from scholars of color, who recognize that the primary formative environments of the white community do not always want to offer them life. As Patrick Reyes puts it, bluntly, "How am I going to live when the world wants me dead?"[23] In his work on vocational discernment, he points to the importance of "elders, ancestors and communities."[24] The communities that Reyes speaks of where the work of education will happen are not necessarily established institutions with budgets. He speaks of the exhausting work of "showing up for each other,"[25] and "building a space where we hold each other authentically, from heart to heart."[26] Because, as he notes, "Even when we follow God's call, people of color still operate in a rigged game,"[27] he imagines formative communities as the struggle to "hold space" for a community to bring together their knowledge for survival and being called to life and share it. Education has a provisional and survivalist quality in Reyes' thinking: "What my education gave me was a set of skills, an ability to navigate multiple worlds so I could hold the space for new knowledge to emerge, and the responsibility to make an impact with what I was learning in the classroom in my own community."[28] At times this means resisting, saying *basta* to the people and institutions that do not call you to life, saying that prophetically and with force.

As Reyes and Francis imagine the community of formative environment, what comes to mind is not established congregations but the kind of commu-

---

22 Leah Gunning Francis, *Ferguson and Faith: Sparking Leadership and Awakening Community* (Chalice Press, 2015), 157.
23 Patrick B. Reyes, *Nobody Cries When We Die: God, Community, and Surviving to Adulthood* (Chalice Press, 2018), 3.
24 Reyes, *Nobody Cries When We Die*, 127.
25 Reyes, *Nobody Cries When We Die*, 145.
26 Reyes, *Nobody Cries When We Die*, 144.
27 Reyes, *Nobody Cries When We Die*, 49.
28 Reyes, *Nobody Cries When We Die*, 145.

nities of solidarity and engagement that require fighting to hold space for in the midst of less-than-ideal conditions. This notion of community as existing short term or for a while, of faith community not as well-resourced and established institution, and of faith community as something that has to be fought to establish and to hold threads throughout these works. They spark a different and important imagination for religious education beyond congregations, embedded in provisional communities of solidarity and engagement. Reading these scholars made me realize that the dependence on well-resourced institutions and the substitution of those institutions for human community may be a lingering assumption of white settler Christianity.

CHAPTER 7

Questioning the Apologetic and Affiliative Function of Practical Theology

Early in my career as a professor of religious education, I was involved with a faculty exercise in sharing syllabi for our introductory classes. After I walked through the learning outcomes and assignments that I engaged in my religious education class, a senior faculty member in theology called into question what I was teaching in my course. She told me that it was her job in theology to teach students the cutting-edge places that the field of theology was going. It was my job in religious education to help students translate this new knowledge so that they could take it to the churches without regression back to the existing theologies more common in church settings. When I suggested that I had my own theoretical content, habits of mind, and practices to engage in the field of religious education, she continued to push back saying that there wasn't enough time in a given term for her to do the important work of teaching theology *and* helping students figure out what it meant for their work as clergy. That was my job in religious education.

This interchange was instructive to me in a couple of ways as a new faculty member. First, I had colleagues who had no idea that the philosophy and practice of religious education was its own topic that also was important to teach rather than a secondary "application" of the primary content that was taught elsewhere. Second, some of my colleagues did not think it was their job to relate the material they were teaching to the professional work of ministry (even when their course was a required course for a professional degree), because they depended upon those of us in the disciplines related to practical theology to do all that work within the curriculum. They could upend and disrupt students' theologies; they could call into question doctrines and modes of biblical interpretation and the very nature of the church as an institution without feeling accountable to supporting the church or defending its orthodoxies. It was our job in the practical fields to help students to make sense of all of this and discern how to take their revolutionized theological worldviews and lead congregations as members of the clergy, how to provide care for suffering people in hospital rooms, or how any of this related to their work in religious nonprofits.

Of course, I am overdrawing the distinction here. I also have colleagues who work carefully with students and always keep in mind that they are ultimately professional students with a sense of vocation that their academic work is meant to support. But this interaction was a strong example of something that I think happens more subtly in many interactions in theological education. Those of us who teach homiletics, spirituality, liturgics, education, leadership, and other courses related to practical theology find ourselves trying to help people headed for professional ministry to be able to function within the institutions they will find themselves, whether that is the church, the nonprofit organization, the military, or the health care system. And, given that we are as much professional education as graduate academic education, this makes sense. Indeed, practical theologian Bonnie Miller-McLemore calls on the other areas of the theological curriculum to learn from practical theological pedagogy about "the marks of excellence in theological education and the nature of doing theology for the sake of Christian life," particularly its focus on integration as "a task that must be shared by the whole faculty."[1]

However, this need to support the work of students in their profession as clergy to upbuild the church also can subtly mute or avoid altogether deep criticism of these same ventures. Can you in the same moment teach someone to preach well while calling into question the legitimacy of proclaiming the word in a non-dialogical fashion? Can you teach someone to educate while also criticizing the unilateral exercise of colonizing power that has all too often been a part of the process of religious education, or the exclusive claims to wisdom presented by a tradition to its young? Can one explore the ways ritual and religious practice has been co-opted to create group cohesion against outsiders rather than to create greater love of neighbor? Can we investigate how notions of improving pastoral leadership have begun in response to demographic changes to blame individual pastors for the decline of the church rather than being honest about the changes in culture and childbearing that reduces the numbers of people in the pews? If the practical fields in theological education are meant to help students adapt the rest of the curriculum to the practices they will engage in leadership of actual communities, is there space in these classes to critique and challenge those communities as well as be supportive of them?

Again, for rhetorical reasons, I am overdrawing the distinctions in these questions. These critiques and challenges to the practices we teach can and are addressed in practical theology classes, but the underlying pressure is to also make these ventures noble and worth learning to do well. Students want

---

[1] Bonnie J. Miller-McLemore, *Christian Theology in Practice: Discovering a Discipline* (Eerdmans, 2012), 206.

to be proficient at the practices they will be called upon to perform in their professional setting. What sense does it make to teach a practice that you are profoundly in tension with? And what sense does it make to be a theology school that doesn't evangelize and apologize for the Christian faith? I have had faculty colleagues who have been called out in social media as "the problem with the church" evidenced by what they are teaching and writing at our seminary when it is critical of white settler Christianity. Theology schools are called upon to graduate students who can be institutional builders and maintainers, who can answer the questions for ordination exams, and who can build a Sunday school curriculum and run a session meeting. Raising deep critiques of the church in the practical theological curriculum is seen by many students and by the institutions with whom we are preparing leaders as counter-productive to the work of the life of the church.

In many ways, the field of practical theology has accepted the challenge to be the place where the institutions of church and academy meet. Indeed, Dorothy Bass and Criag Dykstra talk about practical theology's "special responsibility" to educate and form ministers: "The special responsibility of practical theology for teaching and research on the arts of ministry (including preaching, pastoral care, Christian education, worship, evangelism, and leadership) imbue this field with a crucial role in a theological school's service to church and society."[2] This responsibility sets up the arts of ministry as the connection between the theological school and the church/society, but in a role of servant. Engaging in teaching and research in a practical field has the admissions cost of setting up those ventures in a way that serves church rather than critiques or revolutionizes the form of communities of faith. The "crucial role" may be its own pair of velvet handcuffs. Ours are the classes where students most expect to be inspired, to feel confident in their emerging ministerial identities, to gain an education that is practical and functional. This can lead to internal or external resistance if those classes are perceived as questioning or critiquing the church or the faith.

For religious educators, our research and publications are expected to be easily accessible to those without a theological education, to appeal to a wide market, to include "takeaways" and "concrete practical advice" for practitioners. They may be rejected by denominational presses if they are too theoretical or too theological. As an example, in publishing my first book, which looked at

---

2   Dorothy Bass and Craig Dykstra, "Introduction," in Dorothy C. Bass and Craig Dykstra, eds., *For Life Abundant: Practical Theology, Theological Education, and Christian Ministry* (Eerdmans Publishing Co., 2008), 7.

the deep impact of growing up in consumer culture on the Christian vocation of young people, the publisher asked me to provide hope for how these distortions of vocation could be mitigated or eliminated through youth ministry. In reality, nowhere that I had done research indicated that this was at all possible through congregation-based educational practice. But as an author I was supposed to be defending the possibility of resistance to consumer culture and what the church could do to save their teenagers from the relentless formation of late capitalism in youth ministry.

The norm of offering expertise as a practical theologian focused on youth ministry was to offer solutions that demonstrated the efficacy of the local congregation in ways that didn't feel possible, to engage in a certainty of outcome that did not feel truthful to me as an author and scholar. I was to engage in an apologetics about the power of youth ministry overagainst the formative power of late capitalism in a media-saturated culture that worked in images that inundated the young people with whom we minister. And if I didn't have ten easy solutions, programmatic suggestions, or parenting tips to fix the conundrum of distorted youth vocation, publishers wondered why anyone would buy the book. Couldn't I offer something as an expert in which I could give actual useful advice to my readers about how they could control the outcome of youth formation in consumer culture? To not offer this was, in a way, to fail to offer an apologetic for the practice of youth ministry and its power to form young people. It might, however, have been a truthful assessment of the limited power of congregational formation for young people in the midst of the juggernaut that is consumer culture.

1 What Are Apologetics and How Do Practical Theologians Get Drawn into Them?

I have gone back and forth about using the term "apologetics" for this strong linking between church and academy, or the need to demonstrate the efficacy of the Christian faith in overcoming the challenges and vagaries put to it by real life in the work of the practical theologian. As someone who came up in mainline U.S. Protestantism, apologetics was not something that I was exposed to either in the congregation or in my theological education, other than as a quaint exercise in which other people in history and in other branches of Christianity engaged. The need to prepare an adequate defense for the faith in response to public challenges to its efficacy was the realm of my more evangelical colleagues, who had to be ready to provide their testimony at any given moment that receptivity to it was discerned in the Holy Spirit. Or even more dramatically, to be willing to be martyred or discriminated against due to their fidelity to the faith as a mark of being "in this world, but not of it." I was taught that an incarnational faith, one that was not "Christ against culture" in the overused Niebuhrian scheme, but one that was embedded in creation and engaged in transforming culture, did not require a combative apologetic function. I did not experience myself as someone who needed to engage in apologetics.

In contrast to my bemused distancing from the notion of apologetics as something other people feel the need to do, practical theologian Elaine Graham has suggested the need for "the recovery of a more *apologetic* dimension to our theology, in terms of Christians being prepared to defend their core principles and convictions *in public* (emphasis original)."[3] Graham, too, acknowledges the need to reject the problematic nature of the current practices of apologetics that are held in captivity "by a certain kind of logic-centred, propositional discourse, and recover a sense of a public apologia or testimony, which commends and defends the grounds on which Christians seek the common good, protect the well-being of the city, feed the hungry, empower the poor, work for justice."[4] For Graham, this call to the discipline is about moving the work of apologetics from its role as a "weapon of conversion" to "a gesture of solidarity," with the hope "that in speaking of their own convictions, the churches can model a way of inhabiting public space with conviction, owning their tradition, but regarding that as an invitation to others to share their core values too."[5]

Graham calls for public theology to make itself useful to those who do not share the Christian convictions of the faith but might benefit from the wisdom that commitment to such beliefs might offer to a hurting world:

> The days are gone when the British churches could take for granted an automatic hearing for their cause. They have to earn a place in the public conversation. Nor can they rely on the language of tradition making sense within a secular, pluralist culture. Instead, there needs to be renewed effort to make oneself understood in terms readily accessible to an audience indifferent (at best) to religious concerns. So in the face of widespread skepticism about the value of faith—that it is a source of

---

3 Elaine Graham, *Apologetics without Apology: Speaking of God in a World Troubled by Religion* (Cascade Books, 2017), 6.
4 Elaine Graham, "Showing and Telling: The Practice of Public Theology Today," *Practical Theology*, 9:2, 2016, 156.
5 Elaine Graham, "Showing and Telling," 155.

violence, a breeding-ground for terrorism, a haven for hypocrites, prudes and fundamentalists—ordinary, mainstream people of faith must work hard to show that religion has any positive contribution to make to the common good.[6]

That movement from the assimilationist desire to convert others to one's own way of being towards a humble accountability to explain oneself in terms that make sense to others who hold different perspectives built from different experiences is an important decolonizing shift, and one I can support. I am in alignment with the ways that this kind of public airing and testing of Christian doctrine before those who do not share it as an identity-bearing narrative is something that critiques, renews, and transforms the faith tradition, opening new opportunities for adherents to listen to the Holy Spirit for new direction and to seek how God is moving in new contexts and places. Indeed, many aspects of this book are born of listening to external challenges to settler Christianity and trying to make sense of my own faith and work as a practical theologian in light of them.

In this instance, I am not talking so much about the need to provide a reasoned defense for Christian convictions to potential adversaries in a combative situation where one's belief is challenged. Nor am I seeking to witness appropriately in a postsecular society where the voice of religious persons in public forums can be viewed as controversial or disputed as inappropriate. Rather, the underside of the valid task of making connections between the theological curriculum and real human experiences that is a hallmark of practical theology is the more subtle requirement or expectation that engaging in reflection on the practices of the faith in a theological classroom must also serve the persuasive function of advocating that they are ultimately worthwhile, that they build up faith, and that they serve the church. As Graham notes, "Apologetics is essentially a question of how to engage with a non-Christian interlocutor in order to persuade that person of the validity of Christian faith and practice."[7] In a postsecular era where the "validity of Christian faith and practice" is questioned among those who are affiliated with Christian communities as well as those who are not, Graham notes the additional function that apologetics played historically "in order to uphold those among the faithful themselves who were experiencing doubts or persecution"[8] as a strategy of

---

6   Elaine Graham, "Showing and Telling," 154.
7   Graham, *Apologetics without Apology*, 7.
8   Graham, *Apologetics without Apology*, 7.

Christian conversion, formation, and nurture. Practical theological classrooms are often places where students come with doubts and a strong desire to find validity in the Christian faith that they are training to be leaders within.

In this chapter, I am concerned about something that I have felt as a teacher of Christian practices such as youth ministry and spiritual formation in an academic context where critical thinking and deconstructive analysis are the order of the day in most of the other classes that my students are taking. When students come to the practical theological part of the curriculum, there is an assumption that it is now time not to engage in critique or analysis, but that my task as an instructor in practical theology is as an apologist for the "validity of Christian faith and practice" after so much work that has been engaged to disrupt that in other courses. They are hopeful that finally, in this context, somebody will help them understand why this all matters and remind them why they signed up for this vocation in the first place. So, when I ask students to engage in critical work with the dominating history of Christian practice, the unhelpful notion of youth ministry as saving young people from corrupt external culture, or anything that might undermine the church's legitimation and authority, at times I am perceived as having failed in my special responsibility or critical role as a theological educator teaching in a practical field. Invitations to think critically about or to question certain practices of faith communities are sometimes met with suspicion that undermines my legitimacy as a scholar in a practical field.

Practical theology holds the tenuous curricular ground in theological education of being responsible for the integration of academic theology and the practice of communities of faith, and at times its very purpose as a discipline has been described as the strengthening of the leadership of the church or of faithfulness in believers. As Bonnie Miller-McLemore names it in her essay on the contributions of the field, practical theology has a strategic movement or a "theory of action" for living out faith in daily life: "Finally, in its focus on concrete instances of religious life, its objective is both to understand and to influence religious wisdom or faith in action in congregations and public life more generally."[9] The work of practical theology is meant to undergird the development of discipleship or to increase religious wisdom. As she notes, "Ultimately, practical theology is normatively and eschatologically oriented. In not only describes how people live as people of faith in communities and soci-

---

9 Bonnie J. Miller-McLemore, "Contributions of Practical Theology," in ed. Bonnie J. Miller-McLemore, *The Wiley-Blackwell Companion to Practical Theology*, Vol. 72, Wiley-Blackwell Companions to Religion (Wiley-Blackwell, 2011), 14.

ety. It also considers how they might do so more fully."[10] The field makes itself useful and valid inasmuch as it is able to increase faithfulness in believers in the validity of Christian practice.

The field of practical theology has often claimed this apologetic task for itself as the statement of its value within the theological curriculum, and even as an argument for why it should really be the heart of the theological curriculum. Indeed, in my own setting, over the years I have pushed to have a required introductory class in practical theology, and I have worked to have practical theological methods of reflection as a foundational practice for our internship course, and one of the primary ways that students "do" theology.

This function within the theological curriculum is aligned with a broader goal of practical theology as a discipline. Bonnie Miller-McLemore notes, "Disciplinary expertise is always highly valued. But [practical theology's] ultimate aim lies beyond disciplinary concerns in the pursuit of an embodied Christian faith."[11] In the end, the goal of the discipline is to support the adoption of Christian faith and the ongoing commitment to this faith by everyday believers, as well as training up leaders in achieving this goal:

> To state these four uses again in a slightly different order, moving from practical theology's concrete embodiment to its specialized use, practical theology refers to an *activity* of believers seeking to sustain a life of reflective faith in the everyday, a *method* or way of understanding or analyzing theology in practice used by religious leaders and by teachers and students across the theological curriculum, a *curricular area* in theological education focused on ministerial practice and subspecialties, and, finally, an *academic discipline* pursued by a smaller subset of scholars to support and sustain these first three enterprises.[12]

The subtle mission that academic practical theologians have of "supporting and sustaining" the affiliation of believers and their adoption of Christian belief is what I am questioning in this chapter.

Cameron, et al, in their book introducing theological action research, point to the importance of practical theology in bridging the divide between academic theology and pastoral practice:

---

10   Miller-McLemore, "Contributions of Practical Theology," 14.
11   Miller McLemore, "Contributions of Practical Theology," 5.
12   Miller McLemore, "Contributions of Practical Theology," 5.

> Practical theology has, in a relatively short time, made an important mark on theology and practice. In large measure this 'success' is due to the wide recognition of the problem that the discipline seeks to address- the tendency to split pastoral practice and academic theology, to the detriment of both .... 'Theological Action Research'—while not pretending to be able to answer definitively or exhaustively these questions of practical theology—offers a single methodological and theological vision that aims to hold these questions constructively to the fore, keeping mindful of the claims they have upon us as practical theologians, committed to developing theologies *for* faithful practice (emphasis original).[13]

I find myself both admiring the work of holding oneself accountable to being constructive and to hold together pastoral practice and academic theology as a researcher and scholar and also feeling the dreadful weight that the preposition "for" holds in that final sentence. Theologies that disrupt faithful practice, deconstruct belief, or challenge longstanding traditions might not be appropriate "for" increasing faithful practice. Are they therefore inappropriate directions in practical theological teaching and research?

An interesting case of the limitations that the apologetic and affiliative function of the field plays in the restraint of research was outlined by Tom Beaudoin and James Nagle in reporting their research on "lapsed" or "disaffiliated" Roman Catholics.[14] Noting that former Catholics were the second largest religiously identifying group in the United States, these scholars set out to name what it was that young Catholics leaving the church were learning from their faith journeys in the process of deconversion. Along the way Beaudoin and Nagle learned that it was considered appropriate by funders and the larger church to study deconversion for the service of reconversion or reaffiliation with the religious tradition. Studying deconversion was not considered appropriate if one was seeking to learn what those who had left the church had learned about God and themselves in the process of disaffiliation without the intent of reconversion. Any positive faith development caused by leaving the church was considered problematic and inappropriate to describe.

---

13 Helen Cameron, Deborah Bhatti, Catherine Duce, James Sweeney, and Clare Watkins, *Talking About God in Practice: Theological Action Research and Practical Theology* (SCM Press, 2010), 32.

14 James Michael Nagle, "The Thinker and the Guide: A Conversation concerning Religious Disaffiliation from the Catholic Church." *Journal of Ecumenical Studies* 54, no. 3 (2019): 328–351.

In his later book that arose from this research, Nagle describes how both the language of the field and the subtle coercion of what is expected in practical theological research challenged the direction of this research. He writes, "As teachers in Catholic high schools, my colleagues and I observe that some of our strongest students have taken the faithful but critical reflection we are teaching in alternative directions, including by disaffiliating from the religious communities in which they were raised."[15] He asks what it means to think about religious disaffiliation as a constructive step in religious formation rather than a "definitive loss,"[16] naming all of the negative terms used to describe this response to religious formation such as "lapsed" or "former" Catholics, the "lost" and the "fallen away." Nagle critiques "the hegemonic 'theology of affiliation' view that produces the aforementioned narrative of loss."[17] This seems like such a minor adjustment, but it highlights how much of the scholarship on those leaving religious communities has been committed to recapturing them, in an era where more young people are leaving than not in Roman Catholicism and mainline Protestantism. Nagle notes:

> This mainstream Catholic study concedes that a blind spot has limited the discourse among researchers and pastoral professionals. Why? Because our assumption has been that disaffiliates, and their experience, represent a problem for the church to solve. Such researchers and church professionals see returning to the church as the only faithful option because disaffiliates have 'fallen [a]way.[18]'

Nagle expresses concern that this lens of loss means that the disaffiliated can "never be seen as a source of insight and as potentially contributing something constructive to the faith."[19] They must be experienced as a problem to be solved.

The few scholars who have begun to pay attention to and learn from those who are nonaffiliated and how they frame spirituality, morality, or meaning-seeking do not find a solid place in the discourse of practical theology, perhaps because of what is seen as a lack of rigorous commitment to the normative aspects of practical theological reflection. Those who research the spiritual

---

15   James Michael Nagle, *Out on Waters: The Religious Life and Learning of Young Catholics Beyond the Church* (Pickwick Publications, 2020), xii.
16   Nagle, *Out on Waters*, xiii.
17   Nagle, *Out on Waters*, xiii.
18   Nagle, *Out on Waters*, xv.
19   Nagle, *Out on Waters*, xvi.

lives of nonreligious and/or nonaffiliated people, such as Linda Mercadente, Elizabeth Drescher, Nancy Ammerman, and Lynn Schofield Clark, find homes in religious studies or other affiliated fields because their work is not considered a part of practical theology.[20] Attention to those who are not affiliated with faith communities isn't considered of "real" practical theological concern unless the purpose of the research is how to involve these persons in the institutional life and orthodox spirituality of the Christian faith. Otherwise, they should be in religious studies rather than in conversation with practical theology.

To ask these kinds of difficult questions that I have explored in this book about the history of domination wrapped up in white western Christian practice threatens this special function within the theological curriculum that attends to the life of the church. Yet, because of the potential harm in the Christian practices discourse of perpetuating a subtle form of white supremacy that is alienating not only to other racial/ethnic groups but also subjects our young to a judgmental gaze that deters them from participation in Christian communities, such an investigation must be undertaken. Tom Beaudoin asked rather bluntly whether this legitimating function of practical theology is appropriate, while acknowledging that such a question doesn't make much sense at all within the field: "This sounds paradoxical, but I am no longer sure practical theologians should be encouraging religious practice."[21] It is hard to imagine a world in which the field of practical theology didn't have a role as advocate for and defender of the Christian faith, and yet that doesn't have to be a given for our work. However, because the field has positioned itself in making a bridge between the church and academy and taken on the special function of increasing faithfulness in believers in a normative and eschatological way, the apologetic and affiliative function becomes an essential identifying factor of the work of the field.

2   When Describing Practice Becomes Advocating for Practice

In the field of religious studies, an apologetic or confessional dimension to the study of religious practice is considered suspect at best and undisciplined at

---

20   Ammerman, *Sacred Stories, Spiritual Tribes*; Linda A. Mercadante, *Belief without Borders: Inside the Minds of the Spiritual but Not Religious* (Oxford University Press, 2014); Elizabeth Drescher, *Choosing Our Religion: The Spiritual Lives of America's Nones* (Oxford University Press, 2016); Lynn Schofield Clark, *From Angels to Aliens: Teenagers, the Media, and the Supernatural* (Oxford University Press, 2005).

21   Tom Beaudoin, "Why Does Practice Matter Theologically?," in Joyce Ann Mercer and Bonnie Miller-McLemore, eds., *Conundrums in Practical Theology* (Brill, 2016), 10.

worst. However, scholars wrestle with the reality that describing the actual significance of a practice to those engaged in it can make it compelling in such a way that it can seem like a commendation of it. For example, Robert Orsi, an American religious historian of Roman Catholicism, wrestles with the ways in which even just description of religious practice can subtly communicate endorsement of it. In his work on devotional practices with saints, particularly petitions to St. Jude, he tells the story of an encounter with a liturgist who is horrified that he is studying practices that were carefully abolished by the church's official teaching in an attempt to reduce "superstition" in devotional piety: "You're trying to bring back everything we worked so hard to do away with, the liturgist had accused me."[22] From his colleague's perspective, to simply study the ways that such practices continued to occur and be significant to everyday believers was to acknowledge and validate them as legitimate. Orsi shares how the academic practice of trying to describe what is going on calls the researcher to lean into the religious world that is being described:

> The danger of empirical work in religion on one level is that it appears to endorse, in its initial suspensions of judgments and its refusal of the comforts of otherness—the religious worlds it describes. On a deeper level, however, what may be upsetting about the study of lived religion is that such research appears to align itself with the realness of religious worlds, with presence, thereby threatening to reawaken presence.[23]

Orsi finds himself caught between the kind of distanced observation that he was trained to adopt in the study of living religious communities and their practices and the reality that scholarship about practice that acknowledges its power and meaning to the people engaged in it may come across in the eyes of others as endorsement of these practices, or perhaps more profoundly, as a testament to the reality of the living God.

Of course, Orsi engages in critique of the practices he studies, such as the use of persons with disabilities as objects of pity and moral exemplars and how that impacted his own uncle, or the resonance created between the tragedy of his aunt's life and the story of Gemma Gelgani that I recounted in an earlier chapter. The role that scholars play in adjudicating "good" and "bad" religious practice is concerning to him: "Scholars of lived religion—of religion as people actually do and imagine it in the circumstances of their everyday lives—often

---

22   Robert A. Orsi, *Between Heaven and Earth: The Religious Worlds People Make and the Scholars Who Study Them* (Princeton University Press, 2006), 158.
23   Orsi, *Between Heaven and Earth*, 158.

find themselves called on to judge, which is to say they are called on to reassure readers of the safety and otherness of religious idioms brought too vividly close through empirical research."[24] As a religious studies scholar, Orsi is troubled by the way his role seems to demand that he serve as evaluator of what is safe and unsafe in religious practice if he plans to talk about it in a way that is compelling and truthful. Practical theologians, on the other hand, are called upon to render those same practices useful to the kingdom of God, to the making of disciples, or to the upbuilding of the church as they describe and analyze them. In our discipline, we are not called upon to judge which groups are engaged in good religious practice and which are dangerous and terrible. We are called to construct or renovate those practices so that the impression stands that they are ultimately beneficial and of God. If we cannot perform this apologetic task, our work is considered incomplete or not sufficiently practical theological enough.

As Orsi continues to wrestle with the relationship of scholars to advocating for or even just controlling the narrative on the practices that they study, he notes that perhaps the scholar can never cleanly divorce themselves from those practices. We are implicated in the things that we engage in analysis, and therefore must strive to remain honest, humble, and challenged by their integrity outside of us:

> We may want to include the voices of our sources more clearly—and disruptively—in our texts, inviting them to challenge and question our interpretations of them, to propose their own alternative narratives, to question our idioms from the perspective of their own, and in general to break into the authority of our understandings and interpretations and to reveal their tentative character. We might want to examine openly and critically the emotional and intellectual sources of our own implications in the practices and beliefs we study.[25]

While Orsi's description is a call to religious studies, a place where distancing from the beliefs that one studies is much more common than in practical theology, I believe he has something even more profound to say to practical theologians. While religious studies scholars regularly wrestle with the Scylla of trying to maintain a critical academic perspective on the practices they study, practical theologians regularly wrestle with the Charybdis of hoping to

---

[24] Orsi, *Between Heaven and Earth*, 158.
[25] Orsi, *Between Heaven and Earth*, 175.

have something useful to say to the believing communities they are called upon to support with their expertise. Both moves are dangerous to seeing clearly and describing honestly in our scholarship. As Orsi points out, the halls of religious studies are haunted by the ghosts of minister fathers and childhood religiosity. Willie Jennings also uses the images of haunted halls in theological education, in his case by the white master of self-sufficient masculinity.[26] The disciplinary function of those hauntings is to push the field to advocate for the tradition as an apologist, rather than to be honest about its limitations, its failures, and at times its lack of power as a spiritual technology.

3 Demand for Institutional Loyalty and Assimilation

Like so many other practices engaged in this book, this call for apologetics, for alignment with orthodoxy, and for support of increased affiliation with religious institutions echoes in resonance with the colonial and supremacist origins of white settler Christianity. To question the belief system of the church, to not defend and uplift it, has been a historical practice engaged in by many faithful people. But the overall demand made of challengers and heretics was to align themselves with the interests and purposes of the institutional church, whether you were a dissenter within it or an outsider in need of evangelization. Where the dictates of personal or shared belief were not aligned with the institutional orthodoxy, there was concern and sanction. Where there was refusal to acknowledge the superiority of the dominant Christian worldview, religious and spiritual practices from other traditions were maligned, questioned, and even outlawed. Dissenters were considered treasonous and burned at the stake while indigenous persons were declared savage and massacred. Whether in the inquisition, the alignment of church with monarchy and government in the 16th and 17th centuries in Europe and the persecution of minority sects, or the elimination of indigenous cultural practices in almost every corner of the world where Christian missionaries arrived, the eradication of alternative meaning systems and the call to align with the powerful institution of the church was a regular practice of white settler Christianity. The drive for assimilation in the form of conformity and affiliation is a legacy of white supremacy and colonialism.

The pressures that I am speaking of are much more subtle than the religious wars of Europe that were occurring at the same moment of colonization,

---

26 Jennings, *After Whiteness*.

influencing the kind of Christianity that was carried onto other continents in the process of exploration and conquest. But the sense that the faith is worth defending, that this defense means a deep need for others to confirm and align with it, and that remaining outside the institutional church is somehow a failure of witness is still etched deep in the contours of white Christianity. That belief that, in the end, our role as a discipline is to support and sustain the church and the embodied faith of believers by encouraging affiliation and reaffirming the validity of Christian practice undergirds the work of practical theology.

On a personal level, I find myself wondering if by now the reader of this book is wondering whether or not I am a Christian at all. Part of this lies in my own history as a mainline Protestant who grew up in Alabama and who was forever questioned about whether or not my Christian walk was real because I could not give testimony to the date and time at which I gave my life to Jesus and trusted in him as my personal Lord and savior. But it also points to the demand of faithful witness as an admission ticket to work in the field. Could one be a practical theologian if one did not regularly practice the faith tradition one studies? Could practical theological scholarship exist that was not normative and eschatological? Might there be important insights to be gained within the field by those who do not affiliate with and serve as apologists for Christian practice?

Perhaps no prompt has been more poignant in asking myself about the apologetic function of the field than in teaching LGBTQIA+ and female-identifying students who have been deeply wounded by their upbringing in the church. Many of the students in my institution were raised in deeply orthodox Roman Catholic or fundamentalist evangelical families and faith communities that rejected them when their gender performance or whom they loved crossed wires with the demands and requirements of their homes of origin. Because they were so strongly formed into the faith tradition, they are in seminary to work out their own faith in fear and trembling, often through the study of Christian theology. At the same time, their religious affiliation is often listed as "none." These students are the most sensitive to and the most resistant to the subtle demands to assimilate and to affiliate that are threaded throughout books in the discipline of practical theology. Having been raised in communities that demanded their embodied formation and loyalty to the cultural and religious norms of their faith community, they can sniff it out in a heartbeat. And it was their resistance that began to alert me to the implicit demands for conformity, alignment, and affiliation written into so many of the texts that I assigned.

Institutional loyalty is a deep value of whiteness. While there are white subcultures that challenge institutions for their lack of fulfilling their appropriate purpose, and that resist the intervention of institutions into their individual lives with constraining laws that are seen as infringing upon certain rights, there is also an element of whiteness that assumes that institutions should be serving the interests of white people. Dominant culture thinking anticipates that healthy institutions will be on their side and therefore should be supported and perpetuated. One can see this in deep white support for police and the criminal justice system, for schools (as long as they continue to teach a curriculum in alignment with white supremacy in some cases), for the private medical care industry, and even for the church. Whereas other racial groups have historical experiences of betrayal and trauma generated by institutions, the ones that are powerful in the US were created by and align with white interests. You do not bite the hand that feeds you, and you do not stand against these powerful interests if you want to continue to work in and benefit from them.

The subtle demand to participate in apologetics as practical theologians might be resisted through a commitment to listen to the voices of those who find themselves on the underside of Christian practice and affiliation, whether in historical or contemporary situations. Leaning into radical honesty, or at least authenticity, about the ambivalence of Christian practice and institutions in both cases, resisting full-on apologetics and engaging in truth-telling about the limitations and failures of the church, the Christian tradition, and those who have practiced it, particularly the ways that it has been implicated in colonial projects, seems important. Being as honest as we can possibly be about the tradition we teach and about knowing that sometimes our teaching or our research as practical theologians may be damaging or disruptive of the church in powerful ways challenges the apologetic function of the field.

CHAPTER 8

Questioning Christianity

My experience in teaching practical theology comes in a historically United Methodist related seminary where the second largest religious affiliation is "none." Given its location in the US Mountain West, this reality is not that extraordinary. The region tends towards an independent/social libertarian culture where regular affiliation with mainline Protestant religious communities such as the United Methodist Church is unusual. While Catholics are rather evenly distributed across the US in terms of affiliation (25%, more or less in all regions in 2012), there are far fewer affiliated Protestants in the Western US (16% compared to 47% in the South), and far more declared atheists/agnostics (33% compared to 21–24% in the rest of the country), at least in 2012.[1] A decade later, the numbers of religiously unaffiliated had jumped 10 percent in the US by 2021 to nearly 3 in 10, according to Pew Research, although that report was not broken down by region.[2] Given that I work in a mainline Protestant seminary in Colorado, we are drawing from a small regional population of people affiliated with those traditions, which doesn't necessarily mean a small number of people interested in spiritual or religious matters.

The nones in my seminary tend to be more ex-Christian or alienated Christian than truly outside of formative religious exposure in their religious worldviews, although some do come without religious formation. They are "dones," in the common parlance of many evangelical Christians, those who have left the religious traditions they were raised in because of frustrations from their experiences within them. Who are these students, and why are they in a school of theology getting a masters' degree? Some are what I call "God-haunted," evoking the phrase from the gothic Southern novelist Flannery O'Connor. They grew up in strongly formative Christian communities (often conservative Roman Catholic or white evangelical/fundamentalist churches and families) but were alienated from those traditions, often because of issues of gender

---

1 https://www.pewresearch.org/religion/2012/10/09/nones-on-the-rise-demographics/#region Just to note, the West has far more Latinx Catholics (45% compared to 9–33% elsewhere in the US, and far fewer white Catholics 13% compared to 22–36% elsewhere). So, this is a racialized set of data, including that Black Protestants raise the number of Protestants in the Bible belt.
2 https://www.pewresearch.org/religion/2021/12/14/about-three-in-ten-u-s-adults-are-now-religiously-unaffiliated/, accessed 7/5/22.

identity or sexual orientation. Gender identity struggles might mean that they were women with a call to ministry in a tradition that did not acknowledge women's leadership or ordination, or it might mean that they failed to comply with the strongly regulated gender complementarity values of their communities in their own gender performance. Some are trans, nonbinary, or gender fluid persons who found that their churches and families struggled to acknowledge their sense of true self. Others were ostracized by these home communities because of who they loved, whether that was a same-sex relationship or a sexually-active relationship outside of marriage or other monogamous commitment that challenged strict heteronormative boundaries. While they have felt betrayed by their religious communities, for many their trust in the God they met in those communities has remained more intact, leaving them to sort through the beliefs instilled in their childhoods to see which ones hold up once they are out of its totalizing worldview.

Others among our "nones" came to a non-religiously affiliated spirituality through recovery communities, yoga or meditative practice, mentors/authors who shaped their understanding through individual teaching, or other forms of engagement. They may have switched denominations depending on who they were living with as children or which military base they were assigned to so that none of them feels particularly like home, but don't associate with the nondenominational Christianity that is largely white evangelical in base and don't want to claim that as a label. So, they are Christian, but not affiliated with any particular congregation or denomination after leaving their families of origin. They are not sure they want to affiliate in the future, so they list their affiliation as "none."

My context requires a course in practical theology for students in each of our professional degree programs, even though many of them do not identify particularly as Christian or see themselves affiliated with any sort of religious community at all. Many are resistant to the idea of institutional religion and do not want to be associated with it due to past trauma or the harm that they have seen religious people do in the world. Over the years I have also worked with many students from the Unitarian Universalist Association (UUA), who in the US West tend to be more humanist or Buddhist-informed in their current spiritual path, and who often are also alienated from childhood Christian upbringings that are viewed as intolerant or narrow-minded. And here I am, trying to teach them an approach to theological reflection that implicitly and explicitly asks for correlation between the Christian tradition and the experiences of their daily lives, which requires identification of religious texts, rituals, theologies, and historic materials that are normative to their community. Fewer than a third of my students imagine their vocational context as a ministry professional within a congregation. For those who imagine themselves working in chaplaincy, not-for-profit, and public sector jobs, they struggle to imagine how normative truth claims, particularly from the Christian tradition, ethically function in those religiously plural or nonaffiliated settings, beyond the personal motivation for engagement in the work of the professional. Teaching practical theology in this context becomes a complicated task.

After I had managed to get practical theology on the schedule as a theology class that filled a graduation requirement, I had both a student who was a practicing Wiccan and a student studying to be a military chaplain from the LDS tradition enroll hoping to avoid the more historically focused systematic/constructive theological requirement that worked only out of Christian traditions. The first student was seeking to deepen her theoretical understandings of religion and ritual while serving in a newly emerging tradition made up of people who had largely intentionally left Christianity or were not steeped in it to start with. The other needed an MDiv to be a military chaplain, but also needed to be in a school where other students weren't actively trying to convert him from his religious tradition because they understood it to be a cult, so he ended up in a white liberal mainline seminary. He came from a tradition about which I knew very little, and which does not have an active scholarly tradition of critical engagement with the normative resources of the tradition in conversation with lived experience. The Wiccan student didn't believe that normative resources in her tradition existed. Neither of them found the Protestant Christian-centric readings I offered in practical theology a helpful starting place. In teaching these students, I realized again and again how very Protestant and Christian my own notions of practical theology were.[3]

Given the students that I teach, questioning Christian-centrism in practical theology is a matter of pedagogical urgency as I struggle to help students connect to the practices and modes of reflection within the field. Practical theologian Tom Beaudoin also questions the Christian center as he names a disorientation: "This disorientation has shown me that practical theology (in the USA) has been too untroubled in its Christian confidence. It has not done well enough at letting the religious 'other' into the theological sense it makes of practice; neither has it allowed in much wisdom and experience from non-affiliated/secular persons."[4] While acknowledging the threatening nature of

---

3 Claire Wolfteich, "Reframing Practical Theology," in Joyce Ann Mercer and Bonnie Miller-McLemore, eds., *Conundrums in Practical Theology* (Brill, 2016), 276.

4 Tom Beaudoin, "Why Does Practice Matter Theologically?," in Mercer and Miller-McLemore, eds. *Conundrums*, 12.

his call to "imagine releasing a Christian center for practical theology," especially without a guarantee of what would come next in the discipline without the ties to Christian orthodoxy, his suggestion matches the reality of what it is like to teach practical theology in my context.[5] The mostly Protestant Christian normative assumptions become problematic, and it is difficult to imagine working as a practical theologian without them.

Similarly, Kathleen Grieder has also been a strong voice in questioning the Christian-centrism of practical theology.[6] Greider also has taught for much of her career in the western United States, a context in which religious diversity within families is quite common. She notes that a focus on lived experience has led practical theology to bump up against the religious diversity that marks the contexts of diverse persons living in diverse communities given her context: "[T]he persons, families, and communities practical theologians seek to serve have identities that are religiously multifaceted and the webs of connection in which they interact are weighted by histories, futures, meanings, commitments, joys, and suffering shaped by religious multiplicity."[7] Greider calls for an increased "development of Christian practical theology's reflexively, theologically, and pragmatically honed wisdom" in relationship to this religious pluralism, which will require letting go of its Christian centrism.[8]

However, Greider also notes that acknowledging religious pluralism and releasing a focus on Christian orthodoxy is not an entirely novel move for the field given its attention to actual ministry practice. As an example, Greider talks about how Christian chaplains in the military and health care settings have been called into reflection on interreligious realities due to their roles requiring them to serve both Christian and non-Christian clientele, which has affected their both personal theologies and their practical theological practice.[9] She names that these realities have led to multireligious reflection beyond pastoral care: "History makes clear that some of the field's subdisciplines have resisted the tendency to presume Christian identity and superiority in their attention to practices—especially in centuries of chaplaincy, but

---

5 Beaudoin, "Why Does Practice Matter" in Mercer and Miller-McLemore, eds. *Conundrums*, 12.
6 Kathleen Greider, "Religious Pluralism and Christian Centrism," in ed. Bonnie J. Miller-McLemore, *The Wiley-Blackwell Companion to Practical Theology*, Vol. 72, Wiley-Blackwell Companions to Religion (Wiley-Blackwell, 2011).
7 Greider, "Religious Pluralism and Christian Centrism," 452.
8 Greider, "Religious Pluralism and Christian Centrism," 454.
9 Greider, "Religious Pluralism and Christian Centrism," 458. See also Leah Dawn Bueckert and Daniel S. Schipani, eds. *You Welcomed Me: Interfaith Spiritual Care in the Hospital* (Pandora Press, 2010).

also in pastoral counseling, education, and liturgy and care for persons entering interreligious marriages."[10] Thus, practitioners have sought ways to work across religious difference and with those who are disaffiliated given the experiences of the people to whom they minister, who do not always neatly fit within the boxes of particular religious or denominational affiliation.

In my own subdiscipline of religious education, attention to religious pluralism has caused historic divisions among scholars who wanted to work across religious traditions and those who felt that this move watered down the required fidelity and focus on Christian theology. The Religious Education Association, founded in 1903, began with a focus on the role of both Christianity and Judaism contributing to the education of the public in a democracy, with its practitioner members having over a century of experience of being in conversation across religious boundaries about shared concern for formation and education of both children and adults in relation to the common good in a pluralist democracy.[11] As the neo-orthodox theological movement strengthened in the mid twentieth century, there was a divide initiated from those who focused more exclusively on Christian formation and found the lack of Christian theological attention problematic in the field. This led to the creation of two competing scholarly guilds and journals as the Society of Professors in Christian Education formed to serve those who did not wish to engage with multireligious concerns and thought the field properly should remain situated with a Christian focus rather than the broadness suggested in the name "religious education." This divide remains visible in the naming of academic positions and departments in universities and seminaries, with more neo-orthodox and evangelical protestants more often claiming the name "Christian education" and more progressive Christian and multireligious departments using the term "religious education."

Moving back from the subdisciplines to the disciplinary framing of practical theology, it becomes more problematic to question the dominant presence of Christianity in a field where the second word of the field's name is "theology." Practical theology shares this problem with other disciplinary forms of knowledge creation and educational institutions that include the word "theology" in their names. Although its origins predate the beginnings of various Christianities as religious traditions, the word "theology" itself has been developed

---

10   Greider, "Religious Pluralism and Christian Centrism," in ed. Bonnie Miller-McLemore, *Wiley-Blackwell Companion*, 460.

11   For resources describing the history of the Religious Education Association, an Association of Professors, Practitioners and Researchers in Religious Education, see https://religiouseducation.net/history.

and extended within the Christian tradition since about the third century. As a resource as general as the Britannica encyclopedia puts it: "The problem lies in the fact that, whereas theology as a concept had its origins in the tradition of the ancient Greeks, it obtained its content and method only within Christianity. Thus, theology, because of its peculiarly Christian profile, is not readily transferable in its narrow sense to any other religion."[12] Other religious traditions have at times used the word, particularly in trying to translate their own forms of study of texts and their own tradition into Western universities where historic traditions of Western Christian theology served as the norm for studying religion, but the word "philosophy" or "teachings" is more often used in traditions such as Buddhism or Judaism. The word "theology" itself evokes an assumed relationship with Christianity.

Despite that barrier, some great work is emerging in the field of practical theology from scholars rooted in other traditions, particularly Islam and Buddhism. Some of these scholars have backed into practical theology departments because of their questions and research focus in education and pastoral care. When asked to reflect on how their work is related to the field of practical theology, some perplexity ensues. As Muslim religious educator Amjad Hussain notes: "For a Muslim the question of a 'practical theology' within what could loosely be called Muslim or Islamic Education is a perplexing phenomenon. As a Muslim theologian I am keenly aware that there is no separation between belief/faith and practice in my religion: Islam is recognized by its adherents as a revealed 'way of life' with both a sense of belief and an orthopraxy."[13] Hussain notes that any understanding of theology that is not practical, not related to the concerns of daily life, would not be Muslim because of the utter integration of the two in Islamic understanding.

Other scholars note the more abstract nature of conversations in Islamic studies and call for a move towards practical theology in order to improve chaplaincy and pastoral leadership in Islam, including articles on particular issues related to domestic violence, such as the work of Nevin Reda.[14] A call for an increasing focus on the lived experience of Muslims and the need to put "Islamic theological concepts into practice" comes from Nazila Isgandarova:

---

12 https://www.britannica.com/topic/theology, accessed 7/5/22.
13 Amjad Hussain, "Muslim Theology and Religious Studies: Relational, Practical, and Inter-Faith Dimensions," *Religious Education* 104, no. 3 (May 2009), 239.
14 Nevin Reda, "The Qur'an and Domestic Violence: An Islamic Feminist, Spiritually Integrative Reading of Verse 4:34," *International Journal of Practical Theology* 23, no. 2 (2019): 257–73.

However, if we take into consideration the fact that theological knowledge depends on the context and is sensitive in many ways, there is a need, for an understanding of the 'lived' practice of Islamic theological studies or a greater need for practical theology in Islamic studies to enable both academics and practitioners of the Islamic faith to address issues of power, cultural diversity, and religious pluralism among Muslims.[15]

Isgandarova also notes that increased exposure to contemporary empirical methods to study lived religious practices in diverse Muslim communities will be essential to the development of the field of Islamic studies, linking these methods to practical theology: "For example, if practical methodology provides the perspective of the writer in terms of how she/he reads the Islamic tradition and makes sense of various practices and experiences, the empirical approach promises to make more sense of these rituals and practices from the experience of the people."[16] Isgandarova argues that a more just and complete picture of the nature of Islam in worldwide practice and the diversities of its expression might emerge with a more empirical focus on its expressions in living communities rather than its textual interpretations, and she believes that practical theology might have the research methods to allow this to emerge.

1 Christian Privilege and the Racialization of Religious Identity

As I am writing this chapter, questions of white Christian nationalism are at the forefront of political conversations in the United States. A recent Supreme Court decision, Kennedy vs. Bremerton School District (June 27, 2022) ruled that a high school football coach had the right to lead his football players in prayer on the 50-yard line following games. This reversed a long-standing decision that schools were not allowed to include prayer led by public school employees in classrooms or at ceremonial events like graduations in order to preserve the tradition of separation of church and state rooted in the disestablishment clause in the first amendment to the US Constitution. Many on social media immediately identified that this religious behavior in a publicly funded school would not be considered appropriate if the person leading

---

15   Nazila Isgandarova, "Practical Theology and Its Importance for Islamic Theological Studies," *Ilahiyat Studies* 5, no. 2 (2014), 218.
16   Isgandarova, "Practical Theology and Its Importance for Islamic Theological Studies," 223.

prayer were Wiccan or Muslim, noting that while the current Supreme Court has been named pro-religion, in fact they are pro-Christian. Even now, as the Supreme Court approves teachers leading student in prayer, there are many positive responses from the religious right that indicate that this means Christianity and not just any religious tradition. A relatively new Texas law requires the motto "In God We Trust" be publicly posted in every school building, and a second law trying to achieve the same with the Ten Commandments was only narrowly defeated. A school board in the Dallas/Fort Worth area rejected the use of a sign with the motto written in Arabic and one in rainbow font designed by students in their district, both designed to resist and reveal the Christian theocratic intentions of the law.[17]

This Supreme Court ruling and the local Texas school board's response demonstrate the concept of Christian privilege. Though the United States has a clause in the first Amendment to its Constitution prohibiting the establishment of a particular religious tradition as a national religion, and though there has been a hearty cultural tradition of the separation of church and state practices, Christianity has also served as a de facto established religious tradition in the United States because of its cultural dominance historically. Many workplace and all public school calendars in the United States in both the shape of the work week and in declaring holidays implicitly honor Christian calendars with their Sunday sabbath and major religious holidays such as Christmas targeted for shutdowns. Many US citizens can reasonably assume that other people have heard of their sacred text and have some knowledge of the stories and the rituals involved in Christian practice. These stories and rituals have never been prohibited in the United States, and in fact, they are sometimes referenced in secular discourse, such as the "Good Samaritan" laws that provide legal protections for those who attempt to help someone who has been injured. In contrast, American Indian groups who have sought protection for landscapes and bodies of water based on cultural traditions that name them as sacred have failed repeatedly in legal proceedings to gain the freedom to practice their traditional religious practices in relationship to these sacred lands. Muslim workers who have asked for accommodations to be able to fulfill their rituals of daily prayer in workplaces such as meatpacking plants have faced discrimination and rejection. These contrasting experiences of legal protection for religious freedom demonstrate the Christian privilege experienced in the United States.

---

17 https://www.npr.org/2022/08/31/1120239381/texas-in-god-we-trust-arabic-signs-chaz-stevens.

An additional layer to Christian privilege is its association with whiteness, while other religious traditions have historically been racialized as non-white. The dominant cultural narrative of who belonged in the project of building a new nation included Protestant Christianity as a key identity marker. Waves of immigrants in late eighteenth and nineteenth century from Ireland and from places like Italy and Poland and Germany were mostly Roman Catholic, and it wasn't clear that they should be afforded the legal protections of whiteness, often because of religious belief.[18] Strict barriers against immigration from the Southern Hemisphere targeting non-Christian populations that were racialized as nonwhite were built into immigration policy, such as in the Chinese Exclusion Act of 1882. Extended through the Geary Act of 1892, barriers limiting immigration from Southern and Eastern Europe and all of Asia persisted until they were removed in the Immigration Act of 1965.[19] The combination of race and religion marked persons from these areas as unsuitable for American residency or citizenship.

Both Jewish and Muslim persons have discovered that their religious beliefs have marked them as racially different at various historical moments in Europe and the United States. In Europe, Christian anti-Judaism evolved into a secular racist anti-Semitism in the latter part of the nineteenth and first half of the twentieth century, ending in its most virulent expression in the so-called Final Solution of Nazi Germany.[20] Various white supremacist movements in the United States adopted similar racialized notions of Jewish identity, engaging in violence against Jewish persons and synagogues right up to the present day, with the mass shooting at the Tree of Life (L'Simcha) Synagogue in Pittsburgh in 2018. Likewise, after the terrorist attacks of September 11, 2001 in the United States, racist expressions of islamophobia increased dramatically in the United States, including attacks on persons who appeared to be Arabic or Muslim, attacks on mosques and prayer services, and legislative moves banning Sharia law. Over 200 bills banning the use of Sharia law (a religiously-based moral code already subject to Federal and State laws in the United States) have been introduced in state legislatures in 43 states, with 14 reaching the status of law since 2010.[21] These legislative movements and their attending publicity,

---

18 Noel Ignatiev, *How the Irish Became White* (Routledge, 1995).
19 For more information on this history of discrimination in immigration law, see https://www.archives.gov/milestone-documents/chinese-exclusionact.
20 Warren S. Goldstein, "The Racialization of the Jewish Question: The Pseudo-Secularization of Christian Anti-Judaism into Racial Anti-Semitism," *Religion and Theology* 27, no. 3–4 (December 8, 2020): 179–201."
21 https://www.splcenter.org/hatewatch/2018/02/05/anti-sharia-law-bills-united-states.

along with the anti-Muslim rhetoric voiced by Donald Trump on the campaign trail in 2015, spurred hate crimes against Muslims in the United States to raise by 67% in 2015.[22] Christian privilege linked to white supremacy has powerful material effects in the day-to-day safety of those whose religious traditions have been othered.

2 Struggling with Normativity and Universality in White Theology

In my first year of teaching, I had a student from Cambodia in my Teaching and Learning in the Community of Faith class. Each student taught the class for 30 minutes twice, once on a sacred text and once on a religious or spiritual practice. In the class this particular student led, she taught us many aphorisms or proverbs from her home context in translation, trying to help her classmates understand how the practice of deploying the cultural sayings was an important form of spiritual encouragement and support when people were going through hard times. She had students explore the practice of sharing cultural sayings by having them choose certain ones in response to case-study situations that she had created which might require pastoral or emotional support. For the other, mostly white, students in the class, many questions arose about the practice of utilizing the proverbs in the conversation. How did she know which saying to deploy when, since many of them were directly contradictory in meaning? Ah, she said, well this was the soul of wisdom, to be able to know and understand spiritually and maturely which of the sayings was needed in the moment. We talked about how English-language proverbs were often contradictory and still essentially true, such as "money isn't everything" and "a penny saved is a penny earned." But weren't they just clichés? After a long conversation about what her classmates meant by the term "cliché," she resisted the notion that communally gathered, oft-repeated wisdom should be dismissed so easily because simply it was well-worn or not novel.

What ensued in the class was a lengthy conversation about normative truth claims and how they worked in community. I was amid the charged conversation at the time, so I didn't take notes, but these kinds of questions and answers emerged: Did everybody in her community think the sayings were true? Well, they contained truths, and if deployed wisely in the moment they represented the wisdom of her people. But if they depended on correct deployment by a

---

22   https://www.splcenter.org/hatewatch/2016/11/14/anti-muslim-hate-crimes-surged-last-year-fueled-hateful-campaign.

wise person, wouldn't just the words of the person be enough? Why use the cultural sayings at all? If it had been said by people over generations, wasn't there more comfort in knowing that it captured their gathered wisdom and not just the opinion of the one person, she responded. But what if two people used the opposite sayings for the same situation? It would depend on the three people involved to discern what was most helpful at the time. Wouldn't that sound like Job arguing with his friends in his grief? Finally she answered a question with a question: why would that be a problem, if the situation was so difficult that it required many people gathered to sort out what was the right wisdom, and it was located somewhere between the many ideas captured in the sayings of the elders?

Over the years I have thought about this conversation often. What I think was at work was the status of truth claims that the white students were used to navigating had a much stronger truth/falsity division than the truth claims that the Cambodian student was used to navigating. Whiteness was built around simultaneously emerging modernist notions of truth based on reason, science, and logic. There is Truth, and there are falsehoods, superstitions, emotive manipulations, and political propaganda. More than just normativity, white supremacy stands on universalist notions of truth. The truths that we proclaim aren't just based in the wisdom of our culture or our community; to be significant they must be true across time, community, and place. When met with other cultures with radically different worldviews and practices of social organization, white civilizations declared their understandings of civilization universally true, the apex of human development, worth eliminating others to reinforce and maintain. There was an historic merging of cultural specificity of white Western norms and Christian theological claims in proclaiming that what is true for us must be true for everyone.

One of the regular responses in research from the Barna group about why young people have left affiliation with childhood Christianity is their sense that it is out of step with scientific reasoning or is anti-science.[23] Their notions of truth are steeped in these white universalist standards of how truth works: if science is true these religious stories cannot be. And if some of those religious claims are not true, it must all be suspect. Normative claims from a religious tradition are not truth with power beyond a shadow of a doubt. We are called upon to discern how to deploy them, and there might be several faithful responses, and people might still hurt, and it might not be enough to

---

23 https://www.barna.com/research/six-reasons-young-christians-leave-church/, accessed 7/3/23.

stand on. I think for many students, this is a difficult notion; they might be called upon to proclaim a gospel that is not somehow unassailable.

To bring this into the practice of academics, moving towards universal claims is a habit of white supremacy that takes the experiences of a particular community and paints them as normative for all communities. Courtney Goto reflects on this requirement of whiteness as universal experience to which everyone else becomes a specialized or racialized other within the field of practical theology through her discussion of "coercive mimeticism." Coercive mimeticism requires nonwhite scholars to take on the framings, habitual questions, and approaches to the field as established within whiteness in order to gain legitimacy as a scholar. Goto notes, "Coercive mimeticism is incubated by a larger system of white supremacy that allows practical theologians (and Christians more broadly) to base assumptions about the collective 'we' on white experiences, captured and represented in images that are taken for granted yet have profound power."[24] Holding myself accountable to this reality, I can't even count how many times I have evoked a "we" about the discipline in this book. It is right there in the title: Who is the "our" whose faith I am questioning? White people's faith. This is a hard habit to break while writing within the normative forms of academic discourse that historically required research to be generalizable and replicable across context for it to be worthy or useful. While the practice of making "universal" claims was severely chastened with the important critiques of postmodernism in the humanities, more respect and resources are still granted to academic work that stands confidently as if it speaks truth across space and time and in ways that includes all experiences, not just those from parochial, gendered, racially marked, or otherwise specific communities. However, those who are outside the bounds of whiteness are rarely granted the magic of claiming that their experiences or findings are somehow generalizable beyond their specific communities, whether encountered as courses in theology or books published in the field.

Another struggle with normativity within whiteness is generated by its strong individualism. While the love of reason and science in modernity made the belief that one could explain the universe with certain truth, the belief in the individual and the importance of individual experience simultaneously privileged one's internal knowing over trust in institutions, government, or religious traditions as arbiters of the truth. Whiteness emerged with a strong critique of religious institutions, alongside the emerging sense of the priesthood of all believers and individual conscience in heroically standing over

---

24   Courtney Goto, "The Racialized 'Zoo' of Practical Theology," in Joyce Ann Mercer and Bonnie Miller-McLemore, eds., *Conundrums in Practical Theology* (Brill, 2016), 121.

against oppressive institutions. Well-steeped in white individualism for centuries, my students struggle to imagine that religious belonging or historic traditions could be authoritative or could make claims against the freedom of their lives. Their individual experience or that of trusted others is their go-to source of wisdom rather than anything institutionalized or handed down through the generations.

When we start to work with the part of the practical theological reflection process that draws upon normative claims from a tradition held by a particular community, students get tripped up on how that could be possible. While those who are thinking about preaching within a typical Christian congregation can imagine this practice as one of the places such a thing might happen, they find it harder to imagine doing so with congregants outside of that liturgical setting in a counseling or decision-making situation. For those who are in communities that are intentionally non-creedal, particularly the Unitarian-Universalists with their principled commitment to "the free and responsible search for truth and meaning,"[25] such a normative move in practical theology feels close to violation of granting freedom and responsibility to individuals rather than the tradition. They begin to discuss something like what happened in my class struggling with the cultural proverbs and their use in offering spiritual counsel. The tradition could be used to say anything. It is not a reliable resource of truth like the psychological discourse they deploy without critique on shame and vulnerability and embodied trauma, which is seen to be True. White liberal mainline Christians see their religion as a different thing than white evangelical Christians, and they find it problematic that both groups might deploy the same texts for opposite ends. They begin to recognize that what they have is not a single tradition but really a range of Christianities, radically contextualized expressions of a loosely bounded tradition over time with many sources of authority, contradicting claims, fallacies, and prejudices baked in.

We can then begin to discuss how drawing on a tradition as normative is as much about making that tradition normative as it is creating expressions of faithful life based on it. We do not consult the tradition as if the answers are there if we just make the exact right correlation between a historic text or situation or theological claim and the current situation. The more students come to know about the tradition in their education, the more that they begin to recognize that there are as many answers present within it as there are

---

25 For a discussion of the Seven Principles of the UUA, see https://www.uua.org/beliefs/what-we-believe/principles.

people or communities consulting it, and in fact the different questions that communities ask of the tradition make for constructing different traditions. This complexity is what practical theologian Tom Beaudoin is getting at in his argument based on the concept of "Christianicity":

> 'Christianicity' is meant to remind the reader that 'Christianity' is much less a description of a state or condition (an abstract noun) than a kind of display of identity in a certain time and place, a way of designating and fostering an experience of recognizing one's own or another's essential Christian-ness as resident in beliefs and practices, in an over-against relationship with the 'others' of 'Christianity,' that is neither essential nor unchosen. The idea of there being Christian practice is a political choice for one of many possible 'Christianities' that naturalizes its action by establishing continuity with a Christian past and laying down track towards a Christian future.[26]

To begin to accept the responsibility for making normative claims as a political choice that identifies one in relationship to a tradition that was created in the past and that one futures with their meaning-making work is a lot for students to take in. They believe in a truth that is more substantive than this fragile notion of normativity. They want to be "Right" in a way that feels inextricably linked to the history of whiteness. Some want to find this rightness and stand on its promises within Christianity. Others distrust it in Christianity but believe that reliable truth lies in their own wisdom from experience or in other psychological or cultural sources. Few want to reckon with the uncertain responsibility and use of power that engaging with religious tradition as normative requires.

Beaudoin identifies quite clearly that using the Christian tradition as a source of normative truth is both an exercise in contemporary meaning-making and an attempt to preserve the privileged status of that tradition for the future:

> There is a mutual reinforcement between assigning Christian meaning to an assigned domain called *practice*, feeling relatively at home in a religious world of texts, concepts, and experiences, and thinking the task of the theologian is to keep what feels like forward motion going, to

---

26 Beaudoin, "Why Does Practice Matter Theologically?" in Mercer and Miller-McLemore eds., *Conundrums*, 22.

reproduce its essential characteristics in a new generation and to restore fidelity to it in the present by finding ever-anew a hospitable religious past that funds contemporary practice.[27]

Consulting the tradition as having authority to speak to the current situation, says Beaudoin, ritually invokes a boundary for productive ends.[28] He seems to suggest, however, that it might be possible to do so in a way that does not require one to evoke the stability of a single Christian narrative. Those who spend any time learning about the great variety of Christianities historically recognize that there are many streams of cultural and historical inputs merging in a conversation full of disjunctions, contradictions, and sometimes outright fallacies that constitute what we call "Christian tradition." Beaudoin argues for moving from thinking about the normative consultation with Christianities as addressing current "publics" to engaging in the practice as a conscious attempt to invent "futures": "In opening the theological significance of practice to pre-Christian, Christian, post-Christian and non-Christian meanings, which is a result of seeing Christianity itself as a jerrybuilt pastiche of cultural materials, of cultural practices rendered as religious/faith/Christian practices, practical theology keeps its curiosity permanent regarding the heritage of practice."[29] Working theologically from a position of "exploration" rather than "certitude" is something that practical theologians Patricia O'Connell Killen and John de Beer also advocate in their introductory work on theological reflection.[30] Despite being decades old now, that text continues to resonate with my students because of their concerns about wielding tradition, helping them imagine how they might work with normative tradition in a manner that is not a practice of domination.

Over the years, I have found myself working hard to make a case for the utility of a normative moment in practical theological reflection. I name for students the rhetorical strength of appealing to familiar stories, concepts, and values from a religious tradition in swaying communities, in working with loyalties, hearts, and relational identity-bearing truths. I have also found

---

27 Beaudoin, "Why Does Practice Matter Theologically?" in Mercer and Miller-McLemore eds., *Conundrums*, 23.
28 Beaudoin, "Why Does Practice Matter Theologically?" in Mercer and Miller-McLemore eds., *Conundrums*, 26.
29 Beaudoin, "Why Does Practice Matter Theologically?" in Mercer and Miller-McLemore eds., *Conundrums*, 29.
30 Patricia O'Connell Killen and John de Beer, *The Art of Theological Reflection* (Crossroad, 1994), 13–18.

myself calling on the arrogance and limitations of trusting only on the knowledge tested by an individual or even a single generation in facing struggles and conundrums. I also find myself having to explain how religious tradition and human experience are two sides of the same coin in many ways. Experience includes interpretation and revelation of direct experience of the divine/sacred by communities and individuals. When this experience lasts beyond one generation, gets codified and approved by official bodies or by continual use, it becomes tradition. Tradition can include histories, rituals and liturgies, music, official ethical statements of the religious body or professional guild, artwork and architecture, teachings of key religious leaders, theological writings, interpretations and retellings of scripture, spiritual practices and forms of individual devotion/prayer, poetry, and literature inspired by the tradition. I remind students that different kinds of Christianities use these sources with different emphasis, and they are often used to some extent in other religious traditions as well. Even "outside" of religious traditions, people often appeal to the authority of shared normative values as well, whether that be ethnic or national identity and history, cultural sayings or proverbs, science, human rights discourse, documents such as the US Constitution or the UN Charter on the Rights of Children, the sayings of influential or heroic figures, literature and art, movies/games/mass media, etc. I put scare quotes on "outside" in that final set of sources because I know how influential Christianities have been in many of these documents that are deemed "secular" or "cultural" rather than "religious." But I try to help students notice how they are already appealing to normative sources uncritically, and then invite them to broaden their awareness of how these sources might be useful in working with communities and public spaces.

Does this process of holding normative moves lightly in practical theological reflection ultimately mean that we are abandoning the wisdom that still might be found in the Christian tradition? I have appreciated this statement from Pádraig Ó Tuama, who served as the leader of the Corrymeela Christian community in Ireland, found at the front of the prayer book that they created: "The tradition of Corrymeela is Christian. It is from Christian hope and Christian harm that our witness comes, and to be faithful to our voices of complicity and consolation, we speak from the voice of Christianity. This can be a tense stance; so much pain has come from this particularity of following God and the sacred story."[31] In the same moment that the book stands in the particularity of Christian normative claims, it also acknowledges the harm that those

---

31   Padraig Ó Tuama, *Daily Prayer with the Corrymeela Community* (Canterbury Press, 2017), xviii.

particular claims have caused. That ambivalent faithfulness is a model for how we might continue to make meaning with the Christian tradition while also acknowledging its problematic aspects.

3 Interreligious Practical Theology and Multiple Religious Belonging

My experiences in the increasingly secular Mountain West region of the United States creates one form of question for the importance of privileging Christianity in practical theology. Many colleagues who have their roots in places where multiple religious traditions exist with cultural and indigenous traditions have been challenging Christian dominance in Christian formation and practical theology for years. For example, Wehn-In Ng focused on interreligious dialogue within the self and multiple religious belonging amongst Asian females in North American in her work on developing wholesome Christian nurture and culturally appropriate religious education over a quarter century ago.[32] Similarly, Emmanuel Lartey addresses the importance of honoring indigenous African rituals and practices as a source of healing and life-giving communal gathering.[33] Hye-Ran Kim-Cragg, Cláudio Carvalhaes, Jonathan Tan, and many others have advocated for drawing on resources from multiple religious and cultural traditions and acknowledging the reality of multiple religious belonging in the work of practical theology in many disciplines from homiletics to leadership and liturgy.[34] One thing to learn from these colleagues is the ways that multiple religious belonging feels different in places in the world where Christianity is non-dominant, or where regular interaction with and respect for multiple traditions is the norm, or might have been the norm before colonization or missionized Christianity arrived.

Religious educator Sheryl Kujawa-Holbrook has articulated a passionate plea for the task of interreligious learning in faith communities, not just as an accommodation to the reality of increasing pluralism but as "a sign of Divine activity in our midst, a tremendous gift, and an opportunity for the Christian church to deepen the faith of its own adherents, to participate fully in civic

---

32 Wehn-In Ng, "Toward Wholesome Nurture: Challenges in the Religious Education of Asian North American Females," *Religious Education* 91, no. 2 (Spring 1996): 238–54.
33 Emmanuel Y. Lartey, *Postcolonializing God: New Perspectives on Pastoral and Practical Theology* (SCM Press, 2013).
34 Kwok Puilan and Stephen Burns, eds., *Postcolonial Practice of Ministry: Leadership, Liturgy, and Interfaith Engagement* (Lexington Books, 2016).

life, and to work for the good [of] all humanity."³⁵ Indeed, she argues that it is "only through encounters across differences, crossing borders and coming back, that the creativity of the Spirit is unleashed, faith deepened, relationships formed, and new insights gained."³⁶ Kujawa-Holbrook advocates that engaging well in interreligious learning requires knowing one's own faith more clearly even as we learn about and from other traditions and cultures through relational partnerships and honest engagement.³⁷ While she argues that such learning is available in any faith community, it requires struggle and effort to do so with integrity.³⁸ Engaging with a spirit of hospitality while avoiding the dangers of misappropriation requires the creation of intentional spaces with adequate time for deep conversations to happen and for durable relationships to be formed. Such capacity extends to a revolution in the ways that faith communities are structured, as Kujawa-Holbrook notes: "Faith communities which actually encourage a plurality of voices also tend to be places where power-sharing is critical to the way decisions are made and common life organized."³⁹

Another significant voice in the calls for practical theological reflection beyond Christian boundaries has come from the work of pastoral theologian Kathleen Greider. Similar to the earlier work of Wehn-In Ng in religious education, Greider calls for attention to intrareligious pluralism and intrapersonal religious plurality or "multiple religious belonging" in the work of pastoral care.⁴⁰ However, she notes that such attention to multiple religiosity can often reflect a sense of inadequacy inherent in such religious identities in the judgment of Christian ministers: "At the same time, intrapersonal pluralism, whether created through colonialism, socialization, choice, or being born into a multireligious family, has been judged as lack of mature religious commitment or marginalized as threatening religious syncretism."⁴¹ The notion of "immaturity" is loaded racially, given the hierarchical valuing of peoples in developmental schemas in the nineteenth century where darker skinned indigenous and peoples from the Southern Hemisphere and "the East" were

---

35 Sheryl A Kujawa-Holbrook, *God Beyond Borders: Interreligious Learning Among Faith Communities* (Pickwick Publications, 2014), xix.
36 Kujawa-Holbrook, *God Beyond Borders*, 33.
37 Kujawa-Holbrook, *God Beyond Borders*, xix.
38 Kujawa-Holbrook, *God Beyond Borders*, 149.
39 Kujawa-Holbrook, *God Beyond Borders*, 156.
40 Greider, "Religious Pluralism and Christian Centrism," in *Wiley-Blackwell Companion to Practical Theology*, ed. Miller-McLemore, 458–459.
41 Greider, "Religious Pluralism and Christian Centrism," in *Wiley-Blackwell Companion to Practical Theology*, ed. Miller-McLemore, 459.

understood to be less developed towards full humanity. Participation in traditions that were not monotheistic or even theistic was seen as a sign of lack of cultural development towards "true" religion. Deemed a lack of developed civilization, these practices were deemed impure rather than wise, and were used as justification for the history of cultural genocide within Christian missionary practices. Greider highlights the work of postmodern and postcolonial analyses in recognizing these responses as inadequate caricatures, urging more adequate formation, research, and development of persons who understand this increasingly common aspect of lived religious faith.

On the other hand, engagement by white people with indigenous and religious practices such as Buddhism in the West has also raised important concerns about cultural appropriation. Whether these traditions are distorted through exoticizing them or through their extractive plundering as a response to the alienations of late capitalism for individual wellbeing, the uncritical adoption of elements of other religious traditions out of context is ethically suspect. Practical theologian Mary Elizabeth Moore is aware of these concerns as she advocates learning from Native American peoples about more sustainable relations to nonhuman entities. She questions: "How can people in non-indigenous cultures value and learn from indigenous peoples without abusing and distorting their sacred traditions? The challenges of those traditions to most Western worldviews are so vital that we need to find ways to learn without objectifying and to collaborate without dominating or colonizing."[42] Her apt question is a sober reminder that after colonization and cultural genocide, the capacity of white persons to engage well with the traditions they once denigrated and decimated is diminished. Listening and learning from other traditions requires a practiced humility and the development of mutual relationships before drawing on the wisdom they might be willing to share.

4 A Somewhat Less-Christian Practical Theological Reflection Cycle

As I began to teach practical theology regularly as a required course in my setting, I worked to create a single-page version of what it was that I was asking students to learn as a mode of reflection. Based strongly on Thomas Groome's six movements of Christian shared praxis,[43] I worked to translate

---

42 Mary Elizabeth Moore, "Responding to a Weeping Planet: Practical Theology as a Discipline Called by Crisis," *Religions* 13: 244 (2022), 7.
43 Thomas H. Groome, *Sharing Faith: A Comprehensive Approach to Religious Education and Pastoral Ministry* (HarperSanFrancisco, 1991), 146–48.

the language into my more interreligious and not-religious teaching environment. Several years later, I worked with my colleague Kristina Lizardy-Hajbi to integrate the form of practical theological reflection we were teaching in the introductory class into our internship reflection seminars, meaning that students spent at least four terms regularly practicing with it as they engaged in the core curriculum and professional formation. We later worked with our pastoral care colleague, Carrie Doehring, to begin to refine the method, sensing that the basic outline was missing a layer of communal and reflexive questions that were essential for critical ministerial praxis. These reflexive and communal questions were designed as a way of trying to make this less of a heroic individual leadership process and more of a communal consultation and discernment practice. Finally, Lizardy-Hajbi removed the words "practical theological" because of student and supervisor concerns and misinterpretations of what was meant by the word "theological," calling the process an "integrative reflection" method in internship without substantively changing any of the movements. I am sharing this method here in case there are others teaching in similar contexts who might find it useful:

A Practical Theological Method (with reflexive and communal questions)

Movement 1: Lived experience or a particular event in a specific context generates theological, religious, spiritual, or moral questions or issues. The significance of this experience or event may be marked by deep emotional stirrings or reactions, communal conflict or division, expressed desire for change, a sense of despair or being stuck in repeated patterns, or an increased energy that moves a community to action. In other words, this situation truly matters to you and your community.

> *Reflexive Questions*: Why do I particularly notice this situation as important? What hooks me, and how does that relate to my commitments, social location, or prior experience?

> *Communal Questions*: How might others in my community interpret or describe this experience differently and why? Who else in relationship to this event or experience might have a stake in this situation changing or staying the same?

Movement 2: Describe current practice related to this question or pondering. What is going on? Current practice may include the ritual and spiritual rhythms of the community, structuring of relations of power through spatial and material resources, powerful symbols and stories that hold meaning for the community, habitual social patterns of interaction and relationship, shared values and ethical norms that are expressed through the event or experience.

Reflexive Questions: What is going on in relational dynamics, institutional structures or policies, cultural values or practices that either impacts me particularly deeply *or* that I don't notice or have to engage because of my social location? Where do I get stuck or what bothers me most about our current practice because of my life experience?

Communal Questions: Observe how members of your community think about your issue. What are differences and similarities between your and their understandings about the issue? Who might you need to consult to reach a fuller understanding of what is going on both within the particular context and outside of it? What "expert" or scholarly resources are available to help me understand the biggest picture of what is happening?

Movement 3: Engage in critical reflection on current practice, including its historical, contextual and ideological situation. Why is it going on? Analyze and interpret the situation at a deeper level through interdisciplinary studies by utilizing sociological analyses, historical trajectories that contributed to the current practice, religious and ritual studies, ideological analysis, cultural and gender studies, psychological studies, medical or scientific research, etc. Here you may draw on all of your prior educational training and professional experience as well as what you are learning in other classes.

Reflexive questions: How do I or people in my community hold or experience these histories and ideologies: as authoritative, oppressive, truthful, identity-bearing, troubling? Where have they deeply informed my personal understanding and commitments? What experiences or outside voices helped me come to become aware of or critique them?

Communal questions: Which forms of knowledge are most valued by the community or most commonly used to describe and understand their situation? How do these histories get told differently by other communities or peoples? What happens if we tell the histories with a different starting point or narrator? Who benefits from the continued upholding of these ideologies? How is the context experienced differently by people who are located differently within it? What histories or ideologies are hidden or suppressed in my community and why? What would be the perceived loss to the community if these histories and ideologies were to change?

Movement 4: Engage resources from a religious or wisdom tradition, including sacred texts, historical and liturgical sources, theological resources/visions for flourishing that might be able to speak to the experience or event and its resulting theological questions or issues. What should be going on? Identify particular themes in your analysis in movements 2–3 that your tradition might speak to (e.g., hospitality, diversity, compassion, forgiveness and reconciliation, suffering, creation, mindfulness, healing, repentance, peace, etc.). Be sure to engage these resources critically using the skills you are learning in other classes.

Reflexive questions: How did I come to know these resources in my own history? How were they shared, remembered, ritualized, or proclaimed in communities that helped to form me? What do I find compelling, beautiful, terrible, or tragic about them? Which ones still hold mystery and power for me in their complexity and layered meanings, and which have been domesticated or diminished to me by abusive or clichéd use?

Communal questions: Which theological or religious resources from a shared tradition are held as valuable by others in my community that contradict what I believe to be true, just, or beautiful? How do their interpretations of the tradition relate to their understanding of what is going on, and can I find anything worthwhile in them? How have other communities drawn upon the tradition in ways that my community has not, and could we learn something from what they find valuable in the tradition? What from the tradition has continued power for our community in shaping their imagination of the world, their shared moral values, and their ways of being in the world?

Movement 5: Critical dialogue between present practice and tradition in conversation with one another to see how they speak to each other. Here you are bringing the normative resources of the tradition into conversation with the theological question arising from current practice. The resulting dialogue may call forth new wisdom from the tradition as to how to respond to the contextual question, or it may generate new ways of understanding or holding the tradition because of the fresh insights or failure of wisdom that current practice illuminates within it.

Reflexive questions: Could I gain new insight from the collective wisdom of the tradition, or am I simply seeking to use it to reinforce my individual perspective? What do I find hard to hear in the tradition because of my social location? Where might the tradition call my habitual practice into question, or help me to find renewed depth in my expressions of my deepest values and increased faithfulness in my practice?

Communal questions: How might I seek others whose perspectives differ from mine to deepen the dialogue between the tradition and current practice? Whose work inspires or startles us into new insight and deeper understanding? How do we create the space and time to engage in communal dialogue with diverse voices rather than just limit ourselves to individual interpretive work? What would it mean for our community to hold our traditions differently after this dialogue? What in our traditions needs to be resisted, revised, or renewed?

Movement 6: Decisions/ proposals for lived praxis are made and lived into. What are the next right steps in response given the insight gained through this process of theological reflection? Beyond simple strategic problem-solving, this could also include new visions for how we should be and act in the world; new understandings of the sacred, God, or shared core values; or proposed changes in common life through shared practice and institutional structure.

Reflexive questions: Where am I appropriately relying on my own wisdom and experience to know what to do, and where do I discover I need to know more or to partner with others to respond? What resistances, intuitions, fears and desires does this proposed praxis raise in me and what can I learn from them? How do spiritual practices that foster self-compassion, radical respect, and shared commitments sustain my leadership and the work of our community in this praxis?

Communal questions: What assets and strengths does our community have to respond faithfully in this situation? What kind of changes does the community want or not want in this moment, and what do they need? What needs to be developed relationally, spiritually, skill-wise, and commitment-wise to engage this praxis? How will we share visions, celebrations, failures, and movement towards the praxis we hope to engage? What will be shared markers of living more faithfully into our praxis?

As I am writing this book, I notice something new about the process that we built together in trying to adapt practical theological reflection for a not-entirely Christian setting. Note that at each step there is a constructive, assured move towards analysis and understanding of the situation. There are also two steps that involve reflexive and communal questioning of that analysis and understanding, habitually destabilizing and opening it to the discernment of an assumed community of difference. Rather than making a strong argument or building toward a conclusive Christian normative answer to the question of what we should do, this process invites uncertainty and critical dialogue at each step of the process with both one's own interiority and personal history as well as a diverse community's reflections and connections. The focus is not necessarily on reaching agreement about those things, but about evoking important conversation and engagement in order to discern what might be going on and how to respond.

The process has been difficult not only for our students to engage, but also the practitioner-instructors who lead internship to facilitate. Many have concerns about "analysis paralysis," or the idea that this can lead to great academic discussions, but not actual reflective practice that gets anything done. The outlined process is multi-layered and complex, and it does feel like a lot to internalize as a habit of reflection in leadership and ministry. However, the ongoing practice of consulting reflexively and communally is essential to move beyond a gut or intuitive feeling that often replicates the practices of white supremacy that feel most normal to many of our white students. The reality that "theological reflection" inherently is phrase that privileges Christian worldviews and epistemologies means that it is nearly impossible to engage in practical theology without privileging Christianity. However, there are ways to hold Christianity with more humility and to be in dialogue with significant voices from other traditions and no traditions at all that can serve to de-center white Christian supremacy while engaging in the process.

CHAPTER 9

Questioning Anthropocentrism

As part of my work in teaching doctoral students, I was asked to create a comprehensive exam focused on the outrageously broad topic of "Religion and Human Experience." On the one hand, as a practical theologian for whom living religious communities are the focus of my work, this makes some sense, since I do not study religion beginning with text, image, artifact, philosophy, or theory like some of my colleagues. The kind of theological reflection I engage begins and ends in human experience, religious communities, and the cultural contexts in which they are embedded. The interdisciplinary work of theology and social science had been a part of my doctoral training, and we worked to create an exam that would help students demonstrate working knowledge of this particular intersection, its research methods, and its contours and complications of knowing. On the other hand, my somewhat snarky first question when asked to develop the exam was: "Isn't *all* religion human experience"? I mean, if we even talked about other species having something akin to religious experiences, wouldn't this be a projection of human categories and ways of being onto their experiences?

A focus on human experience is central to practical theology, particularly human meaning-making, ritual, formation, care for suffering, spiritual practices, and communal life. Certainly there is an incredible expanse of things to consider and reflect upon with human religious life, even just in the Christian traditions, enough to keep generations of practical theologians busy for centuries. As my first teacher of practical theology, a peer in my doctoral program at Emory, explained it to me; practical theology is a cycle of reflection that begins and ends in lived human experience. It is about the lives of people, the theological questions that arise from their daily lives, the ways that these interact with the Christian tradition, and the renewed faithful praxis that arises from reflective work in dialogue between tradition and everyday practice.

We humans are having to come to terms with the way that we as a species are impacting other species on the planet we share and the processes that affect the natural elements and climate patterns that are essential to all our survival. That more expansive vision of interdependence and the significance of existence together has been something left to the climate scientists and global corporations and markets to influence. Meanwhile we in practical theology have attended primarily to human experiences of meaning-making and connection with the divine, often imagined in an ethereal and other-worldly locale. We have attended to the natural world as it aids human spirituality. We have attended to environmental justice as it impacts human survival and flourishing. But we have struggled to decenter human experience in our field and move into an expansive, systemic way of thinking that makes us one species among many in relation to the planet and universe that we inhabit.

When I wrote my own dissertation, and later a version of it in my first book, I was focused on the problems of consumer culture and how it distorted the vocation of youth. As I was beginning to write the book, my advisor and other faculty that I discussed the project with pushed me to consider whether I was calling for the end of capitalism, and didn't I need to do more reading in economics in light of that possibility? Knowing that I was a new mother with a young baby, I tried to keep the work as focused as possible on the culture of hyper-advertising and the need to continuously form young people into consumers and how that onslaught shifted their sense of identity, vocation, and imagination of their own lives in the world to focus primarily on acquiring the trappings of the good life promoted by consumer culture. In the entire book, I only name environmental concerns two or three times as an impact of continuously forming humans to participate in a rampantly escalating late capitalism that requires the destruction of ecosystems to support its energy use, easy access to disposable goods, and extractive exploitation of natural resources and pollution of clean air and water. At one point near the end of the book, I sort of mused that only the total collapse of the environment was likely to bring a change to the system of consumer capitalism, and then proceeded to say that it was important to teach young people and ourselves not to depend on late capitalism for vocational meaning making since it wasn't going away anytime soon. I should also confess that in writing this current book, this chapter was also a late addition, because I still struggle to conceptualize the intersectionality of white supremacy and ecological destruction, despite so much work that has made those connections again and again. The mystification and erasure of ecological awareness is deep in me as well as others in the Western parts of the northern hemisphere.

In preparation for teaching a first-year interdisciplinary seminar at my school some years ago, I was reading in ecological literature over the summer. The course, "Food, Faith, and the Land," was to be co-taught with a Hebrew Bible scholar on my faculty, Amy Erickson. She surprised me by declaring that much of the literature she had found useful on the topic had come from the field of practical theology. In particular, she named the work related to food from Jennifer Ayres and Norman Wirzba in practical theology, which we eventually combined with ecofeminism and ecowomanism and work on the land

and understandings of creation in relation to the Hebrew Bible.[1] And then, one beautiful summer day I picked up the Australian climate change report that I mention in the beginning of this book. In this report, the scientists and policy experts writing it agreed to consider that worst case scenarios, while on the extremes of possibility, are within the realm of possibility, and should be deliberated when studying the effects and future trajectories of climate change and its impacts. The report gives as an entirely possible scenario the extinction of human species within this century. By 2050, in fact, when my children are meant to be middle-aged and perhaps raising children of their own.

I had the closest thing to a radical religious conversion experience that I have ever had after reading that report. I hardly slept for two days. I kept thinking, why isn't this the only thing we are teaching about in theological education? The end of human life on earth, which would occur after the great extinction of so many other hundreds of thousands of species due to human behavior, seems like something that those of us in the project of theological education might want to spend our time addressing. The reality that a billion climate refugees will likely be displaced this century due to rising oceans, drought, and increasing daytime temperatures that make human life unsustainable in many places around the globe should capture our attention. I started to feel like there were paltry resources to even begin to address these issues in theological education or in the field of practical theology, and that we were ignoring the very thing that we should spend all our time helping religious leaders and any people of conscience to come to terms with and begin to change. Honestly, I was ready to put on whatever the contemporary form of camel hair is and eat locusts and shout at people that we all needed to repent and live differently for a while.

At the point of my belated conversion experience, Pam McCarroll was already arguing that the field of practical theology is not paying enough attention to environmental crisis: "While creation is groaning, burdened under the consuming habits of the richest among us, the poorest of the world suffer the extremes of the environmental crisis. Given the extremity of the crisis, why is it that practical theologians are not talking about it?"[2] Lisa Dahill, in an essay on rewilding spirituality makes a similar call, echoing a challenge made by former AAR president Laurie Zoloth, suggesting a need to recognize the current situation as a pressing emergency:

---

[1] Norman Wirzba, *Food and Faith: A Theology of Eating* (Cambridge University Press, 2011); Jennifer R. Ayres, *Good Food: Grounded Practical Theology* (Baylor University Press, 2013).
[2] Pamela R. McCarroll, "Listening for the Cries of the Earth: Practical Theology in the Anthropocene," *International Journal of Practical Theology* 24, no. 1 (2020), 31.

the shattering 'interruption' of our ordinary priorities and projects, the shock of our lives jolting all humans into new thinking and leadership and requiring us in whatever roles we serve in church or society to step up into leadership and activism. Each person needs to discern and give their own signal contributions toward turning this gigantic ship that is our shared Western economic system.[3]

The pressing situation that whiteness has created through capitalism, colonialism, and "civilization" are the conditions for our own destruction and that of almost every other living species on the planet. We have, of course, done this before as a species with the nuclear arms race, which caused a similar flurry of theological response. But these two situations of potential self-destruction are also markedly different. While nuclear destruction was in the hand of a few powerful leaders who held the fate of the world and all its species in their hands, ecological destruction is built into the daily living patterns of many of us together. The desires amongst the wealthier nations for easy access to a wide variety of disposable goods, the use of fossil fuels and energy at levels that are unsustainable, the patterns of eating and growing food, current water use, and transporting goods globally cannot be maintained if we want to exist beyond a few more generations as a species. The pushing of some peoples into increasingly harsh environments of famine and death-dealing weather patterns while the very wealthy buy up land deemed to be arable and defensible from desperate refugees once the inevitable human migration for survival begins is the canary of the coal mine of where we are headed as a species.

In the retreat center that my husband directs in Wyoming, the devastating effects of climate change are written in the landscape. Like so many parts of the Rocky Mountains, the trees have been weakened by years and years of drought conditions and warmer winters. The mountain pine beetle, a species native to the region, began to thrive as its larvae and eggs were no longer killed off cyclically in the harsh winters because of a warming climate about 15 years ago, leading to epidemic infestations that destroyed as many as half of the trees in the forest, including on the 400 acres on which the retreat center is located. One year, the trees were green and vibrant. The next summer when we returned, the trees were a rusty brown, an eerie sense of an inappropriate fall, where evergreen trees were turning autumnal in a way that bespoke decay and imminent death. They dropped all their needles by the next year, leaving

---

3   Lisa E. Dahill, "ReWilding Spirituality," in Lisa E. Dahill and Jim B. Martin-Schramm, eds., *Eco-Reformation: Grace and Hope for a Planet in Peril* (Cascade Books, 2016), 179.

the gray skeletal remains of their once vibrant selves, a veritable graveyard forest created by climate change.

Perhaps I need not recount the ways in which climate change is not a future possibility but rather a situation that impacts us now. Whether it is rising average temperatures with record-setting heat occurring on an annual basis in many parts of the world, or increasing natural disasters such as the flooding that just shut down Yellowstone National Park due to unseasonal early heat and rainfall that supercharged snowmelt, or the massive hurricanes that destroy low-lying areas because of increased intensity and the destruction of once protective wetland barriers. I am writing of more protected areas of the world that I am closely related to, areas where these changes in patterns are expensive, and health-threatening, but not yet at extinction level to the humans living there. By contrast, this late summer as I write, Pakistan is experiencing a monsoon season with such excessive flooding that it has killed thousands and displaced tens of thousands. We can see where this is headed, though it is very hard to keep our attention focused on longer-range threats as a species.

Given these conditions, practical theologians might focus less on the intricacies of individual and congregational Christian formation related to specialized technologies of connection with God and begin to lend their energies to helping those who are accelerating this destruction begin to shift their patterns of value and living in meaningful ways that allow for our collective salvation and survival. And of course, many of my colleagues in the field of practical theology have already gone there. Bonnie Miller-McLemore, in an essay reviewing what practical theologians have done in relation to ecology, challenges the critique that the field has ignored the climate crisis or remained entirely silent in response to its challenges, tracing over fifty years of contributions and beginnings to the response.[4] My own mentor Mary Elizabeth Moore wrote her book *Ministering with the Earth* nearly a quarter century ago, and she has also authored many subsequent articles seeking to turn the attention of the field to ecological matters.[5] In a recent essay, she renewed her call for practical theologians to use the practices of reflection central to the discipline in the service of responding effectively to the climate crisis that faces us all:

---

4 Bonnie J. Miller-McLemore, "Climate Violence and Earth Justice: A Research Report on Practical Theology's Contributions," *International Journal of Practical Theology* 26, no. 2 (2022): 329–66.

5 Mary Elizabeth Moore, *Ministering With the Earth* (Chalice Press, 1998).

For example, practical theologians regularly respond to habituated practices with *proactive responses*, encouraging people to examine their habitual patterns for the sake of comprehending, critiquing, and reshaping or reinforcing them. Consider the work of public practical theologians, cultural analysts, pastoral counselors and caregivers, educators, and homileticians. Climate crisis underscores the need for these same theologians to reflect on engrained habits that have contributed to ecological crises, and the habits that are needed to prevent further destruction in the future.[6]

Jennifer Ayres has a trilogy of books that attend to food systems, interaction with the natural world, and the need for social change that all attend regularly to climate crisis as a central theme.[7] Tim Van Meter also has a longstanding commitment to responding to ecological crisis, although his work has understandably been more praxis-oriented in creating a sustainable farm and ecological focus across the seminary where he works rather than in an abundant publishing record.[8] In cognate fields, scholars like Melanie Harris and Miguel De La Torre have focused on ecowomanism and ecojustice concerns, particularly the racialized impact of suffering and now death caused by ecological destruction.[9] Many scholars among us have given us decades of work in trying to shift the focus of the field away from its anthropocentrism.

More common in the field, like in my early work, is acknowledging ecological crisis in a throwaway line here and there in the midst of work that focuses more regularly on human experience. For example, ecological systems might be named at the end of talking about how people in pastoral care are a part of the living web, or in a litany of existential crises experienced by people that ends with "that includes the impact on the earth and its ecosystems." At least it has become a part of a kind of litany. As Pamela McCarroll notes, however, inclusion in the litany of ills and suffering ceases to be enough when facing species extinction, including our own:

---

6 Mary E. Moore, 2022. "Responding to a Weeping Planet: Practical Theology as a Discipline Called by Crisis" *Religions* 13, no. 3: 244.
7 Ayres, *Good Food*; Jennifer R. Ayres, *Inhabitance: Ecological Religious Education* (Baylor University Press, 2019); Jennifer R. Ayres, *Waiting for a Glacier to Move: Practicing Social Witness* (Pickwick Publications, 2011).
8 Timothy L. Van Meter, *Created in Delight: Youth, Church, and the Mending of the World* (Wipf and Stock, 2013).
9 Miguel A. De La Torre, *Gonna Trouble the Water: Ecojustice, Water, and Environmental Racism* (Pilgrim Press, 2021); Melanie L Harris, *Ecowomanism: African American Women and Earth-Honoring Faiths* (Orbis Books, 2017).

However, identifying the environmental crisis as one among many issues facing humans, is not enough. Such framing continues to place humans at the center obscuring the extent to which the mere survival and quality of the living human web is dependent upon (and part of) the health of larger ecosystems. Further, such human-centric methodologies also perpetuate the crisis by ignoring it.[10]

Of course, other social issues such as gun violence, systemic racism, gender and sexuality-based oppression also deserve our focused attention and theological reflection. More importantly, they are linked in significant ways to issues of climate crisis. The differential impact of climate change and environmental destruction by wealth and race globally demonstrates that environmental racism is a central element of systemic racism. The reliance on military might and physical violence to protect our individual and national access and hoarding of the earth's natural resources must be addressed in practical theological reflection. Without attention to the flourishing of earth and the other species who share it with us, practical theology will devolve into sheer irrelevance in the face of the ecological devastation that we are causing. We do not need another paper on how the doctrine of the trinity justifies the idea that humans are relational and interdependent. We need to muster the resources that we have to attend not just to climate change, but climate crisis.

1   Refuting Theologies of Human Domin[at]ion

In order to discuss the anthropocentrism of the field of practical theology, we turn to the ways in which Christian theology has undergirded the focus on human religious lives and experiences without a deep connection to how those lives are placed in bodies within an ecosystem without which they are not sustainable. Theological concepts such as human dominion over the earth and the notion of humans as alone among the species in being created in the image of God have bolstered the entitlement of people in supposing that the other species of the earth, plant, animal, and mineral, have been placed here for our use and pleasure. Practical theologian Pamela McCarroll notes that this focus has been roundly critiqued already by our colleagues in other fields:

> Within the eco-theology, religion and ecology and other like-minded movements, many have critiqued Christendom and the modern west-

---

10   McCarroll. "Listening for the Cries of the Earth," 36.

ern narrative that places human beings at the centre of creation, divinely intended to "image God" by "dominating and subduing" the earth. In the modern era this distorted vocation of mastery coalesced with a dream of progress wherein humans, through their technology and will, were to create utopia—a heaven on earth.[11]

These theologies have undergirded the religious sanctioning of extractive notions of our relationship with the earth and its creatures for centuries, and they are difficult to deconstruct and to transform. Perhaps they align particularly well with the colonialist impulse of white supremacy, as we can trace through the various notions of the "great chain of being" that put European humans on top of all other races and species, linking the racial project of whiteness with the exploitation of other humans as well.

Mary Elizabeth Moore identifies that dominant forms of practical wisdom need to shift in relation to ecological crisis from "justifying social, economic, and ethnic stratifications and human abuses of land and seas for the sake of monetary or techno-industrial progress" to questioning these long-standing habits of extraction. She notes that the values undergirding this practical wisdom have already long been named and challenged by the scientific world:

> Ecologists have long recognized the need to question dominant world views and theologies, seeking to replace individualistic views with communal ones; accents on progress with accents on well-being; anthropocentric views with ecocentric or cosmocentric ones; technological solutions with holistic ecological ones; focus on economic expansion with focus on sustaining and regenerating the ecology; political competition with communal collaboration; and hierarchies of power with deep listening to all beings of creation.[12]

In this second sentence, Moore identifies so many ideologies related to whiteness already discussed in earlier chapters that have impacted the creation of climate crisis: individualism, myth of progress, economic expansion and technocentric approaches, hierarchies of power. It is as if all of these ideologies come together in one mighty force in the climate crisis like the small tremors that synchronize and eventually take down entire bridges with their combined strength. The destruction of our very ecosystem and the ending of the species on the planet may be the ultimate end of whiteness if unchecked.

---

11   McCarroll, "Listening for the Cries of the Earth," 34.
12   Moore, "Responding to a Weeping Planet," 244.

Whereas whiteness advocated dominating the land and other species for our own economic gain, practical theologian Karen Crozier notes that this theology was not equally shared by indigenous persons and those of African descent, who often lived in more direct relationship to the land. Crozier invokes environmental sociologist Dorceta E. Taylor in naming the difference between white and nonwhite peoples in relation to the land:

> Black people and indigenous people espoused a sense of community and belonging to the land while the early white explorers and subsequent conquerors, thieves, colonizers, and settlers saw the land for private, individual use and ownership. What would happen if a sense of community and belonging were recovered as a normative way of relating to humans and the planet instead of humans and the planet being brought into service for a few white men and the ideology of white supremacy?[13]

Crozier declares that these white habits of relation to the land have shown their fruits and demonstrated themselves unsustainable for both human life, other species, and the natural processes that keep the planet alive. She suggests turning away from these habits and towards the wisdom of other peoples whose ideologies did not lead to decimation: "Indigenous, African, and African American cosmologies reflect collective rights, communal, cooperative access and responsibility, and an integrated awareness of all life forms in daily existence, including the divine."[14] These shifts might support a different kind of relation to the earth and its inhabitants.

Crozier turns to the practical theology of Fannie Lou Hamer, an everyday prophet known for her leadership within the Mississippi Democratic Leadership Party and her stirring public leadership in the Southern Freedom Movement. Crozier traces how Hamer believed that land should not be commodified, but rather was a resource to be shared with all who inhabit and commune with it. She notes, "In this vein, preservation of the wild would be inclusive of people, land, place, and space without any race-based, gender-based, class-based, or human-based domination among the inherent biodiversity."[15] A somewhat lesser-known part of her advocacy against segregation included advocating for communal relationship to the land rather than individual ownership, drawing on both African cultural and Christian teachings

---

13   Karen D. Crozier, *Fannie Lou Hamer's Revolutionary Practical Theology: Racial and Environmental Justice Concerns* (Brill, 2020), 92–93.
14   Crozier, *Fannie Lou Hamer's Revolutionary Practical Theology*, 109.
15   Crozier, *Fannie Lou Hamer's Revolutionary Practical Theology*, 84.

as well as her lived experience in rural Mississippi. As Crozier notes, Hamer lived and worked from a deep "sense of belonging to the land, and not owning it."[16] These beliefs played out in Hamer's establishment of the Freedom Farms Cooperative, an interracial effort that particularly supported women as heads of households to be "able to feed themselves, own their homes, farm cooperatively, and create small businesses together in order to support a sustainable food system, land ownership, and economic independence."[17] This material expression of belonging to the land rather than owning land shifted the possibilities of life together and with the ecosystems in which humans exist. Crozier eventually challenges the notion that concern for human and earth can be separated:

> People in community and the space and place in which they inhabit are developed and tended to within a harmonious balance of give and take. In this vein, creation care is never separated from the human nor from the natural environment. Both are acknowledged and necessary for life-bearing opportunities for both human and non-human beings. Put differently, neither any human nor the land are subjugated for the benefit of only a few white men in the land.[18]

Crozier's exploration of Hamer's thought refuses to divorce care for the land and the visibility of African American and other nonwhite people groups, calling for "public displays of confession and commitment to redress and reverse environmental degradation while serving as a counternarrative to historical and contemporary public displays of lynching, killing, displacing, and depleting of black people and their habitats."[19]

This theme of our belonging to the land, or being in deep community with the land is a longstanding theological notion, now being traced by biblical scholars in the Hebrew Bible, but also expressed regularly in the resurgence of ecological writings in the twentieth century. These writings have been fertile ground for practical theological reflection. For example, Mary Elizabeth Moore picks up on this theme of rejecting the commodification of land and moving into relationship with land as community, drawing on the work of Aldo Leopold from *The Sand County Almanac*.[20] She builds on his basic notion:

---

16   Crozier, *Fannie Lou Hamer's Revolutionary Practical Theology*, 85.
17   Crozier, *Fannie Lou Hamer's Revolutionary Practical Theology*, 95.
18   Crozier, *Fannie Lou Hamer's Revolutionary Practical Theology*, 102.
19   Crozier, *Fannie Lou Hamer's Revolutionary Practical Theology*, 109.
20   Moore, "Responding to a Weeping Planet," 5.

"When we see land as a community to which we belong, we may begin to use it with love and respect."[21] However, Moore notes that Leopold and other beloved white environmentalists such as Wendell Berry also required challenging because of their expression of "hierarchies of value" that unequally value white communities over others who lived in relationship with the land long before their arrival.

Similarly, Jennifer Ayres focuses on developing an ecological religious education that nurtures "inhabitance," for her a human vocation requiring moral courage from intentional moments of formation that lead to "ingrained, embodied ecological sensibilities."[22] Being an inhabitant is a deeper connection to the earth and all its species for Ayres than being a mere resident or occupant. The fundamental characteristic of an inhabitant is "a creature who lives well within the context and bounds of its habitat."[23] Humans are unique as a species because they can be "moved to protect their ecosystems and the human communities, even those seemingly unlike their own, who share their ecosystem."[24] Living in such loving relationship and ecological sensibilities requires not only affective dispositions for attunement to God's world, but also the "will and felt responsibility to protect and delight in the ecosystem, particularly those places that are closest; and through participation in intentional and social practices."[25]

2 Restoring Connection to All Our Relations

While the shift from land as object of ownership to an idea that we belong to the land and are in accountable and loving relationship to it sounds lovely, when we scratch the surface of this belief just a little, we begin to see how such a shift to understanding land as community rather than property reaches down to the foundations of the rule of law and the very founding documents and commitments of the United States under whiteness. When I have begun to explore such ideas with students, they grow more uncomfortable than with almost any other ideologies we challenge in class. "But you can't just take land

---

21 Aldo Leopold, *A Sand County Almanac & Other Writings on Conservation and Ecology*, Curt Meine, ed., reprint edition (Library of America, 2013), 16–17.
22 Ayres, *Inhabitance*, 49.
23 Ayres, *Inhabitance*, 49.
24 Ayres, *Inhabitance*, 49.
25 Ayres, *Inhabitance*, 55.

away from people who have worked hard to buy it?" they say in disbelief. Even students who will affirm that the land we live on was stolen from indigenous persons will balk at the notion of undoing the colonial move of theft that allowed the land to become the property of European settlers. Decades of anticommunist rhetoric and practice in the United States, as well as deep belief in human exceptionalism, make any move to hold land communally or to understand ourselves as protectors rather than owners of it is deeply challenging. It upends the fundamental assumptions about land and property on which the founding of the nation-state stands.

However, this notion of land and nonhuman species as being relations rather than commodities is embedded in many indigenous worldviews. One of the examples of public practical theological reflection that I often share in my introductory practical theology class is a speech given by Autumn Peltier, an Anishinaabe woman who was thirteen when she spoke before the United Nations about the work she engaged with her aunt to protect water on World Water Day, March 22, 2018. Peltier grounds her testimony in the cultural traditions of her people:

> I can't stress enough what I have learned about the water from my elders and our ceremonies. Many people don't think water is alive or has a spirit. My people believe this to be true. There are studies now that prove this …. We believe our water is sacred because we are born of water and live in water for nine months. When the water breaks, new life comes. But even deeper than that, we come from our mother's water, and her mother's water, and so on. All the original water flows through us from the beginning and all around us.

She goes on to describe that there are communities around her where people in her province live under boiled water advisories, and she laments the lack of clean water for other peoples in countries around the world. She speaks about how water and land should not be for sale, because it is an issue of honoring elders for her, the need to "respect Mother Earth and honor our sacred water." In a move linked to the normative values embedded in the institution of the United Nations, she attempts to translate this respect for elders and her belief in the sacred agency of water as a relation, arguing: "Our water deserves to be treated as human with human rights. We need to acknowledge our waters with personhood so we can protect our waters. Our waters should not be for sale. We all have a right to this water as we need it. Not just rich people. All people. No one should have to worry if the water is clean or if they will run out of water."[26] The notion of bodies of water as having human rights challenges the very categories of sense-making in a white Western worldview. Peltier attempts to stretch the categories valued by an anthropocentric culture, seeking to expand the cateogries of beings that have agency and who deserve protection well beyond the human species.

In the field of practical theology, Danielle Tumminio Hansen takes such an expansive step in thinking about what it means to show empathy to the earth by thinking about the harm done to the earth as a sexual violation. She attempts to leverage the capacity for human empathy to another violated human in a kind of metaphoric attempt for white people to understand the earth as our relation:

> If we apply the metaphor of the world as God's body to the climate crisis and understand the harm we are doing to the earth is a sexual one, in which the agency and generative parts of the earth are being violated by humans, then perhaps there is a traumatic dimension to the earth's violation. Indeed, framing the ecological crisis in terms of a series of sexual traumas undertaken by humans on the earth's body changes how we understand the earth's response, because it causes us to consider the ways in which the earth is a subject and, as a subject, is exerting agency in response to the horror humans are inflicting upon it.[27]

The notion of earth having agency and being deserving of empathy captures a different sort of relationality and belonging to what has normatively been considered an object rather than a being with agency. Calling for empathy with the experience of the earth seeks to evoke responsiveness to the trauma that the earth is experiencing. In doing so, Hansen anticipates not only that the fullness of relations between human and the earth would be restored, but that such a move portends necessary reconciliation between humankind and God through the respect of agency of the earth as God's body, echoing the metaphor of Sally McFague.[28]

But in indigenous cultures, the notion of land as community is not metaphorical. As Anishinaabe scholar Mark Freeland notes, "Indigenous peo-

---

26 To see the video of Autumn Peltier addressing the UN: https://www.youtube.com/watch?v=A6LcaTWTx8g. For a gorgeous Caldecott Medal winning children's book with similar themes, see Carole Lindstrom, *We Are Water Protectors* (Roaring Brook Press, 2020).

27 Danielle Elizabeth Tumminio Hansen, "The Body of God, Sexually Violated: A Trauma-Informed Reading of the Climate Crisis," *Religions* 13: 249 (2022), 8.

28 Tumminio Hansen, "The Body of God," 10.

ples live in a world saturated with relationships. These relationships form a large connected web of relatedness in which humans occupy a place of equity, not of privilege."[29] Freeland works carefully with linguistic differences that point to a different underlying notion of human relationships to all life. As an example, he discusses the form of life communicated by the word *mitigoog*, translated as "trees" in English. However, unlike in English, *mitigoog* in his cultural narratives can also serve as companions, teachers, and elders to people who find themselves in need of their wisdom. While they may be cut down for use in building, their agency is acknowledged at that moment: "However, when these actions of taking the life of a *mitig* is negotiated, the tree is talked to as a person, the actions are explained to it, and an offering is made to help recognize its life and sacrifice."[30] Freeland compares this to notions of trees as living beings in Eurowestern worldview, but as a lower life form in a hierarchy "with humans on top and trees falling far below other living creatures."[31] That hierarchy of importance does not exist in the same way in Anishinaabe culture, which requires offerings and recognition to restore harmony whenever a life is taken, whatever the species. There is no word for "animal" in Anishinaabe language; rather, all species are people, whether bear people, elk people, or tree people.

Freeland furthers his exploration of the relational nature of all reality with a discussion of another Anishinaabeg word without a direct English translation, *chidibenjigeg*. An essential guiding concept for his people, it has no iconography or other material representation. Freeland notes, "Built within the knowledge of *chidibenjiged* is the simple truth that there is a power or energy that 'makes all things belong.' This is an unconditional mandate that all life associated with Anishinaabe Akiing belongs to that place."[32] Because of *chidibenjigeg*, all life is related in a nonhierarchical way; it all is made to belong: "No one form of life is greater than another, so there is a necessity to make sure that our interactions with other forms of life do not kill them off as a group."[33] Such a principle immediately highlights the enormous ethical failure of the human species in the sixth mass extinction, a massive loss of biodiversity and loss of species largely held to be "driven by human activity, primarily (though not limited to) the unsustainable use of land, water and

---

29   Mark D. Freeland, *Aazheyaadizi: Worldview, Language, and the Logics of Decolonization* (Michigan State University Press, 2020), 87.
30   Freeland, *Aazheyaadizi*, 97.
31   Freeland, *Aazheyaadizi*, 97.
32   Freeland, *Aazheyaadizi*, 99.
33   Freeland, *Aazheyaadizi*, 99.

energy use, and climate change."[34] Freeland notes that recent developments in Eurowestern science have also begun to highlight the fundamental realities of relatedness that have long been evident in the cultural logics and ethical foundations of Anishinaabeg culture: "This trajectory of scientific thought has demonstrated a growing dissonance within eurowestern culture between the longstanding anthropocentric hubris evident in Christianity, capitalism, and much of scientific thought, and the growing theories of interrelatedness in biological and astronomical systems that surround all of us."[35] Ironically, Freeland notes, hundreds of years of scientific development has finally allowed Eurowestern peoples to "finally catch[] up to Indigenous knowledge that has been here since time immemorial."[36]

A promising development in the shift we need in practical theological reflection away from anthropocentrism is the increased teaching of indigenous understandings of human relation to the earth in theological schools. One key example of this is the work of Potowami botanist and genre-crossing essayist Robin Wall Kimmerer, whose blend of sacred storytelling, science, and cultural analysis builds a bridge between environmental science and systems of meaning and ceremony that are more familiar to theological schools. Kimmerer focuses on the need of humans to exist in relationship of gratitude to the earth: "For much of humans' time on the planet, before the great delusion, we lived in cultures that understood the covenant of reciprocity—that for the Earth to stay in balance, for the gifts to continue to flow, we must give back in equal measure for what we are given. Our first responsibility, the most potent offering we possess, is gratitude."[37] While Kimmerer admits that gratitude might not seem like a particularly powerful response, it requires the recognition of the agency and integrity of the other entity that gives, in this case, the living earth. That attention to the earth, and the responsibility to reciprocate the earth's gifts with our own care and responsivity to her needs, is what Kimmerer believes might leverage a change that could reverse our current mistaken relationship with the earth. She notes:

> In the geologic scope of things, the Industrial Revolution that fueled the expansion of the exploitative, mechanistic worldview was only an eye blink ago. For eons before that, there was a long time on this planet

---

34   https://www.worldwildlife.org/stories/what-is-the-sixth-mass-extinction-and-what-can-we-do-about-it, accessed 7/5/23.
35   Freeland, *Aazheyaadizi*, 125.
36   Freeland, *Aazheyaadizi*, 125.
37   Robin Wall Kimmerer, "Returning the Gift." *Minding Nature*, 7, no. 2 (*Spring 2014*).

when humans lived well, in relative homeostasis with biotic processes, embodying a worldview of reciprocity that was simultaneously material and spiritual. There was a time when we considered ourselves the "younger brothers of creation," not the masters of the universe. Our current adversarial relationship with the rest of the living world is not necessarily all that we are as a species. We are a species that can learn from the global mistakes we are making. We have stories to help us remember a different past and imaginations to help us find the new path. We are a species who can change.[38]

Perhaps ironically, and bringing me back to the full strength and history of practical theological reflection in self-critical reflection on human experience, Kimmerer reminds us that what needs to change is not the way that we continue to extract value from this living entity of earth, but ourselves. While we want to focus on new wind turbines or plastic-eating microbes or manufacturing ice and dumping it back into the polar waters, what needs to change is human behavior and understanding. She notes, "The danger is that we have been captured by a worldview that no longer serves our world, if it ever did—a worldview whose manifestation is destroying our beloved homelands, our fellow species, and ourselves."[39]

Practical theologian Mary Elizabeth Moore gives an extended review of Kimmerer's work and its importance to practical theological knowledge about our interrelationship with all of creation.[40] After her close work with Kimmerer's notions, she reaffirms the use of this non-Christian indigenous knowing in the work of practical theology, saying:

> If we are to respond well to a weeping planet, we need to face the limitations of the assumed wisdom that modern/postmodern people have inherited within a techno-industrialized, progress-seeking, individual-focused, capital-oriented society. We need to stretch practical wisdom in order to learn from many ancestors (including our own), many living beings, many language worlds, and the spiritual experiences and instructions of peoples living closely with the earth.[41]

---

38   Kimmerer, "Returning the Gift."
39   Kimmerer, "Returning the Gift."
40   Moore, "Responding to a Weeping Planet," 7–8.
41   Moore, "Responding to a Weeping Planet," 9.

Practical theology needs a renewed cultural humility and expansion of imagination and phronesis, as Moore suggests. She suggested that we minister *with* the earth (not *to* it) because any hope for our future together requires an "interdependent, intersubjective relationship between the human family and the rest of creation."[42] Shifting from an anthropocentric worldview to one that understands the agency and mutuality with all species and processes of the earth requires a fundamental change of worldview. Moore calls for four movements in response to the damage wrought from living out of our current white formation: attending, searching, imagining, and communal living and acting.[43] Through these breadth of approaches to acquiring new practical wisdom that is more attuned to the complexity of our interdependent and intersubjective relationship with the many species and ecological systems of water, air, weather and so on that are essential to our survival, argues Moore, we might begin to create new ways of living that are more vibrant and sustainable.

3 Legacy Fears of Heresy and Syncretism

Attention to indigenous knowledges and listening to those whose worldviews extend back to before industrialization and the colonial project seems like a sensible response to seeking ways forward in our relationship to the planet. However, the Christian disdain for such knowledges hardened into the minds and hearts of many who are part of the white Christian churches often creates a backlash to any ritual actions, storytelling, or policy efforts that take such knowledge seriously. Old charges of heresy and syncretism join with new accusations of politicization and "wokeness" to generate active, vocal, vehement resistance to any such engagement with these wisdoms.

An excellent example is the work of practical theologian Claudio Carvalhaes. As part of his much larger project to create new rituals and ways of engaging the spirit that take the earth and its many peoples seriously, Carvalhaes led the community of students and faculty at Union Theological Seminary in New York City through a ritual at weekly worship. In the ritual, Carvalhaes invited students to confess to plants in an embodied attempt to engage the harm that humans have generated for other species, and to lament the destruction that this harm has created and invite a different way of being related to other species. In an article explaining why he had created the liturgy, he shared the invitation into the liturgy that he had written for the occasion:

---

42 Moore, "Responding to a Weeping Planet," 9.
43 Moore, "Responding to a Weeping Planet," 9–12.

Many of us have a disconnected relationship with nature and relate to nature as outside things, as "it." Today we will try to create new connections by talking to the plants, soil, and rocks and confess how we have related with them. Confessions are also forms of mending relations, healing, and changing our ways. We are all manifestations of the sacredness of life and the "we" of God's love is way beyond the human, so let us confess to "each other" including plants, soil, rocks, rivers, forests.[44]

This way of granting subjectivity to what are considered in Western worldviews as "inanimate" objects feels odd and confusing to many who only grant personhood or agency to other humans. As Carvalhaes reports one student in the moment responding: "I don't know how to relate to you in this subjective way. I am afraid that if I do I might discover a level of pain that I don't know whether I can bear." Carvalhaes also writes about how the ritual was meant to expand the imagination of participants to perceive objects of nature as "subjects having their own life and full experience." He notes:

> Ritual confession involves pausing, listening, and a new way of being. Confession can run the risk of a naïve and sentimental idealizing of the earth and of nature, but this practice sought something deeper—to expand faith as we recognize the interdependence of life and relinquish the death-dealing habits of our human autonomy in relation to our mastery over the natural world.[45]

Much like the practices of gratitude that Kimmerer called for, which require admission of the agency and independent integrity of the earth, Carvalhaes was inviting an intimate ritual experience in which participants experimented with what it meant to related to other beings in a way that granted both their dignity as beings and the interdependence of participants' relationships with them.

The response to this service in other segments of white evangelical Christianity was instructive about the commitments in place that keep many practical theologians focused on human experience outside of the context of its

---

44 Cláudio Carvalhaes, "Why I Created a Chapel Service Where People Confess to Plants," *Sojourners*, September 26, 2019. https://sojo.net/articles/why-i-created-chapel-service-where-people-confess-plants.
45 Cláudio Carvalhaes, "Why I Created a Chapel Service Where People Confess to Plants," *Sojourners*, September 26, 2019. https://sojo.net/articles/why-i-created-chapel-service-where-people-confess-plants.

interdependence with the rest of creation. On the one end of spectrum of responses was the more benign ridicule of the experience, as evidenced in this tweet from Victoria Weinstein (@peacebang): "There's not a thing wrong with having reverence for all of creation & lamenting humanity's disgraceful treatment of it but bringing houseplants into a worship service to confess to them is hysterically funny, condescending & ludicrous #PlantGate." On the willful misunderstanding end, a Fox News article entitled "Liberal seminary students worship potted plants as 'the beings who sustain us.'[46]" Albert Mohler, Jr., the president of Southern Baptist Seminary in Louisville, took up the experience on his podcast:

> We cannot be pleased with the desecration of creation, but we can also not be pleased or ever satisfied with the idea that creation exists unto itself, that human beings are a blight upon creation, and that it is wrong for human beings to exercise dominion over creation .... Plants are not beings, but what you see here is the confusion that happens when the biblical worldview is abandoned.[47]

Mohler deploys the idea of humans having "dominion over creation," the extractive interpretation of Genesis 1:26–28. And he relegates the reverent and interdependent ideals embraced by the water keepers to a "secular worldview."

This controversy brings up the issues from the last chapter about Christian-centrism, with the stronger notion of anti-indigeneity woven in. Carvalhaes explicitly links the notion of interdependence with the earth and the subjectivity of other species to an indigenous worldview, as well as the facing of climate change likened to the devastation faced by first nations peoples when colonial invaders began to destroy their societies and take over with radically different notions of land use and property ownership. Bonnie Miller-McLemore, in an essay reviewing the attention of the field of practical theology to ecological concerns, echoes Mary Elizabeth Moore's categories of imagination and attention as she wonders why white Western Christians resist recognizing nature's intelligence: "Christianity is part of the problem, blinding us from attending to nature; shaming us for love of nature as unorthodox, animistic, and even pagan; and perverting or condoning a sinful exploitation of nature."[48] The conversion needed requires a change of imagination and atten-

---

46 https://www.foxnews.com/faith-values/liberal-seminary-students-worship-plants.
47 https://www.christianpost.com/news/union-seminary-mocked-for-having-students-confess-to-plants.html.
48 Bonnie J. Miller-McLemore, "Trees and the 'Unthought Known': The Wisdom of the Nonhuman (or Do Humans 'Have Shit for Brains'?)," *Pastoral Psychology* 69, no. 4 (2020), 431.

tion more than information, argues Miller-McLemore, noting that literature and spiritual practices of listening to other species are critical for such a conversion.[49] Pam McCarroll further names the resources offered by "minority traditions of panentheism, animism, process theology and earth-based mystical traditions within Christianity," noting that these strands of the tradition entertain the notion of the natural world as sacred and worthy of "reverence, awe and gratitude."[50] Getting more comfortable with the relational practices and connections between humans and nonhumans that white Christianity once deemed heretical and even demonic will be an essential shift in addressing the climate crisis that we now face.

In reflecting on the renewed interest in animism in Christian theology, Chickasaw novelist and poet Linda Hogan notes that what is often seen as a "new" study has been long considered tradition by her people and others:

> For those who have always prayed with, to, and for the waters, and known our intimate relatives, the plant people, the animals, insects, and all our special relations, the field of Animism is a belated study. It has not gone unnoticed that without these relationships, a great pain and absence has been suffered by humanity, an absence and loss we ourselves have felt as a result of the determinations of the Western mind to separate us from our homelands and created great destruction to the living body of the continent.[51]

The forced separation from these practices and epistemologies has long been a source of suffering and estrangement for indigenous persons, who, as Freeland named, now find it ironic that white people are finally coming around to what has already been central to their worldview and way of life.

Often the resistance to such forms of liturgy and spirituality has been imprinted on the souls of those steeped in the traditions of mistrust and denigration of traditions such as animism, indigenous cultural traditions, and nature-based spiritualities that is centuries old. We know in our bones that our ancestors' response to these wisdoms was to eradicate them because they were either superstitions (dismissal) or of the devil (denigration). And so, scholar of Christian spirituality Lisa Dahill describes that her conversion to a more nature-based spirituality raised her suspicious nature about the validity of her own experience. On a sabbatical, Dahill had recognized that the traditional

---

49   Miller-McLemore, "Trees and the 'Unthought Known,'" 440.
50   Pamela McCarroll, "Listening for the Cries," 42.
51   Linda Hogan, "We Call It Tradition" in G. Harvey (Ed.), *The Handbook of Contemporary Animism* (Acumen, 2013), 19.

forms of Christian prayer and sacramental worship that she had studied and practiced from her own tradition made her increasingly uncomfortable. She began to have a radical recognition that the real world outside of the chancel walls was entirely made of sacrament, and began to spend more and more time in the natural world. She notes:

> It's disorienting: Jesus is dissolved, all that's left is the wind ... the *literal* wind, the outdoor wind breathed from trees and cold fronts that fills my lungs and pushes against me on my bike and lifts pollen and petals and termites and spores up and out and this is all I seem to need, ever—but is this Christian? Is it really prayer? It's strange prayer, as it opens, this utter outdoor-ness.[52]

The suspicion that such deep relatedness with awe and reverence to the natural world might not be prayer, but instead pagan idolatry or belonging to a different tradition entirely continues to infect the minds of those whose tradition made a practice of suspicioning and eradicating such belief.

Another major barrier to taking up the anthropocentrism of the field is the deep climate anxiety, despair, and nihilism that can be overwhelming in the face of recognition of the consequences of the ways in which our living has decimated other species and the life-sustaining processes of the planet. Many practical theologians have been attending to the paralyzing effect of this overwhelm and its impact on thwarting collective action, sometimes named ecoanxiety.[53]

When I wrote about consumer capitalism and its impact on faith formation, I was surprised to discover that many of the questions that arose when I presented on it were about my own lifestyle habits, parenting choices, and recommendations for other parents. I had an infant and a preschooler at the time, and felt like I had almost no authority to say anything about how to parent in the midst of this system. I realized that my scholarship rightly had claims on the way I structured my life, and that people I taught or spoke to had some right to expect that my personal commitments and praxis might match my

---

52 Dahill, "Rewilding Spirituality,"105.
53 Joyce Ann Mercer, "Children and Climate Anxiety: An Ecofeminist Practical Theological Perspective," *Religions*, Pamela R. McCarroll and HyeRan Kim-Cragg, eds. 13, no. 302 (2022): 1–15; Panu Pikhala, "EcoAnxiety and Pastoral Care: Theoretical Considerations and Practical Suggestions," *Religions*, eds. Pamela R. McCarroll and HyeRan Kim-Cragg, 13, no. 192 (2022); Pamela R. McCarroll and HyeRan Kim-Cragg, eds. *Practical Theology Amid Environmental Crises*. MDPI—Multidisciplinary Digital Publishing Institute, 2023.

scholarship. That demand for scholarly integrity makes writing about issues as overwhelming as climate crisis daunting. And yet, something that Mary Hess and Stephen Brookfield wrote about working as a white person to be antiracist applies here as well. We will do this work "imperfectly or not at all."[54] Our enmeshment in the systems of capitalism mean that we cannot be perfect examples of ecological responsibility and pristine relationships with other species. As always, that desire for perfection and purity is a remnant of white supremacy that we must question. We are left to do the work of attention to climate crisis imperfectly and collaboratively and creatively, if we hope for our children and grandchildren to have a habitat to live in.

---

54 Stephen D. Brookfield and Mary E. Hess, *Becoming a White Antiracist* (Routledge, 2021), 192.

Epilogue: Living the Questions

I come to the end of this writing project, although certainly not to the end of the life project that it points toward: lending my energies to the recognition and dismantling of white supremacy in the places where I have any power and influence to do so. As promised, I am leaving us without ten steps to take to fix the situation, or without a comforting nod and reasonable explanation as to how we are supposed to live with the ambivalence, disloyalty, and even mistrust that I am bringing to the venture of practical theology as it has developed within white Western Christianity. At times in writing this, I thought maybe I could end each chapter with a virtue or a practiced orientation towards one's own work that might mitigate the tendency towards white supremacy. I hint at play rather than practice, humility, networks and tenuous communities instead of congregations, vulnerability in leadership, authenticity rather than apologetics, rebuilding relationships with other species, and so on. I remain hopeful that constructive moves are available within the field, indeed, are emerging among its current generation of scholars of color and their accomplices. These innovations and new directions are transformative and possess a salvific imagination that extends well beyond the mimicry of whiteness. Images of a different kind of world have been offered by my many conversation partners in this book such as Reyes on networks and community, Jennings on belonging and communion, decolonizing leadership from Lizardy-Hajbi, and revelatory experiencing from Goto. I also come to the end with a continued sense of the incredible weight of whiteness, its ubiquity and entrenchment, and my entanglement and that of my ecclesial and academic communities within it.

Struggling with the narratives and values that formed the field of practical theology within a context of white supremacy feels uncertain. When I have talked with colleagues at various points about the content of this book and the elements of practical theology that I was questioning, inevitably they asked: So, what's the alternative? Hidden under that question were small betrayals and frustrations that I was actively undoing the work that they found most important and had leant their energies to, and I understand that conflict. Given the questions that I was raising, was I just setting out to destroy all their efforts to make the field relevant and useful?

I said in the beginning of the book that I was more about pulling the rug out from under myself then about living the questions in a gentle Rilkian way. To revisit the quote that is often cited from Rainier Maria Rilke in a letter to a young seeker:

> Be patient toward all that is unsolved in your heart and try to love the questions themselves, like locked rooms and like books that are now written in a very foreign tongue. Do not now seek the answers, which cannot be given you because you would not be able to live them. And the point is, to live everything. Live the questions now. Perhaps you will then gradually, without noticing it, live along some distant day into the answer.[1]

The hope at the end of this quote, of living some distant day into the singular answer, is not what I offer here. Living these questions, those that fundamentally upend worldview, purpose, and hope, is neither fun nor comfortable, nor will it resolve into an answer. But that displacement, that discomfort, pushes us towards practicing a different future together with those who have felt dis/ease within white Christianity for much longer. It opens the possibility for true communion as Jennings describes it, and for something closer to solidarity or co-conspiratorship with colleagues already actively about dismantling white supremacy.

The questions that drove this book are the ones that I continue to ask myself: What if the values, institutions, practices, and beliefs of white Western Christianity are so thoroughly corrupted by their pass through the colonizing venture through which they spread onto the continent in which I encountered them that they cannot be redeemed? What if the only response is to lend our voices to disrupting them, to dismantling them, to undercutting and undermining them and then waiting to see what comes next? What if the extractive and supremacist values of whiteness in late capitalism are so capable of coopting any ventures within the institutions created within them that the best response is merely to take them apart and trust that if there is a loving creator at the pulsing heart of all that is, something else might emerge that is more worthy? Is it possible to live within this kind of disruption with joy, with curiosity, with connection and love rather than defensiveness or desperation?

Living with these questions is hard when everything that you are has been formed into whiteness. Even for scholars of color within the worlds of Christian theological education, as Keri Day has noted, the costs of admission for almost everyone in the academy has been "learning to pass."[2] Courtney Goto has written about the demands for coercive mimeticism within practical theology for those who wish to participate who are not white, drawing on

---

1 Rainer Maria Rilke, *Letters to a Young Poet*, translated by M.D. Herter Norton, revised edition (W.W. Norton & Company, 1993), front matter.
2 Day, *Notes of A Native Daughter*, 29.

Memmi's scholarship.[3] Whiteness as a force of gravity orienting the field has been a reality that all of us have reckoned with, adapted to, navigated around, and lived within. In light of that reality, maybe what we are dealing with is not a dichotomy of questions and answers, but instead the ongoing practice of living into the ambivalence and murky reality of this moment. We continue to seek moments of beauty and truth-telling while both desiring and hating what might dismantle whiteness and seeking to believe that its legacy isn't all there is, in the end. We believe, O Lord, help our unbelief.

1 Original Sin, Shameful Hiding, and Right Repentance

When I first wrote about resisting dominant culture two decades ago, I came to rely on the doctrine of original sin as a way of naming my formation into the problematic values of that culture before I even knew that I was formed at all.[4] If I want to name whiteness and white supremacy as part of my understanding of original sin, it might be helpful to say a bit more about what I mean about that labeling. When I write original sin, I refer to a broader corruption of the soul rather than individual acts of wrongdoing. Original sin lost favor and was critiqued thoroughly as a theological doctrine because of the destructive historical interpretations that linked it to human sexuality in misogynist ways, as well as the problematic directions that it generated for God's vision for those who are not part of the Christian faith or for those who die before baptism. However, revisiting the doctrine of original sin allows us to consider an initial state of being that requires transformation because of its thoroughgoing attachment to unworthy objects, such as white supremacy. It is "original" in that it is a "given" operating in our lives because we were born into this culture of white supremacy that impacts who we are, what we believe, how we imagine the world we live in, and how we act in everyday situations.

In her book *The Fall to Violence*, theologian Marjorie Suchocki describes original sin as expressed in a trifold structure of genetic endowment towards violence, the social interdependence of all humans, and "the unique structures of intersubjectivity that mediate the values of one generation to the next."[5] She notes that the particular forms of sin that take form in society's institutions deeply influence the structures of awareness and conscience of

---

3 Goto, "The Racialized "Zoo" of Practical Theology," in *Conundrums* ed. Mercer and Miller-McLemore, 114.
4 Katherine Turpin, *Branded: Adolescents Converting from Consumer Faith*, Pilgrim Press, 2006.
5 Marjorie Hewitt Suchocki, *The Fall to Violence* (Continuum, 1995), 129.

the next generation. Along these lines, the narratives of meaning that support white supremacy are hardwired into the awareness and conscience of those who participate in the legacy of white settler Christianity. The "corruption" of the soul occurs through the unintentional daily reality of living within white institutions, white dominant political systems, and the norms of violent social interaction related to the social construct of race that have developed within this system.

To consider this original corrupting situation in a different way, I turn to the biblical story most linked with the idea of original sin, the story of Adam and Eve in the garden in Genesis.[6] The fall to sin, so the story has been interpreted, happened when the woman offered the fruit of the tree of the knowledge of good and evil to the man, and they both ate of it and came to understand themselves as naked:

> Then the eyes of both were opened, and they knew that they were naked; and they sewed fig leaves together and made loincloths for themselves. They heard the sound of the LORD God walking in the garden at the time of the evening breeze, and the man and his wife hid themselves from the presence of the LORD God among the trees of the garden. But the LORD God called to the man, and said to him, "Where are you?" He said, "I heard the sound of you in the garden, and I was afraid, because I was naked; and I hid myself."[7]

As the story goes, because of this decision and its aftermath, we are cursed, living in enmity with creatures such as the serpent, suffering under heteropatriarchy ("your desire shall be for your husband and he shall rule over you"), the toil to bring forth that which sustains human life will be difficult, and death and dust is our destiny.

This moment of hiding from God and trying to cover oneself with a loincloth is a poignant image for where white settler Christianity is living at this moment. A moment of recognition has come that much of what has passed for faithfulness in US congregations is intertwined with the violence linked to white supremacy, and some are starting to recognize that the whiteness that was once was uplifted as purity and blamelessness may actually be an expression of our nakedness and sense of inadequacy before God. In this story,

---

[6] I am indebted to my colleague, the Rev. Dr. Jennifer Leath, who first pointed me in the direction of this story and the notion of hiding from God while God is still seeking us in thinking about this chapter.
[7] Gen 3:7–10, NRSV.

original sin is not linked to particular acts of wrongdoing that lead to a declaration of guilt, but rather to a state of recognition in which the entirety of who we are is inadequate, so we become defensive and try to cover it up. This is not the guilt of original sin, but rather the shame of it.

If sinfulness and guilt have become thoroughly out of fashion to discuss in contemporary Christianity, shame is considered even more problematic. Judgmentalism and shaming have been named by younger generations as one of the more toxic features of Christianity that have caused them to leave.[8] In the hands of dominant culture, feelings of shame and inadequacy have been a major tool for reinforcing internalized oppression in those who are different than the white cishet male norm. In movements for racial justice, white shame and guilt have been noted as not particularly helpful in the fight for racial equality because of the defensiveness and rigid self-protection that these emotions tend to produce rather than movement towards conversion and different behavior. So, shame has been named as an inappropriate feeling that must be rejected.

Appropriate shame is also essential to prosocial behavior. A sense of shame is what lets us know that we have broken the covenants of human coexistence, recognizing when we have found who we are to be inadequate to the relationships and communities we hope to be a part of. To be shameless is to lack the ability to be called into account by those with whom we desire to reconnect, to reject the connections and responsibilities that living in community demand for peaceful coexistence. The remedy for shame is not continued hiding of ourselves in our nakedness, which leads to ongoing isolation. As shame researcher Brené Brown notes, "Shame needs three things to grow out of control in our lives: secrecy, silence, and judgment. When something shaming happens and we keep it locked up, it festers and grows. It consumes us."[9] Brown notes that shame resilience, or "the ability to recognize shame, to move through it constructively while maintaining worthiness and authenticity, and to ultimately develop more courage, compassion, and connection as a result of our experience," comes from naming shame, sharing those stories and owning them rather than trying to hide them away.[10]

One of the prominent cultural features of reckoning with white supremacy and the shame of its legacy in the United States has been a deep desire from

---

8   David Kinnaman and Aly Hawkins, *You Lost Me: Why Young Christians Are Leaving Church ... and Rethinking Faith*, reprint edition (Baker Books, 2016), 20.

9   Brené Brown, *The Gifts of Imperfection: Let Go of Who You Think You're Supposed to Be and Embrace Who You Are* (Hazelden, 2010), 40.

10 Brown, *The Gifts of Imperfection*, 40–41.

white people to hide it away, to not teach about racism in public schools, to insist that this formation is not a part of the history of the United States, and to deny the ways that it has shaped white Western Christianity by focusing with singular intensity on the good and virtuous gifts of Christian theology and tradition. This denial and secrecy response to the shame of this history is much "more likely to lead to destructive and hurtful behaviors than it is to be the solution."[11] Rather than seeking reparations, actively dismantling the conduits of white supremacy, or relinquishing cultural power, we are in the midst of a moment where heated defense of historically white ways of seeing the world is being mounted.

If we believe that despite our recognition of our inadequate ways linked to whiteness, God is trying to call us out, to reconnect and find us, it is time to stop hiding those ways in which we have found ourselves thoroughly enmeshed in white supremacy. Rather than continuing to prop up the institutions and systems that are thoroughly implicated in white settler Christianity, an ongoing form of hiding from and fearing God because of our nakedness and trying to cover ourselves, we are called to step out and acknowledge what we've been up to, who we have discovered ourselves to be. But this requires a moment of reckoning and repentance.

The work of repentance is difficult when we try desperately to protect our sense of ourselves and our tradition as basically good. If we know at some cognitive level that "white supremacy is bad," then it's hard to face up to the fact that we might still be deeply invested in it through our religious commitments and institutions. So, we engage in vigorous and effective self-deception to maintain our sense of ourselves as basically good and not committed to whiteness. White supremacy has been a closely guarded self-deceit within white settler Christianity, a belief that alignment with whiteness is closely linked with salvation.[12]

From my own tradition, John Wesley includes "repentance, rightly understood" in a list with the practice of all good works of piety and mercy as "in some sense necessary to sanctification."[13] Wesley explains that "repentance, rightly understood" means repentance without guilt, fear of the wrath of God, or sense of condemnation. It is repentance with assurance of the favor of God,

---

11 Brown, *The Gifts of Imperfection*, 41.
12 Willie James Jennings, "Whiteness Isn't Progress: How the Missionary Project Went Horrifically Wrong," *The Christian Century* 135, no. 23 (November 7, 2018): 28–31.
13 John Wesley, *John Wesley's Sermons: An Anthology*, Outler, Albert C., ed. (Abingdon Press, 1991), 377.

repentance in the gracious context of our acceptance by God as we are. Repentance rightly understood takes into account our paradoxical and conflicted nature as both justified and not yet perfected in love. We participate in sin which still remains, though it doesn't reign, in our hearts.[14] An atmosphere of gracious acceptance allows for the seeking out of those places where sin still remains with the recognition that finding them doesn't indicate shameful failure. Rather, identifying the ways in which we are still committed to white supremacy facilitates movement towards fuller expression of the love of God. The simple definition that Wesley most often used for repentance was "self-knowledge."[15] The desired self-knowledge is awareness of the "corruption" of the inner nature, in this case the ways in which we love whiteness with all of our heart, soul, mind, and strength, our affections and passions.[16] The language that Wesley uses here is quite fascinating. Knowledge includes the fullness of desire and emotional life for Wesley: "Thy affections are alienated from God, and scattered abroad over the earth. All thy passions, both thy desires and aversions, thy joys and sorrows, thy hopes and fears, are out of frame, are either undue in their degree, or placed on undue objects."[17] Whiteness is an undue object for our affections and our desires, and trusting in its ways leads to alienation from God, or from the deepest forms of love and communion in the universe.

Right repentance, then, allows us to reckon with the shameful legacy of white supremacy that is at the heart of white mainline Christianity from a posture that is not defensive or protective, that trusts that element of transcendence that does not delimit God to the boundaries of the tradition, that reckons with the prophetic calls for reform that have been calling white Western Christianity to account for its colonizing and earth-destroying practices. In short, it allows us to recognize the legacy of the white church in white supremacy honestly and in all of its nakedness, to tell that story as part of defanging its power that causes us to try to cover it up, and to do so with a belief in our worthiness and belonging that does not require a sense of superiority in relation to others to be maintained. Those of us formed at the center of whiteness will live out our lifetimes in a stance of confession and repentance, for the patterns formed that we are living into have had centuries to adhere to our ancestors and to congeal in our own souls.

---

14   Wesley, *Sermons*, 377.
15   Wesley, *Sermons*, 128.
16   Wesley, *Sermons*, 128.
17   Wesley, *Sermons*, 128.

The confessional stance is a way to refuse to consent to the commonsense values of white supremacy at the heart of our institutions and our patterns of life together. Jennings calls this consent a "surrender of imagination":

> We live in a defeated conceptual moment when so many have surrendered their imaginations to working inside the ideas of race, religion, and nation as the most rational way to think collective existence and for peoples to know and announce themselves. It may be impossible to escape these ideas for thinking collective existence given how they are embedded in the word order formed through modern colonialism and enacted through education, but the more urgent question is whether we should continue to surrender our imaginations to them.[18]

In many ways, this book has been an extended exercise in trying not to surrender my imagination to the calls for efficacy, control, mastery, and embodied formation that are so much a part of white supremacy and then to ask, how does that change the nature of the field of practical theology? I find myself asking if "not surrendering one's imagination" is enough for those of us who are destined to benefit from the unequal hierarchies generated by this system.

Jennings reminds me that this orientation is about being willing to be upended again and again through committed relationship with non-white others, through consistent embrace of vulnerability and critique of one's deepest beliefs and values, through abandoning a sense of mastery and control and embracing risk and failure. It is to be willing to be "changed not by a non-descript other but by nonwhite peoples historically imagined at the sharp point of instruction."[19] It is, as Elizabeth Conde-Frazier and Anne Carter Walker have reminded me with their own work reflecting on Paulo Freire, a lifelong process of constant conversion to these specific others with whom I am in structural and personal relationship.[20]

I have been haunted throughout the writing of this book that maybe I am simply echoing what my colleagues of color have been saying more eloquently before me. The white need to be unique and to be an individual who contributes to innovation in scholarship raises its ugly head and demands that

---

18 Willie James Jennings, *After Whiteness: An Education in Belonging* (Eerdmans, 2020), 137.
19 Jennings, *After Whiteness*, 141.
20 Anne Carter Walker, "Practical Theology for the Privileged: A Starting Point for Pedagogies of Conversion," in *International Journal of Practical Theology* 16 (2), 250; Elizabeth Conde-Frazier, "From Hospitality to Shalom," in Elizabeth Conde-Frazier, S. Steve Kang, and Gary A. Parrett, *A Many Colored Kingdom: Multicultural Dynamics for Spiritual Formation* (Baker Academic, 2004), 176–177.

I somehow add something special and different to this conversation. Echoing what my colleagues have already said beautifully is absolutely what I have done here. The question of whether this has been an extractive or appropriative move remains to be seen through the assessment of nonwhite others. My hope is that this work has been an amplifying and an appreciative move. This is my attempt to witness that their white colleagues are listening and learning from them, even though they do so imperfectly and perhaps with maddening slowness and investment in the continued power of whiteness. I hope you have found my writing an invitation to read and re-read the work of our contemporaries of color in the field and to be inspired and transformed by their courage and insight, to invite them to be your keynote speakers, and to put them in positions of power and influence in institutions and in control of funding distribution.

Many different theories of social change in response to injustice exist, particularly addressing whether reform is possible within the existing structures or whether it is time to blow the whole thing up and start again. Every time that I teach my course "Education and Social Change" I have to plan for the emotional quandary that it puts me in, where I read deeply enough of Paulo Freire, Ella Baker, Myles Horton, Carter G. Woodson, Ivan Illyich and others to remember that I do not think graduate schools are institutions capable of liberative education. And then I cycle back to being inspired to live into a different future in education that is more lifegiving despite being located within historic institutions and structures built to serve the ends of the status quo. My teaching practices change, and I move a little more closely to relationships with students that enable all of us to know more together than we did when we started about the futures we are moving toward together.

A revolutionary mindset opens up space to consider true alternatives by upending and disrupting existing narratives. I have taught with radical colleagues such as ethicist Miguel De La Torre who remind me that the correct response to entrenched injustice is an ethic of *joder* ... to literally screw with the system.[21] Or, for years, teaching with George "Tink" Tinker who reminded anyone who wanted to learn about American Indian spirituality that since that spirituality was based on intimate relationship with the land and all the relatives upon it, it was impossible to understand unless white people first gave the land back. The starting point would have to be the elimination of the notion of property rights upon which the founding documents of the United States were based. In my experience, many white students and faculty colleagues find

---

21 Miguel A. De La Torre, *Embracing Hopelessness* (Fortress Press, 2017), 127.

these stances offputting, to say the least. The radical demands of dismantling structures of power, of refusing to lend oneself to the projects of whiteness in late capitalism, of not accepting the common sense understanding that its values and aims and sense of the beautiful are non-negotiable and fitting, that is crazy talk. It violates central inherited shared understandings of education, of social organization, of leadership and the purposes of human existence. And yet, I think that their radical stance has opened the space for me and others to begin to let go of some of these habituated professional values of control and mastery and to imagine other possibilities.

Having let go of a sense of professional competence and opened myself to the fullness of questioning leaves me in an awkward place. Academics generally frown upon the stance of doubting oneself as an expert in a field. But refusing to surrender one's imagination to whiteness doesn't mean not engaging in practical theology, or even the end of advocating for all the practices and commitments I am questioning in this book. A historic embeddedness of white supremacy in one's field of study is not a unique problem to practical theology, but rather it serves a key role in the Western academic venture as a whole. I hope in the pages of this book you have begun to glimpse what that embeddedness looks like in the field of practical theology and have found some spaces to question your commitments to its values and practices. Together may we have the courage to live into a different future together where salvation is not equated to whiteness and true communion and belonging await.

Bibliography

Aguirre, Roxanne Gaxiola. "Cultural Humility and Intercultural Engagement." *Brethren Life and Thought* 63, no. 2 (2018): 57–61.

Althaus-Reid, Marcella. "Sexual Strategies in Practical Theology: Indecent Theology and the Plotting of Desire with Some Degree of Success." *Theology & Sexuality*, no. 7 (September 1997): 45–52.

Ammerman, Nancy Tatom. *Sacred Stories, Spiritual Tribes: Finding Religion in Everyday Life*. Oxford University Press, 2013.

Andrews, R. 2002. *The dynamics involved in the introduction of cultural diversity into the mission of the evangelical Christian school*. Dissertation. ProQuest Dissertation Publishing.

Ayres, Jennifer R. *Good Food: Grounded Practical Theology*. Baylor University Press, 2013.

Ayres, Jennifer R. *Inhabitance: Ecological Religious Education*. Baylor University Press, 2019.

Ayres, Jennifer R. *Waiting for a Glacier to Move: Practicing Social Witness*. Pickwick Publications, 2011.

Bass, Diana Butler. *Christianity for the Rest of Us: How the Neighborhood Church Is Transforming the Faith*. HarperOne, 2006.

Bass, Dorothy C., Kathleen A. Cahalan, Bonnie J. Miller-McLemore, Christian Batalden Scharen, and James R. Nieman. *Christian Practical Wisdom: What It Is, Why It Matters*. Eerdmans Publishing Co., 2016.

Bass, Dorothy C., ed. *Practicing Our Faith: A Way of Life for a Searching People*. Jossey-Bass, 1996.

Bass, Dorothy C., and Craig Dykstra, eds. *For Life Abundant: Practical Theology, Theological Education, and Christian Ministry*. Eerdmans Publishing Co., 2008.

Bass, Dorothy, and Don C. Richter. *Way to Live: Christian Practices for Teens*. Edited by Dorothy C. Bass. Upper Room, 2002.

Beaudoin, Tom. *Witness to Dispossession: The Vocation of a Postmodern Theologian*. Orbis Books, 2008.

Berthold, Dana. "Tidy Whiteness: A Genealogy of Race, Purity, and Hygiene." *Ethics & the Environment* 15, no. 1 (Spring 2010): 1–26.

Bondi, Roberta C. *To Love as God Loves: Conversations with the Early Church*. Fortress Press, 1987.

Bourdieu, Pierre. *Distinction: A Social Critique of the Judgment of Taste*. Translated by Richard Nice. Harvard University Press, 1984.

Bourdieu, Pierre. *Outline of a Theory of Practice*. Cambridge University Press, 1977.

Bourdieu, Pierre. *Practical Reason: On the Theory of Action*. Translated by Randall Johnson. Stanford University Press, 1998.
Brittain, Christopher Craig. "Can a Theology Student Be an Evil Genius?: On the Concept of Habitus in Theological Education." *Toronto Journal of Theology*, 2009, 141–54.
Brookfield, Stephen D., and Mary E. Hess. *Becoming a White Antiracist*. Routledge, 2021.
brown, adrienne maree. *Emergent Strategy: Shaping Change, Changing Worlds*. Reprint edition. AK Press, 2017.
Brown, Brené. *The Gifts of Imperfection: Let Go of Who You Think You're Supposed to Be and Embrace Who You Are*. Hazelden, 2010.
Browning, Don. *Fundamental Practical Theology*. Revised edition. Fortress Press, 1995.
Brueggemann, Walter. *A Way Other Than Our Own: Devotions for Lent*. Westminster John Knox Press, 2016.
Brueggemann, Walter. 2010. "Walk Humbly with Your God: Micah 6:8." *Journal for Preachers* 33:4, 14–19.
Bueckert, Leah Dawn and Daniel S. Schipani, eds. *You Welcomed Me: Interfaith Spiritual Care in the Hospital*. Pandora Press, 2010.
Butler, Judith. *Giving an Account of Oneself*. Fordham University Press, 2005.
Cahalan, Kathleen A. *Introducing the Practice of Ministry*. Liturgical Press, 2010.
Cahalan, Kathleen A. and Gordon S. Mikoski, eds. *Opening the Field of Practical Theology: An Introduction*. Rowman & Littlefield Publishers, 2014.
Cameron, Helen, Deborah Bhatti, Catherine Duce, James Sweeney, and Clare Watkins. *Talking About God in Practice: Theological Action Research and Practical Theology*. SCM Press, 2010.
Carvalhaes, Claudio. *Liturgies from Below: Praying with People at the End of the World*. Abingdon Press, 2020.
Carvalhaes, Cláudio, Marc H. Ellis, and Daisy Machado. *Praying with Every Heart: Orienting Our Lives to the Wholeness of the World*. Cascade Books, 2021.
Carvalhaes, Cláudio, and Ivone Gebara. *Ritual at World's End: Essays on Eco-Liturgical Liberation Theology*. Barber's Son Press, 2021.
Carvalhaes, Cláudio. "Why I Created a Chapel Service Where People Confess to Plants." *Sojourners*, September 26, 2019. https://sojo.net/articles/why-i-created-chapel-service-where-people-confess-plants.
Cash, Tierian "Randy." "For God and Country." The American Legion. Accessed July 21, 2022. https://www.legion.org/magazine/243950/god-and-country.
Center for Humans and Nature. "Returning the Gift, 2021." *Center for Humans and Nature* (blog), June 15, 2021. https://humansandnature.org/returning-the-gift-2021/.
Chung, YongHan. "A Postcolonial Reading of the Great Commission (Matt 28:16–20) with a Korean Myth." *Theology Today* 72, no. 3 (October 2015): 276–88.
Clark, Lynn Schofield. *From Angels to Aliens: Teenagers, the Media, and the Supernatural*. Oxford University Press, 2005.

Cohen, Rebecca. "Framework for Understanding Structural Racism: The Cult of Purity." *Journal of Ecumenical Studies* 55, no. 1 (2020): 46–62.

Conde-Frazier, Elizabeth. "Religious Education for Generating Hope." *Religious Education* 112:3, 2017. 225–230.

Conde-Frazier, Elizabeth, S. Steve Kang, and Gary A. Parrett. *A Many Colored Kingdom: Multicultural Dynamics for Spiritual Formation*. Baker Academic, 2004.

Cone, James. H. "Theology's Great Sin: Silence in the Face of White Supremacy." *Black Theology* 2:2, 2004. 139–152.

Creamer, Deborah Beth. *Disability and Christian Theology Embodied Limits and Constructive Possibilities*. Oxford University Press, 2009.

Creative Knowledge Resource. "Extraction as White Supremacy | Moving towards Anti-Extraction Practices in the Arts." Accessed June 22, 2022. https://www.creativeknow.org/bopawritersforum/extraction-as-white-supremacy.

Crozier, Karen D. *Fannie Lou Hamer's Revolutionary Practical Theology: Racial and Environmental Justice Concerns*. Brill, 2020.

Dahill, Lisa E and Jim B. Martin-Schramm, eds. *Eco-Reformation: Grace and Hope for a Planet in Peril*. Cascade Books, 2016.

Davie, Grace. *Religion in Britain: A Persistent Paradox*. Second edition. Wiley-Blackwell, 2015.

Davie, Grace. *Religion in Britain Since 1945*. John Wiley & Sons, 1994.

Day, Keri. *Notes of a Native Daughter*. Eerdmans, 2021.

Dean, Kenda Creasy. *Almost Christian: What the Faith of Our Teenagers Is Telling the American Church*. Oxford University Press, 2010.

De La Torre, Miguel A. *Burying White Privilege: Resurrecting a Badass Christianity*. Eerdmans, 2018.

De La Torre, Miguel A. *Embracing Hopelessness*. Fortress Press, 2017.

De La Torre, Miguel A. *Gonna Trouble the Water: Ecojustice, Water, and Environmental Racism*. Pilgrim Press, 2021.

Delgado, Yenny. "The Complicity of the Christian Church: The Creation of White Supremacy Ideology." Unbound, January 15, 2021. https://justiceunbound.org/the-complicity-of-the-christian-church-the-creation-of-white-supremacy-ideology/.

Dewey, John. *Experience And Education*. Reprint edition. Free Press, 1997.

DiAngelo, Dr Robin, and Michael Eric Dyson. *White Fragility: Why It's So Hard for White People to Talk About Racism*. Beacon Press, 2020.

Dilley, Andrea Palpant. "The World the Missionaries Made: They Didn't Set out to Change History: But One Modern Scholar's Research Shows They Did Just That." *Christianity Today* 58, no. 1 (January 2014): 34–41.

Drescher, Elizabeth. *Choosing Our Religion: The Spiritual Lives of America's Nones*. Oxford University Press, 2016.

Dumas, Michael J. "Against the Dark: Antiblackness in Education Policy and Discourse." *Theory into Practice* 55, no. 1 (2016): 11–19.
Dykstra, Craig. *Growing in the Life of Faith: Education and Christian Practices*. Geneva Press, 1999.
Dykstra, Craig R. "Reconceiving Practice." In *Shifting Boundaries: Contextual Approaches to the Structure of Theological Education*, 35–66, 1991.
Ebaugh, Helen Rose, and Janet Saltzman Chafetz. "Structural Adaptations in Immigrant Congregations." *Sociology of Religion* 61: 135–53. 2000.
Farley, Edward. *Practicing Gospel*. Westminster John Knox Press, 2003.
Fast, Anicka. "Sacred Children, White Privilege, and Mission: The Role of Historical Reflection in Moving toward Healthier Relationships within the Global Church." *Missiology* 47, no. 4 (2019): 435–48.
Fawson, Patricia Shawn. "Sustaining Lamentation in Traumatic Grief Through the Contemporary Elegy: A Practical Theology of the Poetics of Testimony." Dissertation. 2019.
Foster, Charles R. *Educating Congregations: The Future of Christian Education*. Abingdon Press, 1994.
Foster, Charles R. *From Generation to Generation: The Adaptive Challenge of Mainline Protestant Education in Forming Faith*. Wipf & Stock Pub, 2012.
Foucault, Michel. *Discipline and Punish: The Birth of the Prison*. 2nd ed. Vintage Books, 1995.
Fowler, James W. *Becoming Adult, Becoming Christian: Adult Development and Christian Faith*. Revised edition. Jossey-Bass Publishers, 2000.
Francis, Leah Gunning. *Ferguson and Faith: Sparking Leadership and Awakening Community*. Chalice Press, 2015.
Freeland, Mark D. *Aazheyaadizi: Worldview, Language, and the Logics of Decolonization*. Michigan State University Press, 2020.
Freire, Paulo, and Donaldo Macedo. *Pedagogy of the Oppressed: 50th Anniversary Edition*. 4th edition. Bloomsbury Academic, 2018.
Fulkerson, Mary McClintock. *Places of Redemption: Theology for a Worldly Church*. Oxford University Press, 2010.
Fulkerson, Mary McClintock. "Theologia as a Liberation Habitus: Thoughts toward Christian Formation for Resistance." In *Theology and the Interhuman: Essays in Honor of Edward Farley*, 160–80, 1995.
Gafford, Jennifer, Tara C. Raines, Sree Sinha, Cirleen DeBlaere, Don E. Davis, Joshua N. Hook, and Jesse Owen. "Cultural Humility as a Spiritually Focused Intervention in Correctional Settings: The Role of Therapists' Multicultural Orientation." *Journal of Psychology & Theology* 47, no. 3 (2019): 187–201.

Goldstein, Warren S. "The Racialization of the Jewish Question: The Pseudo-Secularization of Christian Anti-Judaism into Racial Anti-Semitism." *Religion and Theology* 27, no. 3–4 (December 8, 2020): 179–201.

Gonzalez, Norma, Luis C. Moll, and Cathy Amanti, eds. *Funds of Knowledge: Theorizing Practices in Households, Communities, and Classrooms*. Routledge, 2005.

Goto, Courtney T. *Taking on Practical Theology*. Brill, 2018.

Goto, Courtney T. *The Grace of Playing: Pedagogies for Leaning into God's New Creation*. Pickwick Publications, 2016.

Graham, Elaine. *Apologetics without Apology: Speaking of God in a World Troubled by Religion*. Cascade Books, 2017.

Graham, Elaine. "Showing and Telling: The Practice of Public Theology Today," *Practical Theology*, 9:2, 2016, 145–156.

Graham, Elaine L. *Transforming Practice: Pastoral Theology in an Age of Uncertainty*. Mowbray, 1996.

Gray, John. "The Myth of Progress." *New Statesman* 4/9/1999.

Groome, Thomas H. *Christian Religious Education: Sharing Our Story and Vision*. Jossey-Bass, 1999.

Groome, Thomas H. *Sharing Faith: A Comprehensive Approach to Religious Education and Pastoral Ministry: The Way of Shared Praxis*. HarperSanFrancisco, 1991.

Groome, Thomas H. *Will There Be Faith: A New Vision for Educating and Growing Disciples*. HarperOne, 2011.

Gunn, Dennis. "William Rainey Harper's Founding Vision for the REA and the Rhetoric of American Imperialism." *Religious Education* 117:2. 2022. 125–137.

Harris, Maria. *Fashion Me a People: Curriculum in the Church*. Westminster John Knox Press, 1989.

Harris, Melanie L. *Ecowomanism: African American Women and Earth-Honoring Faiths*. Orbis Books, 2017.

Hauerwas, Stanley, and William H. Willimon. *Resident Aliens: A Provocative Christian Assessment of Culture and Ministry for People Who Know That Something Is Wrong*. Abingdon Press, 1989.

Hersey, Tricia. "Playboy Symposium: Rest is a Divine Right," Feb. 8, 2021.

Hersey, Tricia. *Rest Is Resistance: A Manifesto*. Little, Brown Spark, 2022.

Hogan, Logan. "We Call It Tradition." In G. Harvey (Ed.), *The Handbook of Contemporary Animism*. Acumen 2013. 17–26.

Hong, Christine J. *Decolonial Futures: Intercultural and Interreligious Intelligence for Theological Education*. Lexington Books, 2021.

Horton, Myles, and Paulo Freire. *We Make the Road by Walking: Conversations on Education and Social Change*. Edited by Brenda Bell, John Gaventa, and John Peters. Reprint edition. Temple University Press, 1990.

Horujy, Sergey. *Practices of the Self and Spiritual Practices: Michel Foucault and the Eastern Christian Discourse.* Eerdmans, 2014.

Hovland, Ingie. "From Reading to Thinking: Student Lines of Thought in a Seminar on Christianity and Colonialism." *Teaching Theology & Religion* 22, no. 3 (July 2019).

Hughey, Matthew W. "Racializing Redemption, Reproducing Racism: The Odyssey of Magical Negroes and White Saviors." *Sociology Compass* 6, no. 9 (2012): 751–67.

Hussain, Amjad. "Muslim Theology and Religious Studies: Relational, Practical, and Inter-Faith Dimensions." *Religious Education* 104, no. 3 (May 2009): 239–42.

Ignatiev, Noel. *How the Irish Became White.* Routledge, 1995.

Ingram, Hannah Adams. *The Myth of the Saving Power of Education.* Pickwick Publications, 2021.

Isgandarova, Nazila. "Practical Theology and Its Importance for Islamic Theological Studies." *Ilahiyat Studies* 5, no. 2 (2014): 217–36.

Jennings, Willie James. *After Whiteness: An Education in Belonging.* Eerdmans, 2020.

Jennings, Willie James. *The Christian Imagination: Theology and the Origins of Race.* New Haven: Yale University Press, 2011.

Jennings, Willie James. "Whiteness Isn't Progress: How the Missionary Project Went Horrifically Wrong." *The Christian Century* 135, no. 23 (November 7, 2018): 28–31.

Jones, Alexander Harris, James G Huff, Mandy Kellums Baraka, and Laura S Meitzner Yoder. "A Pedagogy of the Parochial: Pedagogical Imperialism and Mutual Accompaniment in Christian Higher Education." *Christian Higher Education* 18, no. 1–2 (2019): 125–41.

Kallenberg, Brad J. "The Master Argument of MacIntyre's After Virtue." In *Virtues & Practices in the Christian Tradition: Christian Ethics after MacIntyre*, 7–29, 1997.

Karabel, Jerome. *The Chosen: The Hidden History of Admission and Exclusion at Harvard, Yale, and Princeton.* Houghton Mifflin, 2005.

Kauffman, Bill. *With Good Intentions?: Reflections on the Myth of Progress in America.* Praeger, 1998.

Kaur, Valarie. *See No Stranger: A Memoir and Manifesto of Revolutionary Love.* One World, 2020.

Killen, Patricia O'Connell, and John de Beer. *The Art of Theological Reflection.* Crossroad, 1994.

Kim, Grace Ji-Sun, Hilda P. Koster, and Melanie L. Harris. *Planetary Solidarity: Global Women's Voices on Christian Doctrine and Climate Justice.* Fortress Press, 2017.

Kim, Nami. "A Mission to the 'Graveyard of Empires'?: Neocolonialism and the Contemporary Evangelical Missions of the Global South." *Mission Studies* 27, no. 1 (2010): 3–23.

Kim-Cragg, HyeRan. *Interdependence: A Postcolonial Feminist Practical Theology.* Pickwick Publications, 2018.

Kimmerer, Robin Wall. "Returning the Gift." *Minding Nature*, 7, no. 2 (*Spring 2014*).

Kinnaman, David, and Aly Hawkins. *You Lost Me: Why Young Christians Are Leaving Church ... and Rethinking Faith*. Reprint edition. Baker Books, 2016.

Krakauer, Jon. "Greg Mortenson, Disgraced Author of 'Three Cups of Tea,' Believes He Will Have the Last Laugh." *Galleys* (blog), May 4, 2022. https://medium.com/galleys/greg-mortenson-disgraced-author-of-three-cups-of-tea-believes-he-will-have-the-last-laugh-760949b1f964.

Kujawa-Holbrook, Sheryl A. *God Beyond Borders: Interreligious Learning Among Faith Communities*. Pickwick Publications, 2014.

Kwok, Puilan and Stephen Burns, eds. *Postcolonial Practice of Ministry: Leadership, Liturgy, and Interfaith Engagement*. Lexington Books, 2016.

Lartey, Emmanuel Y. *Postcolonializing God: New Perspectives on Pastoral and Practical Theology*. SCM Press, 2013.

Leavitt, Harold J. "Why Hierarchies Thrive." *Harvard Business Review*, March 1, 2003. https://hbr.org/2003/03/why-hierarchies-thrive.

Lee, Boyung. *Transforming Congregations through Community: Faith Formation from the Seminary to the Church*. Westminster John Knox Press, 2013.

Leopold, Aldo. *A Sand County Almanac & Other Writings on Conservation and Ecology*. Curt Meine, ed. Reprint edition. Library of America, 2013.

Lewis, Stephen, Matthew Wesley Williams, and Dori Baker. *Another Way: Living and Leading Change on Purpose*. Chalice Press, 2020.

Lindstrom, Carole. *We Are Water Protectors*. Roaring Brook Press, 2020.

Lizardy-Hajbi, Kristina Isabel. "Frameworks Toward Post/Decolonial Pastoral Leaderships." *Journal of Religious Leadership* 19, no. 2 (2020): 100–130.

Lomawaima, K. Tsianina, and Teresa L. McCarty. *"To Remain an Indian": Lessons in Democracy from a Century of Native American Education*. Teachers College Press, 2006.

Lozang, Trinlae Bhikshuni. "Prospects for a Buddhist Practical Theology." *International Journal of Practical Theology* 18, no. 1 (2014): 7–22.

Lugones, Maria. "Purity, Impurity, and Separation." *Signs: Journal of Women in Culture & Society* 19, no. 2 (Winter 1994): 458.

MacIntyre, Alasdair. *After Virtue*. Third edition. University of Notre Dame, 2007.

Mahan, Brian J. *Forgetting Ourselves on Purpose: Vocation and the Ethics of Ambition*. Jossey-Bass, 2002.

Mahan, Jeffrey. *Church as Network: Christian Life and Connection in Digital Culture*. Rowman & Littlefield Publishers, 2021.

McCarroll, Pamela R. "Listening for the Cries of the Earth: Practical Theology in the Anthropocene." *International Journal of Practical Theology* 24, no. 1 (2020): 29–46.

McCarroll, Pamela R., and HyeRan Kim-Cragg, eds. *Practical Theology Amid Environmental Crises*. MDPI—Multidisciplinary Digital Publishing Institute, 2023.

McLaren, Brian. *Finding Our Way Again: The Return of the Ancient Practices*. Thomas Nelson Inc, 2008.

Mercadante, Linda A. *Belief without Borders: Inside the Minds of the Spiritual but Not Religious*. Oxford University Press, 2014.

Mercer, Joyce Ann. "Children and Climate Anxiety: An Ecofeminist Practical Theological Perspective." *Religions*, Pamela R. McCarroll and HyeRan Kim-Cragg, eds. 13, no. 302 (2022): 1–15.

Mercer, Joyce. *Welcoming Children: A Practical Theology of Childhood*. Chalice Press, 2005.

Mercer, Joyce Ann, and Bonnie Miller-McLemore, eds. *Conundrums in Practical Theology*. Brill, 2016.

Mikulich. Alex. "Whites Live a Fantasy of Innocence." *National Catholic Reporter*, November 7, 2014, sec. Arts and Opinion.

Miles-Tribble, Valerie A. *Change Agent Church in Black Lives Matter Times: Urgency for Action*. Fortress Academic, 2021.

Miller-McLemore, Bonnie J. "Climate Violence and Earth Justice: A Research Report on Practical Theology's Contributions." *International Journal of Practical Theology* 26, no. 2 (2022): 329–66.

Miller-McLemore, Bonnie J. "Trees and the 'Unthought Known': The Wisdom of the Nonhuman (or Do Humans 'Have Shit for Brains'?)," *Pastoral Psychology* 69, no. 4 (2020): 424–440.

Miller-McLemore, Bonnie J. *Christian Theology in Practice: Discovering a Discipline*. Eerdmans, 2012.

Miller-McLemore, Bonnie J. *The Wiley-Blackwell Companion to Practical Theology*. Vol. 72. Wiley-Blackwell Companions to Religion. Wiley-Blackwell, 2011.

Moore, Mary Elizabeth. *Ministering With the Earth*. Chalice Press, 1998.

Moore, Mary Elizabeth. "Responding to a Weeping Planet: Practical Theology as a Discipline Called by Crisis." *Religions* 13: 244 (2022).

Mortenson, Greg. *Three Cups of Tea: One Man's Mission to Promote Peace—One School at a Time*. Penguin Books, 2007.

Mosher, David K., John M. McConnell, Joshua N. Hook, Laura E. Captari, Adam Hodge, Franco Dispenza, Cirleen DeBlaere, Don E. Davis, and Daryl R. Van Tongeren. "Cultural Humility of Religious Communities and Well-Being in Sexual Minority Persons." *Journal of Psychology & Theology* 47, no. 3 (2019): 160–74.

Nagle, James Michael. *Out on Waters: The Religious Life and Learning of Young Catholics Beyond the Church*. Pickwick Publications, 2020.

Nagle, James Michael. "The Thinker and the Guide: A Conversation concerning Religious Disaffiliation from the Catholic Church." *Journal of Ecumenical Studies* 54, no. 3 (2019): 328–351.

Ng, Wehn-In. "Toward Wholesome Nurture: Challenges in the Religious Education of Asian North American Females." *Religious Education* 91, no. 2 (Spring 1996): 238–54.

Niklas K. Steffens and S. Alexander Haslam. "The Narcissistic Appeal of Leadership Theories." *American Psychologist* 77, no. 2 (2002): 234–48.

Orsi, Robert A. *Between Heaven and Earth: The Religious Worlds People Make and the Scholars Who Study Them*. Princeton University Press, 2006.

Osmer, Richard. "Practical theology: A current international perspective" *HTS Teologiese Studies / Theological Studies* [Online], 67:2 (16 November 2011).

Osmer, Richard Robert. *Practical Theology: An Introduction*. Eerdmans, 2008.

Ó'Tuama, Pádraig. *Daily Prayer with the Corrymeela Community*. Canterbury Press Norwich, 2017.

Oyer, Gordon. "Confronting the Myth of Human Progress: Thomas Merton and the Illusion of Privilege." *The Merton Annual* 28 (2015). 149–158.

Palmer, Parker J. *The Company of Strangers: Christians and the Renewal of America's Public Life*. Crossroad, 1981.

Parks, Sharon Daloz. *Big Questions, Worthy Dreams: Mentoring Young Adults in Their Search for Meaning, Purpose, and Faith*. Jossey-Bass, 2000.

Pew Research Center. *2015. America's Changing Religious Landscape*. Available online: http://www.pewforum.org/2015/05/12/americas-changing-religious-landscape/ (accessed on 7 November 2018).

Pew Research Center. "Demographics." *Pew Research Center's Religion & Public Life Project* (blog), October 9, 2012. https://www.pewresearch.org/religion/2012/10/09/nones-on-the-rise-demographics/.

Pikhala, Panu. "EcoAnxiety and Pastoral Care: Theoretical Considerations and Practical Suggestions." *Religions*, Pamela R. McCarroll and HyeRan Kim-Cragg, 13, no. 192 (2022).

Pohl, Christine D. *Making Room: Recovering Hospitality as a Christian Tradition*. Eerdmans, 1999.

Ransby, Barbara. *Ella Baker and the Black Freedom Movement: A Radical Democratic Vision*. University of North Carolina Press, 2003.

Reda, Nevin. "The Qur'an and Domestic Violence: An Islamic Feminist, Spiritually Integrative Reading of Verse 4:34." *International Journal of Practical Theology* 23, no. 2 (2019): 257–73.

Reyes, Patrick B. *Nobody Cries When We Die: God, Community, and Surviving to Adulthood*. Chalice Press, 2018.

Reyes, Patrick B.. *The Purpose Gap: Empowering Communities of Color to Find Meaning and Thrive*. Westminster John Knox Press, 2021.

Richter, Don C. "Religious Practices in Practical Theology." In *Opening the Field of Practical Theology: An Introduction*, edited by Kathleen A. Cahalan and Gordon S. Mikoski, 203–16. Rowman & Littlefield, 2014.

Riley, Cole Arthur. *This Here Flesh: Spirituality, Liberation, and the Stories That Make Us.* Convergent Books, 2022.

Rilke, Rainer Maria. *Letters to a Young Poet.* Translated by M.D. Herter Norton. Revised edition. W.W. Norton & Company, 1993.

Riswold, Caryn D. "Teaching the College 'Nones': Christian Privilege and the Religion Professor." *Teaching Theology & Religion* 18, no. 2 (April 2015): 133–48.

Robbins, Jeffrey W. and Clayton Crockett. *Doing Theology in the Age of Trump: A Critical Report on Christian Nationalism.* Westar Seminar on God and the Human Future. Cascade Books, 2018.

Rosenthal, S.A., & Pittinsky, T.L. (2006). "Narcissistic leadership." *The Leadership Quarterly, 17*(6), 617–633.

Saliers, Don E. "Afterword- Liturgy and Ethics Revised" in Anderson, E. Byron, ed. *Liturgy and the Moral Self: Humanity at Full Stretch Before God.* Pueblo Books, 1998. 209–224.

Scharen, Christian. *Faith as a Way of Life: A Vision for Pastoral Leadership.* Eerdmans, 2008.

Scharen, Christian. *Public Worship and Public Work: Character and Commitment in Local Congregational Life.* Virgil Michel Series. Collegeville, MN: Liturgical Press, 2004.

Schipani, Daniel S. *Religious Education Encounters Liberation Theology.* Religious Education Press, 1998.

Schwarz, Alan. "Study of N.B.A. Sees Racial Bias in Calling Fouls." *The New York Times*, May 2, 2007, sec. Sports. https://www.nytimes.com/2007/05/02/sports/basketball/02refs.html.

Segovia, Fernando F., and Mary Ann Tolbert. *Teaching the Bible: The Discourses and Politics of Biblical Pedagogy.* Fortress Press, 2011.

Shotwell, Alexis. *Against Purity: Living Ethically in Compromised Times.* University of Minnesota Press, 2016.

Slee, Nicola. *Fragments for Fractured Times: What Feminist Practical Theology Brings to the Table.* SCM Press, 2020.

Smith, Andrea. "Heteropatriarchy and the Three Pillars of White Supremacy: Rethinking Women of Color Organizing" in INCITE! Women of Color Against Violence, ed. *Color of Violence: The INCITE! Anthology.* Reprint edition. Duke University Press Books, 2016, 66–73.

Smith, Christian, and Melina Lundquist Denton. *Soul Searching: The Religious and Spiritual Lives of American Teenagers.* Reprint edition. Oxford University Press, 2009.

Smith, Gregory A. "About Three-in-Ten U.S. Adults Are Now Religiously Unaffiliated." *Pew Research Center's Religion & Public Life Project* (blog), December 14, 2021. https://www.pewresearch.org/religion/2021/12/14/about-three-in-ten-u-s-adults-are-now-religiously-unaffiliated/.

Spratt, David and Ian Dunlop. "Existential Climate-Related Security Risk: A Scenario Approach | PreventionWeb," June 12, 2019. https://www.preventionweb.net/publication/existential-climate-related-security-risk-scenario-approach.

Stanton, Graham D. (2019) "A Theology of Complexity for Christian Leadership in an Uncertain Future," *Practical Theology*, 12:2, 147–157, DOI: 10.1080/1756073X.2019.1595318.

Steffens, Niklas K. and S. Alexander Haslam. "The Narcissistic Appeal of Leadership Theories." *American Psychologist* 77, no. 2 (2002): 234–48.

Suchocki, Marjorie Hewitt. *The Fall to Violence*. Continuum, 1995.

Talvacchia, Kathleen T. *Critical Minds and Discerning Hearts: A Spirituality of Multicultural Teaching*. Chalice Press, 2003.

Temple, Katherine. "The Unchallenged Myth of Progress." Sojourners, March 1, 1977. https://sojo.net/magazine/march-1977/unchallenged-myth-progress.

"The Courts and Christian Privilege: The Law Must Grasp a Changing America." Editorial. *Church & State* 72, no. 9 (October 2019).

Tinker, George E. *Missionary Conquest: The Gospel and Native American Cultural Genocide*. Fortress Press, 1993.

Tinker, George E. "American Indians and Ecotheology: Alterity and Worldview." In *Eco-Lutheranism: Lutheran Perspectives on Ecology*, edited by Karla Bohmbach and Shauna Hannan. Lutheran University Press, 2013, 69–84.

Tran, Mai-Anh Le. *Reset the Heart: Unlearning Violence, Relearning Hope*. Abingdon Press, 2017.

Tumminio Hansen, Danielle Elizabeth."The Body of God, Sexually Violated: A Trauma-Informed Reading of the Climate Crisis." *Religions* 13: 249 (2022).

Turpin, Katherine. *Branded: Adolescents Converting from Consumer Faith*. Pilgrim Press, 2006.

Turpin, Katherine. "Christian Education, White Supremacy, and Humility in Formational Agendas." *Religious Education* 112, no. 4 (July 2017): 407–17.

Turpin, Katherine. "Disrupting the Luxury of Despair: Justice and Peace Education in Contexts of Relative Privilege," *Teaching Theology and Religion*, 11:3 (2008), 141–152.

Turpin, Katherine. "Religious Education beyond Congregational Settings." *Religions* 9, no. 11 (November 2018): 1–8.

Unamuno, Miguel de. *Selected Works of Miguel de Unamuno, Volume 5: The Agony of Christianity and Essays on Faith*. Edited by Anthony Kerrigan and Martin Nozick. Reprint edition. Princeton University Press, 2015.

Unamuno, Miguel de. *Tragic Sense of Life*. Translated by J.E. Crawford Fitch. Beloved Publishing LLC, 2018.

US Department of the Interior. "Department of the Interior Releases Investigative Report, Outlines Next Steps in Federal Indian Boarding School Initiative," May 11,

2022. https://www.doi.gov/pressreleases/department-interior-releases-investigative-report-outlines-next-steps-federal-indian.

Van Meter, Timothy L. *Created in Delight: Youth, Church, and the Mending of the World*. Wipf and Stock, 2013.

Veling, Terry A. *Practical Theology: On Earth As It Is in Heaven*. Orbis Books, 2005.

Viau, Marcel. "Practical Theology: Instigator of a New Apologetic: Practical Theology: International Perspectives." In *Practical Theology: International Perspectives*, 39–51. Frankfurt am Main, 1999.

Volf, Miroslav, and Dorothy C. Bass. *Practicing Theology: Beliefs and Practices in Christian Life*. Eerdmans, 2001.

Walker, Anne Carter. "Dreams (a Poem) Indigenous Futuring in the Theological Classroom (Prose)." *The Wabash Center Journal on Teaching* 4, no. 1 (2023): 7–17.

Walker, Anne Carter. "Practical Theology for the Privileged: A Starting Point for Pedagogies of Conversion" in *International Journal of Practical Theology* 16 (2): 243–259.

Warren, John T. *Performing Purity: Whiteness, Pedagogy, and the Reconstitution of Power*. Peter Lang, 2003.

Warren, Michael. *At This Time In This Place: The Spirit Embodied in the Local Assembly*. Trinity Press International, 1999.

Welch, Sharon D. *A Feminist Ethic of Risk: Revised Edition*. Revised edition. Fortress Press, 2000.

Wesley, John. *John Wesley's Sermons: An Anthology*. Outler, Albert C., ed. Abingdon Press, 1991.

Wessels, Tom. *Myth of Progress: Toward a Sustainable Future*. University Press of New England, 2013.

Westerhoff III, John H. *Will Our Children Have Faith?: Third Revised Edition*. Morehouse Publishing, 2012.

Wilhelm, Gretchen M. and Michael W. Firmin. "Historical and Contemporary Developments in Home School Education." *Journal of Research on Christian Education* 18, no. 3 (September 2009): 303–15.

Wimberly, Anne E. Streaty. *Soul Stories: African American Christian Education*. Revised edition. Abingdon Press, 2005.

Winner, Lauren F. *The Dangers of Christian Practice: On Wayward Gifts, Characteristic Damage, and Sin*. Yale University Press, 2018.

Wirzba, Norman. *Food and Faith: A Theology of Eating*. Cambridge University Press, 2011.

Wirzba, Norman. "The Touch of Humility: An Invitation to Creatureliness." *Modern Theology*, 24: 2, 2008. 225–244.

Worthington, Jonathan D, and Everett L Worthington. "Spiritual Formation by Training Leaders in Their Indigenous Cultures: The Importance of Cultural Humility and Virtue Theory." *Journal of Spiritual Formation & Soul Care* 12, no. 1 (2019): 112–34.

Yang, Fenggang, and Helen Rose Ebaugh. "Transformations in New Immigrant Religions and their Global Implications." *American Sociological Review* 66: 269–88. 2001.

Young, Stephen. "Biblical Inerrancy's Long History as an Evangelical Activist for White Patriarchy." *Religion Dispatches*, February 8, 2022. https://religiondispatches.org/biblical-inerrancys-long-history-as-an-evangelical-activist-for-white-patriarchy/.

Zakaria, Rafia. *Against White Feminism: Notes on Disruption*. W.W. Norton & Company, 2021.

Index

Acosta, Jose   65, 70, 73
action/reflection model   81, 83
affiliation
  decreased   41
  theology of   153
agency
  assumed   88, 93
  of children and adolescents   73
  of earth   196, 198, 201
Amanti, Cathy   78
America first ideology   13, 16
American exceptionalism   12–13, 56
American imperialism   66
Ammerman, Nancy   133, 154
Andrews, Dale   14
animism   203
Anishinaabeg language and tradition
    196–198
antiblackness   13
apologetics
  as assurance   149
  as evangelical practice   147–148
  as public conviction   148–149
  for validity of Christian practice   150
  for white Christianity   17
Asad, Talal   93
assimilation   11–12, 51, 63, 68–69, 132, 149,
    157, 171, 207
authority
  for teaching   59, 75, 77
  in James Fowler   26
  internal   27, 38, 172
  questioning of   25
Ayres, Jennifer   5n6, 185–186, 189, 194

Baker, Dori   118, 121, 125
Baker, Ella   119–121
baptism   50–51
Bass, Dorothy   37, 43–44, 47–48, 146
Baudhuin, Paul   138–139
Beaudoin, Tom   15, 22, 152, 154, 162–163,
    173–174
Berryman, Jerome   53
Berry, Wendell   194
Bhatti, Deborah   36n4, 151–152

biblical inerrancy   29
boarding schools   33–34, 65
  Carlisle   34, 64
  Indian   33–34, 62–64
  St. Stephens   33
bodies
  control of   49
  discipline of   44
  dispositions of   46
  as site of learning/knowledge   49
Boesak, Allan   13
Bondi, Roberta   77n51
Bourdieu, Pierre   44–49
Brookfield, Stephen   205
brown, adrienne maree   108–109, 125–126
Brown, Brené   210
Browning, Don   84
Brueggemann, Walter   3, 80
Buddhism   16, 133, 161, 166, 178
Butler Bass, Diana   37, 38–39
Butler, Judith   44

Cahalan, Kathleen   14, 37, 85, 97–98, 103
Cameron, Helen   36, 151–152
capital   46
Carvalhaes, Claudio   176, 200–202
Chafetz, Janet Saltzman   133n5
change agents   85
chaplaincy   20, 100, 162–163
Christian-centrism   162
Christianicity   173
Christian privilege   166–169
Church of Latter Day Saints   140
civilizing   61–62, 69, 85, 86, 89, 136–137
Clark, Lynn Schofield   154
clergy sexual abuse   43, 74, 136
climate anxiety   204
climate crisis   17, 185–186, 190
cognitive structures   45
colonization   23, 25, 35, 52, 54, 59, 61, 73, 76,
    82, 123, 125, 157, 176
common good   85
communal questions   179–183
communion   97, 101, 114–115, 206–207, 215
community   115, 142–143, 193

Conde-Frazier, Elizabeth   78–79, 213
Cone, James   76–77
confession   29, 32, 94, 201, 213
congregational vitality   38, 41
consumer capitalism/culture   47, 185, 204
control   29, 82, 84, 88
    embodied   35
    ethic of   88
    professional   89
conversion
    of imagination   202–203
    teaching and   60
    to the other   77–78, 213
cosmologies   192
Creamer, Deborah   93
Crozier, Karen   192–193
cultural appropriation   8, 177–178
cultural genocide   33, 57, 61, 63–64

Dahill, Lisa   186–187, 203–204
Daloz Parks, Sharon   26
Day, Keri   207
Dean, Kenda Creasy   73
de Beer, John   174
decline of mainline churches   2, 15, 36, 39, 42, 52, 74, 102, 110, 129, 134, 137, 145
decolonial/decolonizing   2, 18, 23, 70, 79, 107, 113, 117, 121, 125, 140, 149, 206
deconversion   152
De La Torre, Miguel   3–4, 88–89, 189, 214
democracy   66–68, 164
denial   211
design   98–99
development   69, 87
Dewey, John   132
dialogical   70, 83, 115–116, 145
DiAngelo, Robin   7n10
disability   93–94
disaffiliation   153–154
discipling/discipleship   60–61, 65
disruption   207
Doctrine of Discovery   28
Doehring, Carrie   20, 179
dominant culture   2, 4, 23, 26, 35, 46, 52, 57, 69, 77, 85, 88, 103, 105, 116, 140, 159, 208, 210
domination   44–47
dominion   190, 202

"dones"   160
doxa   46
Drescher, Elizabeth   154
Dreyer, Jaco   7n13
Dube, Musa   61, 62, 65, 75, 76
Duce, Catherine   36n4, 151–152
Dumas, Michael   13
Dykstra, Craig   42–44, 146

Ebaugh, Helen Rose   133n5, 133n6
ecojustice   189
ecological destruction   187
efficacy   100
efficiency   9
embedded knowledge   26, 46, 49
Erickson, Amy   185
eucharist   50–51, 132
evangelization or evangelizing   34, 35, 51, 52, 56, 60, 65
experience
    and religious traditions   175
    human   184
extractive   8, 87, 191

faith
    defining   28
    losing   24–25
    questioning   3, 4, 5–7
faith development theory   26–27
Farley, Edward   41
feel for the game   45, 47
Ferguson, Missouri   141–142
Firmin, Michael   72n42
fixing   88, 94–95, 147
followers   104–106, 122
formation
    character   41, 72
    Christian   15, 65, 71, 73
    dominant culture   4
    embodied   53
    faith   36, 39, 134–135
    identity   132
    spiritual   48, 133, 141
Foster, Charles   131, 134–135
Foucault, Michel   44
Fowler, James   26–27
Fragmentation   124
fragment workers   123

framing questions   23
Francis, Leah Gunning   141–142
Freeland, Mark   196–198, 203
Freire, Paulo   75, 78–79, 132, 213
Fulkerson, Mary McClintock   51, 82, 85
funds of knowledge   78

generational trauma   33–34
gentrification   30–31
Gerkin, Charles   53
Gonzalez, Norma   78
Goto, Courtney   14–15, 21, 52, 171, 206, 207–208
Graham, Elaine   57, 148–149
"Great Commission"   60
Greider, Kathleen   163, 177
Groome, Thomas   37n5, 73, 79, 83, 131, 178
Guenther, Margaret   53
Gunn, Dennis   66–67

Haaland, Deb   62–63
habitus   41–42, 44–45, 47, 54, 56
Hamer, Fannie Lou   192–193
Hamman, Jaco   53
Hansen, Danielle Tumminio   196
Harper, William Rainey   66–67
Harris, Maria   131
Harris, Melanie   189
Haslam, S. Alexander   121–122
Hauerwas, Stanley   39, 49, 139n20
Hawkins, Aly   210n8
Heifetz, Ronald   104
heresy/heretics   157, 200
Hersey, Tricia   107
Hess, Mary   205
heteronormativity   11
heteropatriarchy   209
hierarchy   10–11, 191
Hiltner, Seward   104
Hogan, Linda   203
homeschooling   72
Hong, Christine   18, 69, 70, 79
hopelessness   88
Horton, Myles   78
hospitality   43, 177
Hughey, Matthew   87n12
humility   59, 74, 76–79
Hussain, Amjad   165

imagination   125
   *dis*imagination   136
   surrender of   213
immigration   133, 168
imperialism   75
implication   55
improvisation   53
indigenous knowledges and traditions   62, 167, 178, 192, 195, 197, 198, 200, 203
individualism   8, 135, 171, 191
Ingram, Hannah Adams   58–59
innocence   51, 55–56
interreligious learning   176–177
intervention   81, 90, 94–95
intuition   25–27, 29, 45, 182
Isgandarova, Nazila   165–166
Islam   133, 165–166, 167, 169

Jennings, Willie James   12, 17–18, 60, 65, 70, 76, 96–97, 101, 106, 114, 123, 125, 157, 206, 211n12, 213
Jinkins, Michael   102–104, 109
Judaism   10, 164–165

Kang, S. Steve   78–79
Karabel, Jerome   10n16
Kaur, Valarie   10n17
Killen Patricia O'Connell   174
Kim-Cragg, HyeRan   18–19, 86, 176
Kimmerer, Robin Wall   198–199
kingdom of God   85, 98
King, Jr., Martin Luther   3, 120
Kinnaman, David   210n8
Kristof, Nicholas   67
Kujawa-Holbrook, Sheryl   176–177
Kwok, Puilan   176n34

labor   105–107
lament   11, 94, 125, 195, 200
land
   belonging to   193, 196
   relationship to   196–197
Lartey, Emmanuel   176
leadership
   constellations in   122–123
   corporate models of   103
   heroic   118
   leaderships   117

leadership (cont.)
　liberating　118
　servant　109–111
　shared models of　108–109
　transformational　111
Leavitt, Harold　11
Leath, Jennifer　209n6
Lee, Boyung　9n15, 134–135
Leopold, Aldo　193–194
Lewis, Stephen　118–119, 121, 125
living the questions　19, 206–207
Lizardy-Hajbi, Kristina　116–118, 179, 206
Lomawaima, K. Tsianina　62
Lugones, Maria　55

MacIntiyre, Alasdair　40–41
Mahan, Jeffrey　132n3
mass extinction　197
mastery　42, 82, 113, 114, 116, 121, 191, 213
McCarroll, Pamela　182, 189–191, 203
McCarthy, Teresa　62
McFague, Sallie　196
McLaren, Brian　37
meaning-making　90–93
Mercadente, Linda　154
Mercer, Joyce　47
Mikoski, Gordon　14n24, 37, 85
Mikulich, Alex　56
militarized pedagogy　63
Miller-McLemore, Bonnie　83, 102, 145, 150–151, 188, 202–203
misrecognition　48–49
mission/missionizing　60, 137–138
Moll, Luis　78
Moore, Mary Elizabeth　178, 188, 191, 193, 199, 202
Mortenson, Greg　67–68
Moultrie, Monique　114
multiple religious belonging　177–178

Nagle, James　152–153
narcissism　121
nationalism　12–13
　white Christian　3, 72
　See also America First ideology, American exceptionalism
Ng, Wehn-In　176–177
Niebuhr, H. Richard　26, 103

Nieman, James　118
nones　153–154, 158, 161
normativity　169, 172, 175
nuclear family　11

O'Connor, Flannery　160
original sin　208–210
Orsi, Robert　90–93, 155–157
Osmer, Richard　41, 83–84, 103, 110–112
Ó Tuama, Pádraig　175
Oyer, Gordon　95

Palmer, Parker　115
Park, J.S.　140
patriarchy　10–11, 29, 63, 124
pedagogical eternalities　70–72
pedagogic violence　49
pedagogies
　decolonial　79
　liberative　79, 214
　multicultural　77
　nonmutual　61, 74, 75
Peltier, Autumn　195
perfection　28, 205
Pew Research　160
phronesis　38, 84, 200
Pittinsky, T.I.　121
Plantgate　200–202
play　52–53
poetry　125, 175
Pohl, Christine　43–44, 57
post-Christendom　39, 139
postcolonial　1, 18, 19, 23, 86, 116, 178
power　3, 8, 10, 12, 42
　fields of　45
　relations　46, 48
　teaching as act of　59
practical theology
　as apologetics　147–152, 157
　as predominantly Protestant　162
　bridging church and academy　146, 151–152, 154, 158
　bridging theory and practice　81, 150
　interreligious　176
　methods of reflection　179–183
　teaching of　144–145, 150, 158, 161, 183

practice
  ambivalence of   34–35, 42–43, 47–51, 54, 91, 159
  and domination   35
  best practices   36, 56
  characteristic damages in   51
  description of as legitimation   155
  embodied   44, 57, 73, 74
  evaluating religious   155–156
  normative   173
  political theories of   35
  recovery of   43
  spiritual   133
  virtues-based   35–44, 54
  See also embodied control
pragmatic task   83
Pratt, Richard Henry   34*n*1, 64
prayer   166, 204
private Christian schools   71
productivity   99–101
progress
  Ideology of   67
  myth of   82, 94, 95, 97, 191
proverbs   169
purity   28–29, 51, 54–56, 209
purity movement   54–55

questioning
  authority   25
  faith   4, 24–25, 27
  white Protestant Christianity   1

racialization
  of practical theology   14
  of religious identity   10, 166, 168
racial purity   55
racial segregation   71
Ransby, Barbara   120
Reda, Nevin   165
reflexive questions   179–193
relations   197–198
religious abuse   74
religious education   15, 18, 35–36, 47–48, 53, 59, 75–77, 141
  teaching of   22, 128, 131, 138, 141, 144–145
Religious Education Association   66, 164
religious institutions
  as educational community   140

gender conformity   158, 161
  in late capitalism   138–139
  loyalty to   157–159
  resistance to   129, 138
religious pluralism   163, 176
repentance   94, 211–212
resistance   2, 147, 158, 200, 203
rest   107
revolutionary mindset   214
Reyes, Patrick   79, 98–99, 122–123, 142, 206
Reynolds, Kim   8*n*14
Richter, Don   37, 40
Ricouer, Paul   27
Riley, Cole Arthur   52
Rilke, Ranier Maria   206–207
risk   89
Roman Catholicism   140, 152–153, 155–157, 160
Rosenthal, S.A.   121

Saliers, Don   51
salvation
  through education   59, 68
  through whiteness   17, 95–98, 211
Scharen, Christian   49
Schipani, Daniel   79
school vouchers   72
second naivete   27
self-deception   211
self-sufficient man   105–106
shame   210–211
Shotwell, Alexis   55, 89–90, 100
Slee, Nicola   124–125
Smith, Andrea   63
Smith, Christian   73
social change   82, 214
social gospel   85
socialization   36, 40, 46, 73, 177
social space   45
Spivak, Gayatri Chakravorty   86
Stanton, Graham   114–116
Steffans, Nicklas   121–122
strategic task   84
Suchocki, Marjorie   208
suffering   4, 13, 86, 91–95, 99–100, 189, 203
Sweeney, James   36*n*4, 151–152
symbolic violence   44–47

Talvacchia, Kathleen   77
Tan, Jonathan   176
taste   45
Taylor, Barbara Brown   139
Taylor, Dorceta   192
theological education   110
    practical theology in   150–151
theology   164–165
Tinker, George   62, 76, 88, 136n18, 214
tradition   25, 172, 175
tragic   91, 93–95, 100
Tran, Mai-Ahn Le   53, 135–136, 141–142
transformation   22, 57, 82, 86, 89, 94, 96–98, 100–101, 111

Unitarian Universalist Association   161, 172
United Methodist Church   17, 24, 60, 134, 160
United Nations   195
universalist notions of truth   170–171
unlearning
    violence   53–54
    white supremacy   18
uplift   61, 68, 73, 86–87

Van Meter, Timothy   189
Veling, Terry   41
Volf, Miroslav   37

Walker, Anne Carter   18, 79, 213
Warren, Michael   16, 47
WASP   10
water rights   195–196
Watkins, Clare   36n4, 151–152

Welch, Sharon   88–89
Wesley, John   132, 211–212
Westerhoff, John   73
white advantage/privilege   18
white fragility   7
white Western, settler, or colonizer Christianity   1–3, 28, 65, 209, 211
whiteness   3
white savior   82, 86–87, 89, 94
white supremacy   6, 11–12, 18
    anti-blackness   13
    anti-indigenity   14, 202
    anti-Muslim   168–169
    anti-Semitism   168
    great replacement theory   16
    ideologies of   70
    patriarchy   16
    unlearning   18
white theological gaze   65, 70
Wilhelm, Gretchen   72n42
Williams, Matthew Wesley   118–119, 121, 125
Willimon, William   39, 139n20
Wimberly, Anne E. Streaty   37n5, 131
Winner, Lauren   35n2, 50–51
Wirzba, Norman   76, 185–186
worldview   7–9, 26, 28, 64, 87, 95, 132, 161, 170, 178, 183, 191, 195, 199

Yang, Fenggang   133n6
Young, Stephen   29n51

Zakaria, Rafia   68–69
Zoloth, Laurie   186

www.ingramcontent.com/pod-product-compliance
Lightning Source LLC
Chambersburg PA
CBHW051220300426
44116CB00006B/646